THE KUKIS OF MANIPUR

A Historical Analysis

THE KUKIS OF MANIPUR

A Historical Analysis

Thangkhomang S. Gangte

GYAN

Published by

GYAN

Gyan Publishing House
5, Ansari Road
Daryaganj, New Delhi-110002
Phone: 011-47034999, 9811692060
E-mail: books@gyanbooks.com

Distribution Network
gyanbooks.com
India, USA, Canada, UK, Australia, France

ISBN: 978-81-2120-400-2 (HB)

Reprint in India, 2024
First Published, 2012

Printed at: Gyan Press, Delhi.

The Kukis of Manipur: A Historical Analysis
Author: Thangkhomang S. Gangte

Dedicated to my father

LALJALIEN

(LALKHO GANGTE)

Whom I could not see when he breathed his last

PREFACE

The purpose of this Thesis is to focus on the unexplored wealth of Anthropological and Sociological potentials that are available which have not yet been given proper emperical studies to the extent modern scientific knowledge would have achieved. The present study relates to a microscopic aspect of a vast perspeetive.

This piece of work tries to project that every walk of life of the Kukis, be it social, economic, political, religious , etc., is a manifestation of their social structure based on cultural heritage. Changes have been brought about in their social matrix by modernism, western education, Christianity, etc.. Notwithstanding, some aspects of their social institutions withstand the onslaught of such changes, of course, not without conflict between traditionalism and modernity.

Such a study as could be seen in the pages that follow herein was possible with the kind permission of the University of Calcutta. I am indeed thankful to the Department of Anthropology, University of Calcutta, for the same. I owe immensely Prof. P.K.Bhowmick, Head of the Department of Anthropology, University of Calcutta, for having accepted me to work under his supervision. His visits to my field braving all the discomforts and inconveniences were of great help that made my work easier than would have otherwise been. Words fail me to express my indebtedness and gratitude to Prof. Bhowmick in commensural terms. I will ever remain grateful to him.

I am indebted to Thangkhosei Chongloi, Chief of Khengjang village, without whose help, initiative, knowledge and insight on the subject, my task would have been much more formidable. My thanks are also due to all the villagers under study for their affection and co-operation extended to me during my field-work.

I greatly appreciate the critical appreciation, reviews and corrections on my manuscripts by my younger brother, P.Gangte, IPS, Deputy Inspector General of police, Manipur, which had given a qualitative lift to my dissertation.

Without requisite maps, illustrative plates, binding, photographs, etc., this dissertation would not, indeed, have the look of authencity and reliability. For this, the credit entirely goes to Dr. M. Balaram Singh, Vice-Principal, Y.K.College, Manipur. I cherish such help and contribution immensely.

The added works of making the dissertation more attractive and informative with photographs during the field visits were mainly the contribution of N. Surendra, Vice-Principal, Liberal College, Luwangsangbam, Manipur, for which I am much indebted. My thanks are also due to Dr. R.K.Ranjit Singh, Sr. Lecturer, D.M.College of Science for his help in preparing the final plates of the photographs that added to the authencity of the materials.

Had it not been for diligence, unstinted support and excellence of work given by N.Nobinchandra Singh in typing out this dissertation many times over, it would have taken me much longer time for materialising this in its present form. My confidence in his capability in giving me an attractive and typed out dissertation has been commensurated. I am indebted to him very much.

For all said and done, it may be incomplete if mention is not made of my mother and my wife without whose loving hand and care, understanding and encouragement, this piece of work would not have seen light of the day.

THANGKHOMANG S. GANGTE.

CONTENTS

LIST OF MAPS AND ILLUSTRATION

LIST OF MAPS

ILLUSTRATION

LIST OF TABLES

LIST OF CHARTS

CHAPTER 1

INTRODUCTION

I North-East India

The North-Eastern territory of India comprising Assam, Manipur, Meghalaya, Mizoram, Nagaland, Tripura and Arunachal Pradesh was carved out gradually from the original Assam Province of British India except the Princely States of Tripura and Manipur. It had been termed as the 'Land of Seven Sisters'. This region covers an area of approximately 2,55,000 square Kilometres with a population of 2,65,13,685 as per Census of India, 1981.[1]

Its geomorphological location offers three distinctly different regions, viz., (1) hills and valleys of the North and North-East, (2) plateau in the South and (3) the plains in between (1) & (2) above. Practically, the Great Himalayan Range runs towards and continues through Patkoi, erstwhile Naga and Lushai Hills to the further South in Burma. The Brahmaputra valley is the Easternmost extension of the Great Plains of the Ganga of North India. There are also some dwarf hills here and there. China lies to its North, Burma to the East, Bangladesh to the South, and Bhutan to the North West. A narrow corridor from Siliguri in Darjeeling district of West Bengal opens up to negotiate this region with the mainland of India.

Ample evidences of stone-age implements found in this region, specially in Meghalaya and other adjoining areas, signify existence of the earliest human civilization. These have resemblance with those of the tool

---

1. Detailed figures of population of the states including the size of each state are shown in Table 1:1.

types unearthed in Burma and other nearby areas. The find of a typical example of shouldered celt (T-shaped) indicates that there was the beginning of agriculture here in human history. Use of this type of tools extended even upto Bihar-Orissa border suggesting the probability of movements or migration of people from one place to another, from the hoary past traversing this obscure and tortuous path of protohistory and history. We find its vibrating corroboration reflected in various ways. The *Purana* (scriptures) refers to Kamarupa *Janapada* having its capital at Pragjyotispur. Kalidasa and Kautilya referred to all-these places in their writings. We also come across the name of *Nagakanya* 'Ulupi' in the Mahabharata, the great epic literature of India. The famous Chinese traveller, Hi-eun T sang, also visited Kamrupa in 640 A.D. Of course, infiltration of Brahmanical system with waving varnas penetrated into some of the areas of North-East India which moulded the life-style of the people. A good number of principalities ruled by the autochthonese - derivative communities of which the Chuta, Koch, Kachar, etc. are significant. Invasion of the Ahoms from Shan tribal groups of Burma on this land approximates to the 13th Century and their continuity was disturbed only during the 18th Century (sometime in 1772) when the British stepped into this tract. The British colonial administration encouraged the Assamese to form a province with their administrative Headquarters at Shillong. But before Independence, Sylhet, a populous district of Assam, was ceded to East Pakistan, now Bangladesh, due to its Muslim Majority residents and afterwards the Union territories and States were reorganised to satisfy emotion and sentiment of the local people as well as to have a strongly built administrative units as shown in Table 1 :1 below :

TABLE 1.1

Area and Population

Sl.No.	Name of State	Areas	Population (1981 Census)
1	Assam	78,523Sq.Kms.	1,99,02,826
2	Manipur	22,346 "	14,33,681
3	Nagaland	16,488 "	7,73,381
4	Meghalaya	22,489 "	13,27,874
5	Tripura	10,477 "	20,60,189
6	Mizoram	20,090 "	4,87,774
7	Arunachal Pradesh	83,578 "	6,28,050
	TOTAL	2,54,991Sq.Kms.	2,65,13,685

II The People :

The entire North-East India is populated by variegated groups of people. Migration of people from Burma to these areas was very common and, as such, we find people of Mongoloid strains in respect of their physical features, culture and language. The autochthones who settled in the hill tracts were subsequently identified and differentiated one from the other based on various historical processes of stress and strains; communication difficulties, to a great degree, had contributed to their being in isolation for a number of generations. These adjustmental processes, in course of time alienated some groups from the bigger ones, while other groups found themselves in aligned condition with some groups to compose a larger social identity or aggregate. Such alienation and alignment of different groups came to bear various ethnic appellations identifying themselves as distinct tribes. This is a common feature in many places, but this is very significant to this tract of land.

Academically speaking, there are a number of definitions about the word 'tribe'. The Dictionary of Anthropology (Charles Winick : 1957) describes a 'tribe' as -

> A social group, usually with a definite area, dialect, cultural homogenity and unifying social organisation. It may include several sub-groups as 'Sibs' or villages.

It is true that they are not a permanent crystal line structure in the stage of historical and social development and all the time, due to interaction and adjustments, these groups of people are found to accommodate themselves in different degrees to varied situations. It is also expected that their society has less and less of hierarchy and less and less of economic specialisation. Thus we find :

> In course of such travels and shifting for security following clashes with other groups have been transformed to a considerable extent or blended according to the demands of the situation or circumstantial exigencies. As a result, present day culture of these groups bear such mark of incorporation into the core of their cultural matrix (Bhowmick : 1980)

But in order to make them eligible to merit the constitutional benefits from our Welfare State, which has been declared after the Independence, these groups have generally been capsulized as 'Weaker Sections' and listed separately as 'Scheduled'. In this part of India, there are altogether

131 Scheduled Tribes with identifiable characteristics and traits, distributed in different areas of this region (Sharma :1978).

These groups of people have different economy, agriculture (Swiden, terraced and plough), industries and some of them, having received higher education, are competing with their neighbours in white collar jobs. In respect of social organisations there are matrilineal tribes, like Khasi, Garo and Rabha, and Double-discent tribes, like Dimasa and Semasa. The others are patrilineal tribes. Owing to the change in religion through conversion, these groups are changing in different degrees. As regards language, Chatterji (1943:4) says :

> Particularly when we talk to her (India) languages and dialects - 179 and 544 respectively, according to the *Linguistic Survey of India* - these have to be taken with a good deal of reservation. For, of these 179, 'Languages' (the separate enumeration of 'dialects' is irrelevant as they come under 'Languages'),116 are small tribal speeches belonging to Tibeto-Chinese speech family which are found only in North-Eastern fringe of India.

It is true that the enchanting land known as the North-East Region of India attracted waves of diverse racial groups through ages. It has come to stay as the confluence of the most colourful mosaic of ethnic, linguistic and cultural diversity (Govt. of Assam,1976:30).

The culture and tradition of the people often overlap the man-made political units of the region. Political loyalty mostly transcends the boundary of each political unit. The Kukis living in Nagaland, Assam, Tripura and Manipur have closer cultural, traditional and ethnic affinity with the people of Mizoram, Chittagong Hills of Bangladesh and the Chins of Chin-hills in Burma, rather than with their immediate neighbours. They yearn to remain under a single political unit. Sometime ago movements with this end in view were started in Chin Hills of Burma under the leadership of Vumkhohau on the eve of Independence of Burma from the yoke of the British rule and for the unification of Zomi (Gougin, 1984:180) under the banner of Zomi Revolutionary Army covering the areas now inhabited by the Kukis and the Mizos in Manipur,Assam. Tripura, Nagaland and Mizoram.

The same holds good with the Nagas. Despite conspicuous nature at the height of diversity in ethnicity, culture, tradition, language, their peculiar emotional upsurge to integrate themselves, burying their hatchet of age-old war of attrition, under the nomenclature of 'Naga' and a language called 'Nagamese',which is pidgin Assamese, is indeed exemplary. This is solely due to the belief in the myth that all the Nagas have a common origin. This encouraged them to demand for a separate State for Nagas which eventually materialised.

With the exception of the Khasi and the Jaintia tribes of Meghalaya, who belong to the 'Mon-Khmer' culture with their Austric dialect, all other tribal ethnic groups of the region are basically Mongoloid in their ethnic origin belonging to the Tibeto-Burman sub-family of the Tibeto-Chinese linguistic group.

The Kuki-Chin speech of Manipur, Mizoram and the adjoining areas of Tripura and the North-Cachar hills of Assam, the Bodo Non-Aryan language spoken in the Brahmaputra valley and the Garo hills of Meghalaya and a host of dialects spoken by the numerous tribes in Nagaland and Arunachal Pradesh belong to the Tibeto- Burman sub-family. The Indo-Aryan language of the Brahmaputra valley, known as Assamese, is also distinguished by its pronounced Mongoloid bias.

These groups of people came to the region at different periods of history. Some of them came in the prehistoric days and the others came at different point of time of history. Thus, even though some of them belong to the same ethnic group, time-gap in the waves of migration between different groups contributed greatly to their present wide-range of divergence and multiplicity, as mentioned earlier.

In Nagaland and Arunachal Pradesh, the tribal dialects are so numerous that one tribe cannot understand the dialect of his neighbouring tribe. Assamese (pidgin) has, therefore, been adopted as a language of communication among themselves, and they are called 'Nagamese' and 'Nafamese' in Nagaland and Arunachal Pradesh respectively. Comparatively, the language diversity in Meghalaya is far less pronounced than in Nagaland and Arunachal Pradesh. Though the Khasis and the Jaintias, with their Austric speech, do not speak the same dialect, the Khasi dialect has emerged as a more dynamic and acceptable one. Both the Khasis and the Jaintias use it as their common language. In fact, Khasi language has become sufficiently developed. It has been accepted as one of the major Indian languages in almost all the Boards of Secondary Education and regional Universities, upto the first degree examinations. The other major tribe in Meghalaya is the Garo. Their dialect is 'Bodo' which is exclusively used in the Garo Hills of the State. Interestingly, these tribes of

Meghalaya are identified by their distinctive matrilineal system prevailing in the society of the entire region.

In Mizoram, with the exception of a few tribes, like the Chakmas and the Lakhers, there appears to have no diversity in use of language among them and it is *known* there as the Mizo language. This language is not only used in Mizoram, but is also widely used in Chin-Hills of Burma, Chittagong hill tracts of Bangladesh, Tripura and Manipur in India. The Kukis of Manipur, Nagaland, Assam, Tripura, Chin Hills of Burma, Chittagong hill tracts of Bangladesh also use it progressively as a medium of communication amongst themselves as well as between them and the Mizos.

It may be mentioned here that the most contrasting nature between the Nagas on the one hand and the Chinkuki-Mizos on the other, is the fact that despite diversity in language among the Nagas, their sense of unity and solidarity in the name of Naga is spectacular, whereas the Chin-Kuki-Mizos could not have a common political platform like the Nagas, despite advantage of the language at their command. As a matter of fact, the Mizo literature has been so highly advanced that it has been recognised as one of the major Indian languages both at the Boards of Secondary Education level and upto the first degree standard at the Universities of the region.

In Manipur, the Meiteis and the Muslims generally use 'Meitei-lon' as their language. The Naga tribes of Manipur can be broadly divided into the Tangkhul Naga, the Kabui Naga[2], and the Mao Naga. These Naga tribes do not have a common language for their benefit through which they can communicate among themselves and also identify themselves exclusively different from the others. They have to communicate among themselves in "Meitei-lon" alone. There is no other language for their common use. In case of the Kukis, however, despite divisions into many tribes and sub-tribes, they have no language barrier. They are able to communicate in their respective dialects, or use one of the dialects of any tribe depending on the person who uses the dialect.

---

2. In recent past the Kabui Nagas attempted to change their nomenclature by an acronym, ZALIENGRONG-ZA for Zaliang tribe, LIENG for Leingmei tribe and Rong for Rongmei tribe, which was considered more respectable. However, of late there arose controversy amongst them in that Zaliangrong was not extensive enough to cover all tribes, and the nomenclature 'HAOMEI' was considered to give sufficient coverage.

As for the religion of the State, while the Meiteis, living in the valley, are predominantly Hindu Vaishnavites, the tribals in the hills are increasingly embracing Christianity.

In Tripura, the aboriginal Tripuri tribals, who are divided into as many as eighteen groups, preponderated over the non-tribal population till 1947 (Sarin, 1980 :126). These tribal groups have identical ethnic affinity. They inhabit not only in Tripura, but also are found to settle in areas covering the North spurs of the Patkoi range upto the Southernmost part of the Chin Hills of Burma. The major tribes that occupy the areas are the Kukis, the Chins, the Lushais, the aboriginal Tripuris, the Chakmas and the Mugha. Through constant social contacts, these groups have influenced one another despite mutual estrangement in diverse ways.

The aboriginal Tripuris belong to the Bodo groups of Indo-Mongoloids, which form a solid block. They occupy the whole of Brahmaputra Valley, North Bengal, Tripura and East Bengal (now Bangladesh). But due to heavy influx of Bengali migrants, the indigenous inhabitants of Tripura were reduced to an insignificant minority of 29 per cent of the total population of the State.

The class composition of the population of Assam still continues to be the most colourful in all the seven units of the region. The Kukis, the Cacharis, the Dimasas and the other tribes inhabit the North-Cachar Hills District. The Karbis, the Kukis and other minor tribes live in the Karbi Anglong Hill District. There are also numerous other plains - living-tribals who inhabit in some pockets of Brahmaputra valley. The Bengalis are the most predominantly large group in Cachar District adjoining Mizoram. There are many Muslim strongholds in the Districts of the Brahmaputra valley. Most of the Muslim population in Assam are immigrants from the erstwhile East-Pakistan (now Bangladesh). A host of people of other castes and creeds mingle with the Assamese of the Brahmaputra valley. Thus, Assam becomes virtually an unrivalled state in regard to demographic diversity.

Notwithstanding the numerous dialects and spoken languages in the State, Assamese is the lingua-franca of the people there. Even the indigenous and the immigrant Bengalis have taken to speaking Assamese which closely resembles Bengali.

Arunachal Pradesh is very much known for its backwardness and isolation from the outside world until the Chinese aggression into the

Indian territory upto the foothills of Assam in 1962. A large number of tribes of different socio- cultural and religious sects inhabit the Union Territory. There are Buddhist tribes in Kameng, North Siang and Lohit Districts, Hindu Vaishnavite Noctes in Tirap District, who live along with other tribals belonging to indigenous tribal religions (Sarin, 1980-167).

The Mijis, the Sherdukpens, the Khowas, the Akas, the Solungs, the Bangais and the Monpas, who are divided into the Dirang Monpas, Tawang Monpas and Kalaktung Monpas, live in the Kameng District. In Sibansiri District, the Apatanis, the Daflas, the Hill Miris, the Nisla and the Tegins live. In Siang District, besides the two Buddhist tribes of Khambas and Mombas, the Adis, who are divided into Padams Bokers, Pailibos, Ashings, Rangams, Shimongs, also inhabit. In Lohit District the Khamptis, the Shingphos, the Jakhrings live along with a small group of the Padams of Siang District and the Mishmis, who are divided into Idu, Digaru and Mizu., Tirap District is inhabited by the Tangsas, the Noctes, the Wanchos and the Singphos of the Lohit District.

All these tribes have their own dialects, customs, dresses, manners, religions, ornaments and traditions; and together they contribute to the varied culture and religion of the region. With the exception of the Buddhist tribes, they have some common traits in domestic types, agricultural practices, observances of taboos and other soico-cultural rites. The composition of religious groups is as much diverse as their ethnic composition in the region. There are Buddhists in Arunachal Pradesh,and Hindus in the Brahmaputra Valley of Assam,Tripura and Cachar Districts of Assam, the Tirap District of Arunachal Pradesh, and the centrally located Imphal Valley of Manipur. The Hill areas of Manipur constituting nine-tenth of the total areas, where tribal people inhabit, are the homelands of various denominations among the followers of Christianity. The States of Nagaland, Meghalaya and Mizoram are Christian dominated areas among the tribals. There are a large number of Muslim pockets in Assam, Manipur and Tripura, living mixed-up with the Hindus in the plains. The Nepali Hindu infiltrators from the bordering areas of Nepal have cooked up various problems in some hill regions,particularly in Manipur, and more so, of late, in Meghalaya.

III Introducing the Research Topic

Attempts have been made in this section to introduce the research hypotheses which have manifested by field work and through in-depth study in some villages. The life-style of the Kukis has been examined with a view to grasping the operating forces playing in their day-to-day living, with special reference to the Kukis of Manipur. Their institutions-economic, political, social and religious-in the face of the changing pattern of life with the introduction of modern education system, spread of Christianity and onslaughts of various other changes brought about by the developmental programmes of the Government, present significant materials for study.

The Kukis here had been the dominant tribe spreading their authority over a wide range of hill areas surrounding the valley of Imphal during the hey-day of the Maharajah of Manipur and subsequently during the British period. The Kuki Chiefs were in supreme command over their respective domains in the hills. This was specially so with the Thadou Kuki Chiefs. The Hao-kip Thadou Chief, under the leadership of their senior most clan, known as the Chahsad Haokip, was the overlord of the hills to the East of Imphal valley exercising his power and authority on the Tangkhul Nagas, and his influence was extended upto the Burma Border, contiguous to the Thongdut State and part of the Somra Tract. The Doungel Kuki chief was the monarch of the North-East of Imphal valley extending his area of influence to the unadministered areas of Somre which lie in between the Naga Hills of the erstwhile Assam Province and the Burmese territory, which later became a bone of contention between the Doungel Chief, better known as the Aishan Chief, and the British Raj resulting in a protracted war that ended in 1919, after the subjugation of the areas concerned by the British who placed the same partly under the then Naga Hills of Assam and partly under Burma.

Likewise, the Sitlhou Thadou Chief, known as the Chief of Jampi, ruled the Western and North-Western part of Imphal valley bordering the Angami country. The Singson Thadou Chief ruled the areas contiguous to the Sitlhou country and the Lushai Hills of Assam. Pulverised in between the Sitlhou in the North- West and the Imphal valley in the North-East was the country of the junior clans of the Haokip Thadous, belonging to the Lunkhel, Songthat and Telngoh clans where they ruled the roost. To the South of them, bordering the Tiddim of Chin Hills of Burma, the areas were occupied by the Manluns (Zou), while the South-East of Imphal Valley extending up to the areas of Kabo valley and Sukte country, were ruled by the Mangvung Haokip Thadous.

Thus, the hill areas of Manipur were the domain and the head-hunting ground of the Thadou Kukis until they were subjugated and controlled by the British in 1917-19 Anglo-Kuki War. The most permanent and lasting effect of this war of Independence by the Kukis was not only the suppression of the Kukis, but marking of permanent boundaries of Manipur, which exists till today. Prior to this, there was no boundary of Manipur as such. The Maharajahs of Manipur were contented with periodical massacre and extension of their influence for specific purposes. The Kuki Chiefs were their allies. After 1919, however, the British assumed direct administration over the hill tribes in general and on the Kuki Chiefs, in particular. The opening of the first sub-divisional offices in Tamenglong, Ukhrul and Churachandpur was made with the sole object of checkmating the Kuki Chiefs and also to avoid recurrence of their insurgency against the British rule. This apart, the British rulers ruled the hill areas through the effective machinery of the Chieftainship and its Council of Ministers. This helped the Chiefs to maintain their authority and hold over the people, thereby, unifying the clans that composed the Kuki Tribes called KUKIS, and to express their identity as such. The authority of the Chiefs also greatly enhanced the strength of their custom, for they were the perennial sources of the Kuki custom, tradition, culture, language, etc.

In contrast with the introduction of western education through the Christian missionaries, spreading from the Lushai hills, the idea of being dominated by the Chiefs and being identified as 'KUKI' were considered as a derogatory foreign design. The authority and leadership of the Chiefs thus began to erode gradually. Ultimately, with the advent of Independence of India, the idea of Chieftainship being thrown out of power was supplanted by a new set-up of administration known as 'democracy' which in a resurgent India was spontaneously accepted by the leaders and the commoners. Besides this, the term 'KUKI' was rejected mainly in the previously known Lushai hills and Manipur. Recognition of tribes as listed in the 'Scheduled Tribes' in various states hastened the process of disintegration among the Kukis, for the new Constitution of India accorded special privileges to such recognised tribes. Along with this, tension, enmity, conflict, factionalism between and among the erstwhile Kukis became the common feature of their life. The people became crazy for being listed as a Scheduled Tribe so as to be able to enjoy the fruits of the Constitutional privileges. Indeed, the immediate adverse effect of all this was telling heavily on the unity and solidarity of the Kukis. The seeds of disintegration thus burgeoned among them. Therefore, in a system of administration where counting of heads and majority rule prevail, the Kukis were the worst sufferers. They are now in a minority wherever they live, because they have become very badly divided and too widely scattered in different administrative units in the entire North-East region of the country.

The empirical study of such people would no doubt open up a new vista leading to the store-house of knowledge for the Social Anthropologists and Sociologists. Many aspects of life of the Kukis which could not be easily uncovered or appreciated with a superficial knowledge of their social system would aptly have misled an outsider. An in-depth study of their life would not only enrich knowledge but also help the people concerned understand them in a better way.

The villages under study were inhabited by the Chongloi, the Sitlhou, the Kipgen, the Haokip, the Singson, the Gangte and the Lhungdim clans. They provide both similarities and diversities and reflect ethnic relationship or otherwise. The areas covered in the selected villages are mainly within the Churachandpur District and the Sadar Hill sub-division of Senapati District of Manipur. The locations of the villages[3] afford accessibility from the National and State Highways. These are not, however, within the areas that can be considered as urbanised or at the outskirts of the growing towns of different Districts. Nevertheless, the villages are not absolutely without the tough of modernity, albeit modern amenities and avenues of modern employment etc. are scarcely available. Though urbanisation is a part of inevitable result of civilization and planned development requiring bringing in of all facilities of upto-date living at the door-step of rural population, and despite changes in the matter of administration with the introduction of Village Authority Act,1956 coupled with negation of the authority of the KUKI Chiefs, the traditional system of village administration continues to hold stage.

The institution of 'Tucha-Songgao' and 'Becha' is the basis on which study of the Kuki society can be made. This institution is vital to a Kuki family, being the nucleus unit, in as much as to the whole social system. Perhaps, this can be said as one of the excellent arrangements of division of labour, responsibility and an extension of public relation in an egalitarian society where the golden rule of the olden days still prevailing. For the study of any aspect of life of the Kukis, this institution is inevitable, be it their social life, or political life, or economic life or religious life. The institution of 'Tucha-Songgao' and 'Becha' is a projection of a typical Kuki institution for their love of orderliness and propriety without which no life appears possible among the Kukis.

---

3. The villages studied in the Churachandpur, district are, 'Chengkonpang' a Gangte village, 'Lhangjol' a Haokip village, 'Songgel' a Lhungdim village and 'Bethel' a Singson village and that of Sadar Hills are, 'Khengjang', a Chongloi village, 'Motbung' a Sitlhou (Lhouvum) village, 'Seloi' a Kipgen village and 'Gelbung' a Haokip village.

The life-cycle of a Kuki, beginning from birth to death, is nothing but a manifestation of the social structure. The alternate-generation naming system is basic and conspicuous in its singular system in all the societies of the world. This system has greatly helped the Kukis maintain their tradition and in reckoning their genealogy. It also shows how important is the relationship between a grandfather and a grandson in manifesting the easy manner of joking relationship. Likewise, the practice of mother's brother's marriage, known as 'Neinu',has a role to play in building the institution of 'Tucha-Songgao and 'Becha' as a living organ. The peculiar joint family system of the Kukis is also another revealing singular aspect in the study of social life of the numerous communities and tribes all over the world. The family of the eldest son of the Kuki parents called UPA, which must necessarily have a joint family comprising his parents, unmarried brothers and sisters, and sometimes with married brothers, who have yet to establish themselves, is called 'Inherent Joint Family',consisting of vertical generations. The other joint family system is that of the younger brothers of the UPA, which is known as the family of NAOPA. It forms the nuclear family of his own. This family ultimately becomes a joint family of UPA when his first son is married and lives with him. This kind of joint family is called 'Earned Joint Family'.

'Luongman'or Corpse Price is another peculiar system of the Kukis. This is the price for a woman when she dies, and also for her sons. The price is claimed by her father, or elder/younger sons, in father's absence, as a token of love and affection between the uterine kinsmen. This also reveals the important position held by a women in a family life, and the weightage given to propagation of the descent through male line. If a woman does not give birth to a son or sons, as her spring promises, it is considered a disgrace to her father and brothers and, as such, here 'Luongman' cannot be claimed.

The institution of 'Sawm' as the dormitory of the ablebodied youngmen of the village as the primary means of initiation and education plays a significant role among the Kukis, and it is the manifestation of the style of life they lead. Subsequent changes of the 'Sawm' system in a decentralised form speak more about its importance. In the like manner, the 'Lawm' institution, as the basic economic life-giving system, is a revelation of the basic concept of community-base economic system of the Kukis. In other words, 'SAWM' is a socio-agro bias social institution whereas 'LAWM' is basically agro-bias institution.

The 'Chang-Ai' festival of the Kukis speaks volumes of the important part played by the women of the family. It is also indicative of the nature of division of labour. 'Sa-Ai' festival is another such example, because of its association exclusively with a man who claims to have achieved fame and bravery in life. The festivals of 'Chang-Ai' and 'Sa-Ai' also reveal lack of conception of saving in the economic life of the Kukis. Consumption is community oriented, and is, therefore, very conspicuous. The distribution system of the Kukis is based on a certain set pattern of social hierarchy. Giving of the 'Salu', head of the games, brought by an individual villager, to the Chief is the manifestation of the position of the receiver as the head of the village community and also an expression of the giver's attitude of loyalty towards the Chief. Similarly, 'Sating',the topmost portion of a hunted animal, which is carved out of the backbone of the kill, known as the 'Ating-Sa', Spinal Flesh, indicates that the man who receives such a portion of meat from a person is senior to him and is his elder or UPA. The share of TUCHA is taken from the waist portion of the prize, 'Sakong', indicating that the person who receives such meat marries a woman from the ego's family or clan or from his exogamous group. It is also indicative of the fact of survival of the system of marriage by service which is called Kong-Lo, i.e. earning the waist of a women. The receiver is 'TUCHA', relative of the giver who is 'SONGGAO' to the former. In the like manner, a man who is a 'Becha' of an ego receives the rib portion, 'Anah', of the hunted animal indicating thereby that the man represents the ego. The rib is closest to the heart of the animal and, therefore, it is meant that the man who receives the 'rib' portion is the closest to the man who gives him the rib portion.

Similarly, among the Thadous and their cognates, 'SANGONG', the neck portion of the animal killed is given to the SONGGAO,mother's brother. Though it is the chest portion, called SA-AWM,given to the SONGGAO relative among the Gangte and Vaiphei Tribes.

A door-to-door study of some villages by participant observation covering 236 families, substantiated with case history reveals various life-style of the Kukis. Some of the genealogies clearly show how they have adhered to their traditional systems, and, also, in many ways, deviated from them. These are very helpful in analysing their social system. This study is expected to enhance a great deal of new knowledge in the social systems operating in the life of the Kukis of Manipur in North-East India.

CHAPTER 2

FACTS AND FABLES

I Origin

The origin of this group of people is shrouded with myths and mythologies. One of such was the traditional accounts that had been handed down through generations in that the Kukis came out of the bowels of the earth or a cave called Chinlung or Sinlung or Khul, the location of which was believed by some to be somewhere in China. But others claimed it to be in Tibet (Ginzatuang, 1973 : 5).

McCulloch (1959:55) contended that the Kukis were known as Khongjai also in Manipur, and that they :

> .... bring their progenitors from the bowels of the earth, and they relate the manner of their reaching its surface thus : One day their King's brother was hunting hedgehogs, when his dog in pursuit of one, entered a cavern, and he waiting for its return remained at the mouth. After lapse of sometime, the dog not having returned, its master determined to go in and see what had become of it. He did not find the dog, but observing its tracks and following them, ;she found himself suddenly on the surface of the earth. The scene presented to his view both pleased and astonished him. Returning to his brother, he related about his adventure, and counselled him to annex the new country to his territory, which the king did.

By way of explanation of their amalgamation with the tribes who speak different languages, they relate :

> ... the three grandsons of the chief, while one day all playing together in their house, were told by their father to catch a rat. They

> were busy about it when, being suddenly struck with a confusion of tongues, they were unable to achieve their object. The eldest son spoke the Lamyang, the Second the Thado, the third, some say, the Vaiphei and some the Manipore language. Thus, they broke into distinct tribes.

Shaw (1929:24) had his own version of the origin of the Kukis which he recorded from the collected verbal information as follows :

> The story of their origin is that they used to live under the earth, or rather inside it. Noimangpa was the Chief of this subterranean region. One Chongthu, a relative of Noimangpa, went a hunting porcupines in the jungle with his dog and discovered a large hole. He perceived through this that the upper crust of the earth was un-inhabited and there was a great darkness. This darkness, which lasted for seven days and seven nights is called "Thimzin" by the Thádous. Chongthu so rejoiced at this discovery that he gave up his hunt and went back to his house. He conjured up ideas of forming a village of his own on the earth and planned accordingly. Just about then, Noimangpa, the Chief of the underworld was performing the 'Chon' festival in which everyone had to attend, including Chongja, elder brother of Chongthu. Noimangpa's son, Chonkim, was also present. During this feast Chongthu started waving his sharp sword so vigorously that he injured some of the folks present, at which all became angered. This action of Chongthu was premeditated as he thought that by doing so he would be turned out from the underworld and thus have an excuse for going out to the upperworld and forming a village of his own. The news of Chongthu's behaviour became known to Noimangpa who said : *Chongthu had better live in Heaven*, meaning thereby that he better be killed. Chongthu hearing of Noimangpa's wrath at once prepared to migrate out of the hole in the earth which he saw and which is spoken of as 'Khul' by the Thadous. So, Chongja and Chongthu killed many pigs, fowls, etc. and feasted in preparation for their departure.

There are many more stories about it. The above story further relates that somehow Chongja's party was delayed, but Chongthu's party moved on followed by Chongthu himself. On reaching the 'Khul', the leaders found that a great snake called Gulheipi was in possession of it and when they endeavored to pass over it, the snake killed them with its tail. Chongthu, on reaching the spot, was not to be thwarted in his ambition. He tied his cloth around him and placed a Phoipi, a thick cotton cloth, over his head and attacked the great snake which he cut into seven pieces. At the same time, a Lhaw, a lion also attempted to block the way of Chongthu's egress. The lion withdrew and Chongthu's party moved upto the 'Khul'. They found that it was covered with a stone and one of Chongthu's party, called Vangalpa, lifted it up. While he could do so, only seven persons were able to get out and then the stone dropped and all further attempts to raise it ended in a fiasco. The seven persons who thus emerged were Chongthu, Vangalpa, the stone-lifter, Khupngam, the keeper of the dog, and four others whose names are not known. These four persons are said to be the progenitors of the Manipuri, the Naga, the foreigner and the Burmese. However, they are not definite about the last three although they are quite emphatic about the number being seven.

In the genealogical tree from Chongthu to Thadou, the persons are mythical and, therefore, when festivities entailing repetition of the genealogical tree of the Thadous became necessary, the Thempu starts from Thadou and not from Chongthu.

Further, from Chongthu to Thadou there were no different languages, and animals and spirits, as well as the mythical ancestors lived in peaceful co-existence.

The hole in the earth called 'Khul' is said to be at the source of the 'Gun' river which seems to be identical with the Imphal river in Manipur State. Etymologically, the word'Gun' in the Thadou means the 'Imphal river'. In all the stories and legends of the Thadous, the river 'Gun' is frequently mentioned and is of great fame (Shaw, 1929:24-26).

Hutton (1929:14) said:

> .... the story of Thimzin with slight variation is found in Shakespear's Lushai-Kuki clans, Chapter V, Mills'-The Ao Nagas, p.314. The Lhota Nagas, pp 176, 193. Molola, in Man in India, 11,100 had similar story of the Chang Nagas, and versions are found among the Hos and Santals of Bengal, the Shans, and the Ami of Formosa, while similar stories pervade the Indian Archipelago generally in Frazer's Folk-lore in the Old Testament, I, iv, which said that the Thadou version of Thimzin story is- "he knew of was that"...the great darkness was preceded by fire and accompanied by flood, and it was this flood which drove the ancestors of the Thado proper to take refuge in the hills, where they found Lenthang, whom they forbore to kill as he, and his, knew the gods of the country : accordingly, it was Lenthang who

caused a white cock detainer of the sun to come and look, whereby the sun escaped and came out again restoring light to the darkened world.

The story is obviously suggestive of a separate racial origin for the Thadou proper, the Changsan and allied clans, who presumably were in occupation when the Thadou arrived in the hills. Hutton further contended that such cultural diversion of the Kuki affinity was found in Naga Hills among the Sema tribe who "speaks a Naga language which is something of a 'pidgin type',lacking the inclusive and exclusive duals and plurals and similar subtleties of most Naga languages". It has a political system turning on an automatic secular chief, with followers, who are house-guards, serfs or similarly bound retainers, known as 'Mughemi' (literally, Orphans). It has other cultural items strongly suggestive of Kuki affinities and has lost the institution of the bachelor's house. It lacks in for the most part the sentiment which binds most Naga villagers so strongly to some particular site, or at least to stones, earth or water brought from that site.

II Migration

It was generally believed that the Kukis came out of China during the reign of Chinese Emperor Chinglung or Chie'nlung, around 200 B.C. Zawla (1976 :2), a Mizo historian, claimed that the Kukis came out of the Great Wall of China in about 225 B.C.,during the reign of Shih Hungti whose cruelty was then at its height. A number of other theories have been advanced in this connection. But in the absence of any written corroboration of existence of historical evidence to support them, such hypothetical theories are considered as highly subjective and conjectural. These are, therefore, taken with a pinch of salt. They remained only as legends.

Nevertheless, Enriquez (1932:7-8) was emphatic in his claim, in that : he thought he had ample scientific data at his command to prove that Mongolian races, who now occupy South-East Asia, and also the North-East India, originated from the Western China lying between the sources of the Yangtze and the Hoang-Ho rivers, and migrated in three waves as follows :

1. The Mon-Khmer(Talaing, Pa Lung, En Riang, Ma, Pale,Khais and Annimite) which included Khasis.

2. The Tibeto-Burman comprising Pyu-Burmase-Kachin, Kuki-Chin and Lolo :

3. The Tai-Chinese which included Shan, Siamese and Karen.

The route-chart of the Mon-Khmer group was that they followed the Mekong valley towards South into Campuchea and Thailand until they reached Burma wherefrom some of them went further Westward upto Bay of Bengal and then turned towards North. It is believed that the Khasis are the remnants of the Mon-Khmer group.

The Tibeto-Burman group initially moved towards the West and thereafter subdivided themselves into several groups. They followed different routes, one group reaching Tibet on the North where some of them stayed behind, while others moved on Northwards until they reached Burma in three waves. These people were the Kuki-chin and the Pyu-Burmese-Kachin groups. While the latter stuck to this place, the Kuki-Chin group moved further towards South-West following the Irrawady and the Chindwin rivers and continued to do so till they reached the shores of the Bay of Bengal. From here they turned back North and eventually fanned out along the mountains down the whole length and breadth of the hilly region, on either side of the existing Indo Burma boundary lines. Thus, when the British came here in the eighteenth century, they found the groups scattered about, and the British officers started keeping records of the various clans or groups of Kukis at different places wherever they were found to have settled.

Hutton (1929) in one of his monographs described the migratory routes of the Kukis in a lucid manner, and was more specific in regard to the scattered settlements of the Kukis.

> For a very long time the Kuki-Chin groups of tribes, pressed from behind Kachins moving Southwards from Chins, and been migrating down the course of the Chindwin River, and some turned back perhaps by the Bay of Bengal, had then moved slowly North-West and North wards again, driving out or incorporating previous inhabitants of what are now parts of the Chittagong Hill Tracts of East Pakistan, the Chin Hills of Burma, the Lushai Hills of Assam, parts of the areas of Manipur State of the North Cachar Hills and the South of the Naga Hills.

Lehman (1963 : 11) observed :

> History shows, however, that both hills and plains peoples have moved about within the general region of South-West China and

South-East Asia over considerable distances for many centuries until the recent past.

III

Speaking further about the Kukis, different scholars and British administrators unanimously described them as belonging to the Mongolian stock, but they did not specify to which particular Mongolian group they belonged. While Yule (1855), Col. Phayre (1866) and Mc. Cabe concluded that the Kukis belonged to the Indo-Chinese family, Captain Forbes and Dr. Grierson differed and called them as a part of Tibeto-Burman group. Taw Sien Kho, a Burmese lecturer at Cambridge classified the Kukis as Turanean (Carey & Tuck, 1932:2) which included the Chinese, Manchus, Japanese, Annamese, Sianese, Burmese, Turks, etc. and further said that their habitat included the whole of North Eastern India before the Aryan conquest.

Regarding the term 'Kuki', which denotes a particular type of people, Lieut. Col. Reid (1893 :5) said :

> Previous to the expedition of 1871-72 the wild tribes, which had been in the habit of raiding our North-Eastern Frontier, were generally spoken of as 'Kukis', a Bengali word meaning hillmen or highlanders. The word was originally applied to the tribe or tribes occupying the tract immediately to the South of Cachar. It is now employed, in a comprehensive sense, to indicate all those living to the West of the Kaladyne river, while those to the West are designated Shendus. On the other hand, to anyone approaching them from the Burma side the Shendus would be known as China, ... of Col Woodthrope, synonymous with Khyen and pronounced as 'Chin'.[1]

He further propounded that the Chins called themselves as 'Lai'. Considering their distinctive characteristics in dress and dialects, there can be little doubt that the Chins, the Kukis, the Lushais, and the various tribes are practically of one and the same race and were included under the term 'Kuki' since the days of Warren Hastings. It is further learnt that their first attack against the British and their subjects dated as far back as 1777."When the Chief of Chittagong a district which had been ceded to the British under Clive by Mir Kasim in 1760, applied for a detachment

---

1. It may be noted that in Burmese a combination of alphabets 'Kh' is pronounced as 'CH'

of sepoys to protect the inhabitants against the incursions of the Kukis as they were then called" (Reid, 1893 :6-7).

Lalthangliana (1975:69) claimed that the word 'Chin' in Burma was synonimous to the word 'Kuki' and 'Mizo' in India. He further contended that though the reason was not known,the Burmese called the people living in the North-West Burma and the North- East India as 'Chin'. In explaining the reason why the Burmese called the Kukis as Chins he inferred:

> Perhaps they were always found carrying on their backs bamboo baskets called Chin by the Burmese. But this particular Burmese word also means friendship and by a stress of imagination one could say that once these two people live very closely together. Since there were relations not partaining strictly to friendliness, I think the explanation "Man with the basket" is most reasonable.

Captain Lewin (1970:130) said that on the Chittagong side the Kukis were described as:

> ... men who live far in the interior parts of the hills, and have not the use of fire arms, and whose bodies go unclothed.

Later, when he became the Deputy Commissioner of Hill Tracts in 1870, he described :

> The Loosei, commonly called the Kookies, are a powerful and independent people, who touch the borders of Chittagong Hill Tracts. They extend in numberless hardes in North and North-East, until they reach Cachar on the one hand, and the frontiers of Burma on the other, ... They are known to the Bengalees by the name of Kookie, and the Burmese as the Lankhe.

Col. Dalton (1872 :44),Commissioner, Chutis Nagpur (Chotanagpur) and a member of the Asiatic Society of Bengal, in 1872, said that the Kukis were first known from an article which appeared in the Asiatic Researcher's journal, volume VII, 1799 contributed by Superintendent Mc-Cres wherein he described the Kukis as :

> ... a nation of hunters and warriors, rules as a nation by their principal hereditary chiefs or rajahs, but divided into clans, each under its own chiefs.

Soppit (1893 :2), who was Assistant Commissioner, Burma and later Sub-Divisional officer, North Cachar Hills, Assam, in his study of the Lushai Kukis remarked :

> The designation of 'Kuki' is never used by the tribes themselves, though many of them answer to it when addressed, from knowing it to be the Bengali or plains term for their people.

Lt, Col. Shakespear (1912 :Pt.I,7), who was one of the authorities on the Kukis, said that the term 'Kuki'

> ... has come to have a fairly definite meaning, and we now understand by it certain closely allied clans, with well marked characteristics, belonging to the Tibeto-Burman stock. On the Chittagong border, the term is loosely applied to most of the inhabitants of the interior hills beyond the Chittagong Hill Tracts; in Cachar it generally means some family of Thado or Khawtlang clan, locally distinguished as new Kuki and old Kuki. Now-a-days, the term is hardly ever employed, having been superseded by Lushai, in the Chin Hills and generally on the Burma border all these clans are called Chins... that these Kukis are also closely allied to the 'Chukmahs', and that the Lushais are more closely allied to the Chiru, Kom, Khawtlang families and are also related to their eastern neighbours who are known as Chins.

He concluded by saying :

> Nevertheless, there is no doubt that the Kukis, Chins and Lushais are all of the same race.

Meerwarth (1919 :29), a noted Ethnologist from Russia, while giving an instructive illustration on the civilisation of the tribes in his comprehensive work on the Andamanese, Nicobarese and Hill Tribes of Assam, observed :

> ... under the term 'Kuki' we comprise a great number of clans ... the most important of which are those which inhabit the mountain ranges known as the Lushai Hills.

Both by language and race they are closely connected with their Eastern neighbours, the Chins, and form a part of the Tibeto-Burman family. There is no doubt also that the Manipuris are closely related to them.

Carey and Tuck (1932 :2) while dealing with the Chin tribes of Burma said :

> Without pretending to speak with authorities on the subjects, we think we may reasonably accept the theory that the Kukis of Manipur, the Lushais of Bengal and Assam, and the Chins, originally lived in what is now known as Tibet and are of one and the same stock; their form of government, method of collection, manners and customs, beliefs and traditions, all point to one origin.

Hutton (1928 :24) while describing on the work of Shaw on the Thadou Kukis said that the origin of the word Kuki is not known, "but it first appeared in 'Bengal',"in the Asiatic Researcher' journal, Vol.II, 1872. Likewise, Maj. Gen. Sir Johnstone (1971 :25), the then Political Agent, Manipur, gave his findings from a different angle wherein he observed :

> The Kukis are a wandering race consisting of several tribes who have long been walking up from the south. They were first heard of as Kukis, in Manipur, between 1830 and 1840.

Shaw (1929 :16), a Civil Servant, whose work on the Thadou Kukis became the most controversial one that led to the disintegration of the Kukis in modern day stated :

> The Koms, Aimols, Khawtlangs, Thadous, Lushais, Chins, Pois, Siktes, Paites, Gangtes, etc. are undoubtedly all connected and are Kukis, and that the language alone has many similarities and the syntex is not dissimilar. Again, there are their customs which have a common principle running through them all.

Majumdar (1944 :127), in dealing with the cultures of India concluded that the Lushais are Kukis and are of Mongoloid stock. He also recorded:

> The Kukis are known by various clan names. Those of the North Cachar Hills are called Biete Kukis and Khelma Kukis. To the North of the Lushai range in the forest-clad hills dwell the Darlung.

IV Where the Kukis Settled :

It has been amply described in the foregoing section as to who are the 'Kukis'. It is now to be ascertained where they settled or are living presently. Captain Pemberton (1835 :15), Joint Commissioner in Manipur in his report on the Eastern Frontiers of British India wrote ;

> ... The Khongjuees, who under the more generally known names of Kookies, Koo-chungs and Kuci, stretch from the Southern borders of the Muneepoor valley to the Northern limit of the province of Arracan, ... that the Kookies have been gradually advancing for years in a northerly direction, and have hitherto established themselves on the ranges which are originally occupied by more northerly tribes or committed such fearful aggressions upon the latter, as to compel them to retire and leave an unoccupied tract between themselves and these formidable opponents.

In this connection Dalton (1872 :44) observed :

> ... The Kukis are now found as neighbours of the Nagas in Assam and in contiguity with the Mugs of Arracan. The hill country occupied by them extends from the valley of the Koladyne, where it touches on the Khumis, to Northern Cachar and Manipur, a distance of about 300 miles.

But studying the Kukis, from their experience, mainly in Burma, in the Chin Hills, Carey and Tuch (1932 :2) remarked :

> As far as the Chins are concerned, we know from our own experience, that the drift of migration has changed and is now towards the North, The Nwite (Gwite), Vaipe (Vaiphei), and Yo (Zou) Chins, who within the memory of men resided in the Northern Chin Hills, have now almost entirely recrossed the Northern border, either into the hills belonging to Manipur or to the South of Cachar and their old village sites are now being occupied by the Kanhow (Kamhow) clan of Sukte Chins, which also is steadily moving Northwards.

Maj. Gen. Johnstone (1871 :25) said :

> The Kukis were now immigrants and were believed to have caused a great deal of ..... anxiety about the year 1845, and soon poured

> into the hill tracts of Manipur in such number as to drive away many of the older inhabitants.

Col. McCullah (1859 :55), the then Political Agent, Manipur, prior to Sir Johnstone, whom the later described as a tactful and generous officer and who often went out of his way to help the Kukis at his own expense said :

> The Khongjais or Kookis until lately occupied the hills to the South of the Koupooes (Kabuis). Whilst in this position, little or nothing of them was known, but they caused fear from their numbers and the bloody attacks they sometimes made upon their neighbours.

Similarly, Shaw (1929 : 11) found that the Kukis of Manipur as having lived :

> .... in a large area of hilly country bounded by the Angami Nagas of Naga Hills District in the North, the Province of Burma in the East, the Chin Hills and Lushai Hills in the South and the District of Cachar in the West. Mainly, it may be said, they occupy the Hills of the State of Manipur on all sides of Imphal valley.

Meerwarth (1919 :29) in his study on the Andamanese, Nicobarese and Hill Tribes of Assam observed that the Kukis occupied :

> ... hill ranges South of the Naga Hills. Their neighbours to the North are the Nagas and the Manipuris, to the East the tribes of the Upper Chindwin and the Chin Hills, on the South those living on the hill tracts of Chittagong, while on the West they are bounded by the plains of Sylhet and the hills of North Cachar.

He went on to remark :

> The Kukis are very migratory, and their settlement can be found dispersed among other tribes, such as, the Nagas, the Cacharies etc. They are split up into a great number of tribes.

Majumdar (1944 : 127) demonstrated that the Kuki Chiefs :

> ... rule over the country between the Karnafuli river and its main tributary, Tuilampai, on the West, and the Tyao and the Koladyne rivers on the East. While their Southern boundary is roughly a line

drawn East and West through the junction of the Mat and Koladyne rivers and their most Northerly villages are found on the borders. of the Silchar district. The Lushai and others with distinct Lushai affiliates are found scattered over wide areas : they are found in the Southern borders of Sylhet, in Tipperah and in the North of the Cachar Hills, and the Chittagong Hill Tracts also contain some Lushai villages.

V Disintegrated Kukis

From the facts stated above we have an idea about the Kukis, their origin and where they live in. With the advent of Indian Independence, however, the situation has taken a sea- change among the Kukis and nobody can differentiate for sure between a Kuki and a Manipuri. These people have now become more politically conscious and socially sensitive. The new Constitution of India ensures an individual the right to equal opportunity for all citizens, along with all other fundamental rights etc. with special provision for safeguarding the interest of the Backward classes, including the people who have been listed as Scheduled Castes and Scheduled Tribes. Thus, in accordance with the Notification of the Ministry of Home Affairs, Government of India, published in the Extra -Ordinary Gazette of India,there are 29 recognised tribes in Manipur. But not a group designated as 'Kuki' is listed there. Therefore, in so far as official matters are concerned, after the publication of the above mentioned orders of the Government of India, no tribe could be referred to officially as 'Kuki' in Manipur, nor, the nomenclature 'Kuki' is recognised for all practical purposes.

It may be said here and now that the Kukis were the monarch in the hills surrounding the valley of Imphal and their relationship with the Raja of Manipur till the outbreak of Anglo- Kuki war in 1917 was one of mutual respect and understanding on equal terms which was well depicted by Hutton (1928 :3) in the following words :

> .... the administration in the hill areas of Manipur State is not very close, and ... as they (Kuki) were ruled by their own organised chiefs and treated as they had been in the past, at any rate, by the Manipur State as allies ......

All the same, the contribution of the Kukis, who were hand in gloves with Juvaraj Tikendrajit Singh, in the uprising of 1891, was great. The changes brought about by the Anglo-Kuki war of 1917-19, formed a watershed for modern Manipur with a permanent territory that still exists. Their virtue of sacrificial spirit probably prompted them to join the Indian National Army in hundreds in response to the call given by Netaji Subhash Chandra Bose of the INA. They were a gallant and martial lot who, among the people of the North-East India, could challenge the invincible power of the British empire then.

But, alas, those glorious days of the Kukis are gone, and gone with them are the existence of these brave tribesmen now. The main factor leading to their extinction was political. The class composition of the Kukis and their political organisation were so independent of each other that the Kukis were obsessed with the idea of inter-clan rivalries, being helped and fomented by the designing political organisation. As a consequence, despite their being one and the same, clan-rivalries for supremacy over each other strained their relationship. But such polemic could not raise its ugly head during the British administration which recognised the Kuki Chieftainship and administered the hill people through these efficient functionaries. However, after Independence of India, when the public in general had became conscious of the modern political trend that espoused the principles of democracy, the inherent but hitherto latent clan-rivalries began to manifest themselves among the Kukis with the result that the process of their disintegration came to a head. This process occurred in quick succession among the Kukis.

Another important factor leading to this disintegration was social which was inextricably inter-twined with the political factor mentioned above. According to their culture and tradition, the social system of the Kukis was so segmentary that every individual was made consciously aware that he or she belonged to a particular clan or sub-clan. Thus, a Kuki cannot be free from such idiosyncrasy, be an educated person or not. Obviously, this became a fertile breeding-ground for discontentment, competition, jealousy, hatred, factionalism, etc. When afterwards, the Government of India started preparing the list of Scheduled Tribes in Manipur, every imaginable group or clan aspired to get the recognition by inclusion in the list as a separate tribe. In the process, no one appeared to have claimed, consciously or unconsciously, to belong to the Kuki tribe and, as a result, no Kuki as such had been Scheduled in Manipur. Surprisingly, however, in Meghalaya, Assam and Mizoram, there are

Kukis[2] who have been included in the recognised list of Scheduled Tribes.

Despite the terminology 'Kuki' having not been scheduled listed in Manipur, the same is being employed for the purpose of this work, meaning thereby the people who claim to belong to the 'Chin', 'Kuki' and 'Mizo' groups.

---

2. Fourth Schedule Section 26(1) of the Amendments to the Constitution (Scheduled Tribes) Order, 1950 Part XIV for Manipur and Part XV for Meghalaya as amended under clause (b) of section 2 of the North-Eastern Areas (Re-organisation Act, 1971 and under the fifth Schedule Section 26(2) of the amendments to the Constitution (Scheduled Tribes) Union Territories Order 1951 as amended under clause (b) of Section 2 of the North-Eastern Areas (Re-organisation) Act, 1971, Part II- Mizoram.

CHAPTER 3

THE SETTING

I.

Manipur, a tiny state in North East India, has an area of approximately 8,628 Square Miles (22,346 Kms), out of which nearly 8,000 Sq. miles are covered with hills. It lies between latitudes 23°50' N, and longitudes 93°10' and 94°30'E. The State boundaries are : Nagaland by the North, North-Cachar hills and Cachar Districts of Assam by the West, Mizoram by the South and the Kabow valley and the Chin hills of Burma by the East - the international boundary being extended approximately by 352 Kilometres. The hill ranges of Manipur are the offshoots of the mighty Himalayas and these are comparatively younger in geological formation. The hill range in the East includes Saramity, Somrat,Kossom, Nupital, etc., while the range to the West includes Nung-jaitung, Kalanuga, Chak-ha, Nungba, Kanpur and Kaprulaimal and that to the North includes Kunhospars, Thumion, Mayangkhong, Laisiom and Sirohifara.

All the rivers in the valley have their sources in the hills lying to the North and North-East of the valley. The most important river is the Imphal river which is locally known as 'Imphal Turel'. The other rivers include the Iril, the Thoubal, the Nambul and the Nambol. All the rivers run from North to South except Khuga river, which runs from South to North into Loktak lake. In the Eastern hills, there are the Lokchao river which drains into the Kabow valley and a number of small streams which flow into the Yu river and thence into the Chindwin. The most important river in the hill areas is the Break which originates from Taphou area of Senapati District. The Loktak is the biggest natural lake situated in the Eastern part of India. It is located at Moirang in Bishnupur District.

Series of rolling ridges with varied undulations and clothed with forests are a picturesque sight to see in Manipur. The forest area falls into four distinct and well-defined zones, Viz., (a) Burma border, (b) Ukhrul pine forest, (c) Forest overlooking the valley and (d) Barak drainage forest.

Manipur enjoys more or less an equable climate, though due to different degree of elevations, some variation is noticed in various parts. Most of the places in the valley and also in the hills have cool and pleasant climate. The rainy season starts from June and lasts upto September, and the winter makes its presence felt from November to February. In fact, there is no distinctive hot season in some of the hill areas of Manipur. The state receives adequate amount of rainfall, but its distribution is higher in the hill area than in the valley. Imphal records 55.63" (approximately).

Regarding the existence of fauna, they include leopard and elephant in Jiribam sub-divisional forests. Jungle cats and wild pigs are commonly found here. Bears, sambars, deer (both spotted and barking) are found in some places. The world-famed rare species called Antlered-deer, locally known as 'SANGAI', is found in the wild sanctuary of Keibul Lampak at Loktak lake , now a National Park.

The rugged terrain of the State makes communication difficult with the rest of the country. Only Imphal- Dimapur road and a few other roads constructed recently have kept the life- line of communication throbbing in Manipur.

II.

In the days of Yore, many of the places of the North-East India were incommunicado with its mainland. But Roy Burman (1970 :21) writes :

> Manipur has a very old history, Arjun, the hero of the Mahabharata, is supposed to have fallen for Manipuri Princess, Chitrangada. In 1630, during the reign of Khagemba, Manipur was invaded by the Chinese. In 1714, Garib Nawas, the famous Manipuri King, ascended the throne. He adopted Vaishnavism as State religion. In 1763, the king of Manipur entered into treaty with the British for protection against Burma. But in the last decade of 19th Century, Manipur came under the rule of the British.

Manipur faced several acute political upheavals, even during the British rule. This had been due to multi-ethnic composition of its people. The Kukis are one of the dominating tribal groups in Manipur. There were Kuki uprisings before and during the World War I of which the Kuki war of Independence (1917-19) had far reaching consequences in the history of Manipur. Thus, Manipur was exposed to the outside world politically.

It is clear that the animistic tribal population and the so called other Hindu groups of people started occupying the valleys. Thus Hinduism slowly but surely penetrated into this region in a diluted form at different degrees. In course of time, the Bhakti cult came to Manipur through Assam and the people of Manipur were slowly drawn towards it. There are evidences to this effect (Constantine, 1981 : 55) :

> In 1704, the ruling prince Rongba embraced Vaishnavism through the influence of one Krishnacharya. This school of Vaishnavism centred1 around the Radha-Krishna Worship. During the reign of Charai Rongba's son, Pamheiba (Garib Niwaz), the Chaitanya Schools also devoted to Krishna, came to Manipur... They captured the imagination of Garib Niwaz who along with a number of his palace retinue and nobles, joined the Ramandi School, which became the state religion. However, the Vaishnavism by which the valley Hindus of Manipur order their lives today still looks upon Krishna and not Rama as Prime deity.

As a result, casteless social condition prevails in Manipur in which the Maitais have a distinctive role to play. The Meiteis claim as early settlers in the tract. Though the Muslims came from outside, slowly they found their wives from among the local women-folk and settled down there. Actually they were not treated as aliens. Ultimately, in course of time, Meitei religion struck its roots (Constantine, 1981 : 41) on this soil :

> Even so, the Meitei religion survived in the Sanamahi Worship, while the Manipuri language languished yielding place to Sanskrit and Bengali, because the bulk of the Brahmin community was originally Bengali and the source of Vaishnavism is in Nabadwip.

However, the World War II changed the geo-political situation of Manipur, Japanese bombed and the Indian National Army (INA) of Netaji appeared on the scene. Thus, with people's co-operation, INA was able to liberate Moirang (April, 1944) where the INA set up an intelligence head-quarters. Manipur came nearer to Pan-India politics with a bang. After Independence, this State gradually merged into the Indian Union, though there existed a little hesitation in the minds of a few people for some time in the matter of such a merger with the Indian Republic.

III.

The people of Manipur constitute varied ethnolinguistic traits, though e autochthones can be divided into only two broad categories, viz., (1) Naga group of tribes and (2) Chin- Kuki-Mizo group of tribes.

Table 2 : 1 below shows details of the recognised tweny nine tribes of Manipur with the population of each tribe shown against each :

TABLE 2:1

The Tribal Communities Inhabiting Manipur and their Population[1]

Sl.No	Name of Tribes.	1971 Population	1981 Population
1	2	3	4
1	Aimol	836	1,100
2	Anal	6,670	8,770
3	Angami	70	82
4	Any Mizo (LushaiTribes)	7,483	9,845
5	Chiru	2,785	3,664
6	Chothe	1,905	2,507
7	Gangte	6,307	8,298
8	Hmar	23,312	30,672
9	Kabui		
(i)	Puinei:		
(ii)	Rongmei:	40,257	52,966
10	Kacha Naga		
(i)	Zemei:		
(ii)	Liangmei:	13,026	17,138
11	Koirao	1,620	2,132
12	Koireng	458	603
13	Kom	6,550	8,618
14	Lamgang	2,622	3,450
15	Maram	4,539	5,972
16	Maring	9,825	12,927
17	Mao	33,379	43,917
18	Monsang	930	1,224
19	Moyon	1,360	1,989
20	Paite	24,755	32,570
21	Purum	N.A	N.A.
22	Ralte	154	203
23	Sema	3	5
24	Salhte	3	5
25	Simte	4,177	5,496
26	Tangkhul	57,851	76,115
27	Thadou	59,955	78,883
28	Vaiphei	12,347	16,245
29	Zou	10,060	13,236

The projected Figures for 1981 are made on the basis of average growth rate of State of Manipur. There may be minor variations from actual.

1. Directorate for Development of Tribals and Backward classes, Tribes of Manipur at a glance, 1981.

Table 2:1 shows their categorisation very clearly and it also indicates that the Naga group of tribes can be counted as Angami, Mao, Maram, Sema, Tangkhul, Kabui (Puinei, Rongmei), Kacha-Naga (Zemei, Liengmei), whereas Chin-Kuki-Mizo comprises Aimol, Anal, Mizo, Chiru, Chothe, Koirao, Gangte, Hmar, Koireng, Kom, Lamgang, Paite, Purum,Ralte, Mayon, Simte, Sukte, Thadou, Vaiphei and Zou. Of course, there are a few non-categorised tribes distributed at different parts of the state. They are Maring and Monsang. It may be said of the Marings that they are closely affined to the Lakhers (Pois) of Mizoram. Thus, altogether twenty nine tribes are scheduled in Manipur to merit constitutional benefits. It has been stated earlier that the hill areas of Manipur state covers 90 per cent of the total geographical area - the hill districts comprise of 20,089 Sq.Kms. and the valley districts comprise of 2,238 Sq. Kms.

For the purpose of analysis and convenience, hereafter the Chin-Kuki-Mizo groups would be referred to as 'Kuki' or 'Kukis'for individuals or groups.

Table 2:2 shows the number of each tribe to indicate as to what are the tribes that can be categorised as Major. Out of tweny nine Scheduled tribes in Manipur, only six tribes, namely, Thadou, Tangkhul, Kabui, Mao, Paite and Hmar, with a population of at least 20,000 could be categorised as Major tribes.

IV

Manipur was originally one district State which was later converted into a six district State. The districts were:

1. Manipur North
2. ManipurWest.
3. Manipur South
4. Tengnoupal.
5. Manipur East
6. Manipur Central.

Five of the above districts except Manipur Central District are hill districts. These districts were redesignated as follows :

1. Manipur North as Senapati District.
2. Manipur West as Tamenglog District.
3. Manipur South as Churachandpur District.
4. Manipur East as Ukhrul District.
5. Tengnoupal District as Chandel District.

Table 2.2

Table 2 : 2

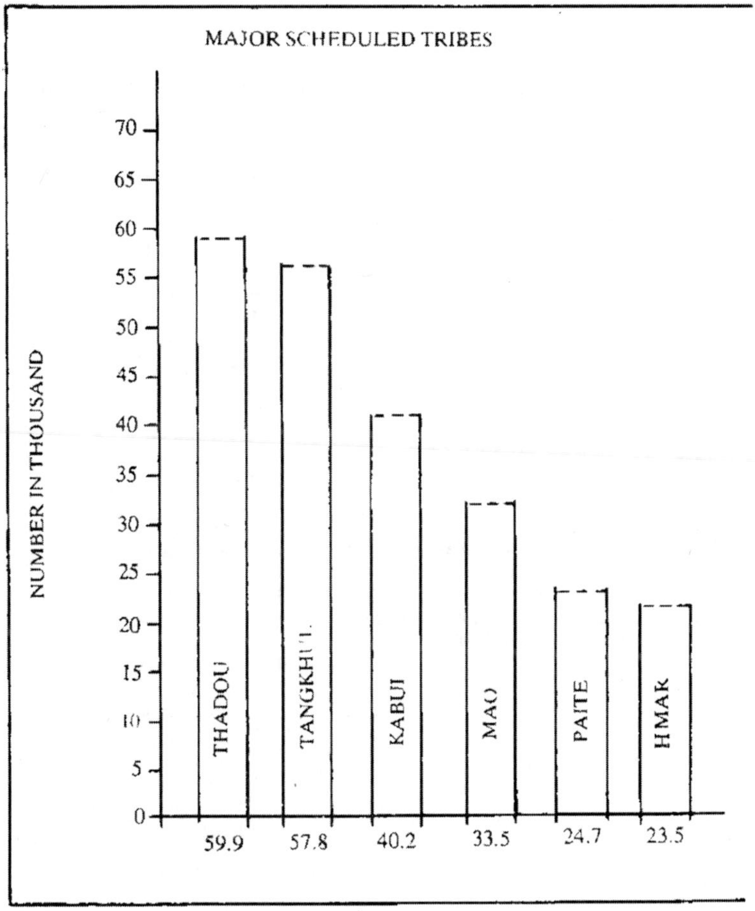

Along with this, the Central District was reorganised and bifurcated into three districts as follows thereby, increasing the number of districts from six to eight:

1. Imphal District.
2. Bishnupur District
3. Thoubal District.

The nature of distribution of the tribals is indicated in Table 3.1

TABLE 3.1

Territorial Distribution of Scheduled Tribe Communities In the Districts of Manipur

Sl.No.	Name of District.	Name of Communities.
1	2	3
1.	Manipur North (Redesignated as Senapati District.)	1. Mao (Major Group) 2. Maram (-do-) 3. Thadou Kuki (-do-) 4. Kabui (Minor Group) 5. Tangkhul (-do-) 6. Maring. 7. Chiru (-do-) 8. Kom (-do-) 9. Koirang (-do-) 10. Vaiphei (-do-) 11. KachaNaga (-do-) 12. Sema (-do-) 13. Keirao (-do-)
2.	Manipur West. (Redesignated as Tamenglong District.)	1. Kabui (Major Group) 2 Thadou Kuki (Minor Group) 3. Gangte (Minor Group)
3.	Manipur South (Redesignated as Churachandpur Dist.)	1. Hmar (Major Group) 2. Paite (-do-) 3. ThadouKuki (-do-) 4. Anal (Minor Group) 5. Chothe (-do-) 6. Kabui (-do-) 7. Kom (-do-) 8. Vaiphei (-do) 9. Zou (Minor Group) 10. Mizo (-do-) 11 .Gangte (-do-) 12. Simte (-do-) 13. Ralte (-do-) 14. Salte (-do-)
4.	Tengnoupal District. (Redesignated as Chandel District.)	1. Anal (MajorGroup) 2. Maring (-do-) 3. ThadouKuki (-do-)

(Contd....)

Sl.No.	Name of District.	Name of Communities.
1	2	3
		4. Lamkang (Minor Group) 5. Zou (-do-) 6. Gangte (-do-) 7. Moyon (-do-) 8. Monsang (-do-) 9. Aimol (-do-) 10. Chothe (-do-) 11. Purum (-do-) 12. Mizos (-do-) 13. Tangkhul (-do-) 14. Kom (-do-)
5.	Manipur Central : (Redesignated and bifurcated into three districts as follows: (i) Bishenpur District. (ii) Thoubal District. (iii) Imphal District.	1. Kabui (Major Group) 2. Representatives of most of the tribes are found in small number
6.	Manipur East : (Redesignated as Ukhrul District.)	1. Tangkhul (Major Group) 2. Thadou (Minor Group)

In spite of distribution and concentration of the tribes, in general, in specific areas, the question of 'alienation and alignment' (Bhowmick, 1989:31) is the major problem in Manipur. Some of them have Burmese affiliations and historical facts corroborate these views. Even their relationship, social connections, etc. are with tribes of Burma especially with those in Chin Hills State which is being inhabited by the 'Kukis' (Chin-Kuki-Mizo) and partly by the Nagas. The Kuki groups of tribe are broadly divided under two sections on the basis of their periods of arrival -(1) the old Kuki group, who came and settled earlier and (2) the New Kuki group, who came later and settled there. Some Kukis, as subsequent events showed, came from the jungles of Tippearah, South of Cachar, and some again came from Burma, the neighbouring country.

Table 3 :2 shows such division of the Kukis into Old and New based on the contention of Sakespear (1912) depending on their arrival.

TABLE 3 :2

Kuki Division on the Basis of Arrival

Old Kuki	New Kuki
Aimol, Anal, Chiru, Chothe, Gangte, Koirao, Koireng, Kom, Lamgang, Paite, Purum, Simte, Vaiphei, Zou, Hmar.	: Thadous (and their other Kin : groups, such as, Dongel, Misao, : Lupheng, Lupho, Ngoilu, Lamhao, : Thengeo, Touthang, etc.etc.which : are not in the list of recognised tribes).

The term 'Kuki' is generally used as a loose connection in this country. Das (1984 :6) says :

> The erstwhile Kuki tribes show their apathy to this term. Only among the Thadous it is used in the context of a larger political identity.

The Meiteis sometime call the Kukis as 'Khongjai'. Many scholars specially Shakespear (1912) used the term Old-Kuki and New Kuki. Now-a-days the blanket term 'Kuki' is not appreciated by many of the sub-groups, and as per recognised list of the Scheduled Tribes of Manipur, there is no tribe as 'KUKI' or 'NAGA',. In a broader sense, the Naga group and the Kuki group are the tribal substratum, and non-tribal entities are the Meiteis and the Muslims. Gradual historical processes of contact and acculturation contributed to the growth of Christianity in this region through conversion from these groups. Despite all these historical factors, conversion to Christianity and the new revival movement of the Meiteis, modern Manipur offers an ethno- centric problem which is not unknown to other parts of India also. The very word 'Mayang' is a term used by the local people to refer to the non-Manipuri people, which is equivalent to 'Diku' (Santal), meaning aliens or outsiders. Likewise, in Meghalaya the Khasis use the word, 'Dakhar',the Kukis in Manipur use 'Kol' and the Mizos in Mizoram use 'Vai' to mean non- indigeneous people. This feeling is dominant among the local people and it is expressed in more than one way when the tribals are in search of pin-pointing their identities for forming alignment or alienation to gain some political benefit.

V Spread of Christianity in Manipur

The tribals in Manipur were happy with their animistic faith and were slowly adjusting themselves with the nature and economy they pursued. But in course of time the Christian Missionaries made some in-roads into their existing faith. The advent of Christianity was an epoch-making event there. It made its way into Manipur through two gates viz., (a) the Silchar Gate and (b) the Aizewl Gate. Reverend William Pettigrew, an educationist, entered through the Silchar gate, and Watkin Roberts along with Dr. Peter Fraser, a medical man, entered Manipur via Aizawl.

(a) The Silchar Gate

The Arthington Mission began to function after the arrival of William Pettigrew in Manipur. This was named after Robert Arthington, a millionaire at leeds in U.K. (Goodwin, 1971 :55). The mission was purely a private organisation, and Arthington himself was the sole contributor to it. Thirteen missionaries entered India by the end of 1890 and Pettigrew was one of them (Laldena, 1985 :36).

The Mission for the aborigines by Arthington was not very keen about denominational affiliation of its missionaries, nor was it concerned about consolidating its ministry at one place. It preferred to withdraw from a place normally after three years when the foundation for the ministry was laid to continue its work. Revd. William Pettigrew was not alone at Silchar. He was assisted by Revd, P.W. Savidge and J.H.Lorraine from the Arthington Mission. They stayed at the residence of a Welsh Missionary at Silchar, Miss Laura Evans. It was here that Pettigrew came in contact with some Manipuris and learnt the way the British administration was conducted by the Political Agent in Manipur. He began to learn Manipuri language with the hope that some day he might be allowed to enter Manipur (Down, 1971 : 75-76). Not long after his colleagues, Savidge and Lorraine, secured the permission and left for Aizawl, Pettigrew also got his permission from the Acting Political Agent, M.A.Porteous, to enter Manipur. Thus, Pettigrew entered Imphal on 6th February, 1894, which later proved to be a Red-letter Day in the history of Manipur in so far as it relates to the establishment of the Christian Church. The missionary lost no time in setting up schools and starting its ministry. In this way, Pettigrew did the pioneering of the missionary work in Manipur through the Silchar-Gate'.

With the return of Major Maxwell, the Political Agent, from Furlough, the course of events changed. The orthodox Hindus started resenting the idea of the Government's allowing a Christian missionary to function freely. They suspected that the Government was trying to impose its religion upon the Meitei Hindus. At the same time, the manner in which the officiating Political Agent acted without consulting higher authorities was regarded as a deliberate attempt to impose Christianity in Manipur. Major Maxwell, therefore, instructed Pettigrew to quit Imphal or to go to hill areas and work among the tribals for his evengelical mission. The fact that generated suspicion among the Meitei Hindus was the liberal policy pursued by the Political Agent, Sir James Johnstone, who made arrangements for any Missionary willing to work among the people of the State. This led to the permission granted by Porteous

In February, 1896 Pettigrew moved to Ukhrul (Luikham, 1988:13) which was more than 40 miles on the Eastern side of Imphal, and resumed the work of his ministry. The Government granted him a plot of land known as *Phungyo* on which he built the Mission Bunglow. The first work Pettigrew took up was to establish a School, as he had done earlier in

Imphal. In fact, he was well-versed in Bengali and Manipuri languages and wrote the Manipuri Primer and Manipuri Grammar, Text-books in Manipuri and an English-Bengali-Manipuri Dictionary. Earlier, he had already established three schools in Imphal - (1) Thangmeiband L.P.School, which was subsequently changed to Pettigrew School, (2) the Tera-Keithel U.P.School and (3) Pettigrew School, Moirangkhom. By 1901, Pettigrew was able to baptise 30 believers in Christianity, which number grew to 70 in 1907 (Pettigrew, 1923:7). The first Baptist Church called the Phungyo Baptist Church was started in Ukhrul. Pettigrew was then made the Inspector of Schools by the Government in 1910-11, a position which enabled him to tour Manipur extensively.

(b) The Aizawl Gate

Thirteen years after Pettigrew arrived in Manipur, Mr. Watkin R. Roberts left England and sailed for India on October 14, 1908. Along with wife and Dr. Peter Fraser of the Welsh Mission he reached Aizawl, the then British outpost towards the end of the same year. Dr. Fraser, who came as Welsh Missionary took charge of the Medical Clinic and Mr. Roberts acted as a dispenser of medicine and a private helper of Dr. Fraser. While Pettigrew had started great work in the North and the East, the Southern part of Manipur remained uncovered. It was from Aizawl that Watkin Roberts heard about the area and explored the place for evangelization.

The above mentioned medical clinic became the centre of evangelical operations. Many people from far and near appeared there for treatment and the performance of the Missionaries was excellent. According to Rochunga Pudaite, Dr. Fraser during his first year attended twenty-four thousand patients. The Ministry also provided good opportunities to the natives to observe their life-style and thereby change their own.

Six months after the Missionaries reached Aizawl. Mr. W. Roberts received a gift of five pounds from a presbyterian Minister from Welsh in support of his work. With the money Roberts purchased a few copies of the Gospel of John in Lushai and sent those to all the ruling Chiefs of North Lushai Hills and the adjoining districts with a letter stating in brief the way to salvation. Those were sent through the callers at the clinic as there were no postal service in those days. At the relevant time two young men, named Thankai and Lungpau of Vaiphei tribe in Manipur reached Aizawl and met Watkin Roberts through one Dala to ask Roberts whether they could be taken as their students in the Hostel. The two youngmen also told Roberts that the people in Manipur South had never heard the Gospel and that no one had taken up any work in the areas. Roberts accepted the invitation and decided to take the journey to Manipur South, much against the advice of his friends at Aizawl. Towards the end of January, 1910, Roberts accompanied by a few Lushai Christians, e.g.Sawma, Taitea (Thangchhingpuia) and Vanzika, and the two natives from Manipur named Thangkai and Lungpau, left Aizawl for Manipur. The journey to Manipur was hazardous one and it took them about six days to reach Senvon from Aizawl. They passed through several villages and reached there on Saturday, the 5th February, 1910 (Laldana, 1985:9).

Having returned to Aizawl, the two natives joined the Hostel for studies, but the three students, namely, Savawm, Vanzika and Thangchingpuia, volunteered to go to the new land of Christianity and became the first national missionaries. Through the Ministry of these three Lushais, the area began to be exposed to Christianity and the number of followers soon multiplied. Watkin Roberts felt that the time was ripe for him to start a mission. Thus, he set up a mission organisation called the *Thadou Kuki Pioneer Mission*. Later, its name was changed to North-East India General Mission. Thus, Watkin Roberts became the second pioneer missionary through the Aizawl Gate.

Clashes took place between the Chiefs and some Christians who, under the guidance of Pettigrew, refused to follow the non- Christians. Under the circumstances, many back- slided to their former religion. However, some Tangkhul Christain leaders, like Honlei, Leishisan, M.K.Shimray, T.Luikham, Kuishon and Machonthei stood firm and remained faithful to Christianity. A.Porom Singh was the only Meitei Christian (Luikham, 1948:24-25).

In 1913, the missionary work was extended to other areas through the efforts of the students who were studying in Ukhrul School. R. Ruichumhao, a product of Pettigrew School, became the first Tangkhul who had his high school education at Jorhat. He even went to France to join the Labour Corps during the First World War. Ngulhao Thomsong was the first Kuki to become a Christian. He was a resident of Taning village in Nagaland before he came to Manipur in 1910. He wrote the first Thadou Kuki New Testament Bible which has a very high standard of literary flow that has not yet been surpassed. He also founded the first Kuki Baptist Church at Tujangvaichong village.

In 1912, nine Kuki students were baptised at Ukhrul Church. They became important leaders in the succeeding years. Among them only four are known. They were Teba Kilong, Longkhobel, Helkhup Kuki and Jamkithang (Luikham, 1948:27 & 51). According to Luikham, Nahseh was the first convert among the Thadou-Kukis in Manipur and through his efforts, Makui church, the oldest church in Manipur came into existence. While Aizawl was the operational base of the newly formed Thadou Kuki Pioneer Mission, Senvon gradually became its sub-centre where R.Dala was appointed as Field-in-charge in 1913 (Vaiphei, 1986 :27). From Senvon, Christianity continued to spread steadily not only in its surrounding villages, but also as far as Khawpibung, near Saikot in Manipur, where a school was opened at the instance of the local people. During those days, some Lushai Christians migrated to Tripura and the work there also began to progress with the first missionary, Thangkunga who was posted there in 1916. In the later part of the same year, Pastor Zabiaka was deputed as the Field Superintendent. After two years, H.K.Dohnuna replaced Zabiaka and put things in a more organised manner. The call to evanglise the Maru, Mogh and Chakma tribes in Chittagong Hill Tracts also came. Under these circumstances Roberts changed the name of the mission to North-East India General Mission.

In conclusion, and in retrospect, it may be stated that today the things that had happened, and are happening are incredibly true. If any religion can play a vital role in changing the life-style of a society, it is the Christianity and its mission that have effected this miraculous change among the Kukis in Manipur.

VI

Attempts have been made in this dissertation to describe the core social and economic institutions of the Kuki life. Examples have been cited from many villages, out of which eight particular villages have been chosen for case study. The villages are as follows :

Songgel Village is situated at the foot-hill of a small hillock, a few Kilometres away from Churachandpur town by the side of the Imphal-Churachandpur Highway. To go to this village, there is a non-metalled road and the road is lined up with rows of shady trees, besides small bushes and shrubs. From the main road of the village there are some feeder lanes and bye-lanes. Semi-pucca houses are located on both sides of the main road. At the middle of the village there is a big playground around which some huts have sprung up. Behind these huts there lie sprawling cultivable lands. There are two rivulets and a church, but the rivulets are almost dry during dry season. Existence of a school in the village for the children is a sure sign of the increasing rate of literacy in the village. The village has only fifteen households. Some villagers of Molnom village, a nearby big village, have migrated long ago, as it could not keep up the growing population there. The villagers of Songgel and Molnom villages are of Lhungdim Kuki, who are otherwise also known as Tungdim among the

Zou Kukis. The second village is Lhangjol which is situated on the same district of Churachandpur on a hill-top that over looks the town of Churachandpur. Here, Haokip Thadou Kukis are the only inhabitants of the village. They have only thirteen households here. The third village is Bethel which is situated in the same region. The only communicating road to this village through is mud built lane, the main road being Imphal-Churachandpur state highway. There are fifty four households, most of which belong to the Singson Thadou Kuki mixed with Hmar Kuki. Bethel is part of Molnom village. It was established by the Chief of Senvon when he was driven away from his village, in the interior hills, during the Thadou-Hmar inter- tribal feud in the late 50s. The fourth village is Chiengkonpang which is located in the identical region and within the Municipality area of Churachandpur town. There are 51 households. A church, a school, a playground, etc. are the important features of the village. The village belongs to a Gangte Chief with Haokip, Paite, Simte, Meitei communities as his villagers in addition to the dominant Gangte villagers.

All these villages have regular connections with Churachandpur town which caters to the day-to-day needs of the villagers.

Seloi is located about a furlong away from the Dimapur- Manipur National Highway in the Senapati District of Manipur. It is a village inhabited dominantly by the Kipgen Thadou Kukis. As for Motbung, it is a village located on the Dimapur-Manipur, 39 National Highway. The village belongs to the Sitlhou Thadou Kukis mingled with other collateral Kin groups, such as, Misao, Singson, Chongloi, Hangsing, etc. The village has a church, a Government M.E. School, a Government High School and one Government College and also a big playground. It is a fast growing urbanised village with a police out-post in the village. There are large number of villagers of which thirty three households have been selected for sample survey and study.

Khengjang is the seventh village. It is located in the Senapati District and is 2/3 Kilometres from the Dimapur-Manipur National Highway. The chief and most of the villagers are of the Chongloi Kukis, a collateral Kin group of the Thadou Kukis. A small stream outside the village at its entrance flows which blocks passages during rainy season to go to the National Highway. It is located at the foot-hill slope connected with the National Highway by a kutcha village bridle path.

Gelbung, the eighth village, is located about one and a half miles away from the Manipur-Dimapur National Highway in the Senapati District, and is of Haokip Thadou Kuki village. The Chief and most of the villagers belong to the Haokip Thadou belonging to the Songthat family. There are fifteen households in the village. The village has a church and a playground. There are other nearby villages belonging to the collaterals of the Chief of the village. Such villages are Songlung, Saitu, Motjang, Sipijang, etc.

Thus, the villages have constant social and economic mix-up with the urban life. Naturally, therefore, the urban influences have moulded their style of life, in varied degrees. The population structure with age-group distribution, marital status and family-size can be visualised out of the eight sample villages. From this we can project the general demographic condition of the Kukis.

TABLE 3.3

Population Distribution as Per Age-group and Sex

Village with No. of families : Total :	Age Group 0-14 : M	F	15 – 30 M	F	31 – 45 M	F	46 – 60 M	F	61 – Up M	F	Total
Songgel (15)	18	21	14	9	8	15	6	1	2	2	96
Lhangjol (13)	7	20	21	15	8	5	3	2	1	1	83
Bethel (54)	47	68	53	57	29	25	14	7	4	6	310
Cheingkonpang(51)	93	87	60	58	34	31	18	15	9	6	411
Seloi (25)	32	20	22	22	8	15	10	3	8	3	143
Motbung.(33)	40	30	25	38	28	10	13	10	3	2	199
Khengjang (30)	45	25	28	40	25	30	5	6	2	3	209
Gelbung (15)	15	19	22	18	10	10	9	5	5	3	116
Total : (236)											1,567

These villages are located in Churachandpur District and Senapati District, four villages belonging to each district. The villages are located in compact areas of each district, and can be considered as representative villages of different tribal groups among the Kukis.

These eight villages with 236 families are having a total population (Male & Female) of 1567. The villages are shown in the tables given below in alphabetical order which are to denote the villages hereafter as indicated against each:

Village A = Songgel Village E = Seloi

" B = Lhangjol " F = Motbung.

" C = Bethel " G = Khengjang.

" D = Cheingkonpang " H = Gelbung.

TABLE 3.4

Marital Status

Village	Population Total	M	F	Unmarried M	Unmarried F	Married M	Married F	Widowed M	Widowed F	Divorced M	Divorced F
1	2	3	4	5	6	7	8	9	10	11	12
1. Songgel	96	34	30	14	17	X	X	X	1	X	X
2. Lhangjol	83	24	26	16	16	X	1	X	X	X	X
3. Bethel	310	83	92	60	60	4	8	X	3	X	X
4. Cheingkonpang	411	142	116	70	70	2	11	X	X	X	X
5. Seloi	143	47	40	32	22	1	1	X	X	X	X
6. Motbung.	199	54	42	54	46	1	2	X	X	X	X
7. Khengjang	209	55	45	50	58	X	X	X	1	X	X
8. Gelbung	116	25	27	36	28	X	X	X	X	X	X
Total :	1,567	484	418	332	317	8	23	-	5	-	-

TABLE 3 :5

Literacy Level

District	Village	Population Total	M	F	Illiterate M	Illiterate F	Literate Primary M	Primary F	Seco-dary M	Seco-dary F	Univer-sity. M	Univer-sity. F
1		2	3	4	5	6	7	8	9	10	11	12	13
	Song-gel	96	48	48	12	27	28	18	8	3	X	X
	Lhangjol	83	40	43	10	28	17	14	10	1	3	X
Chura-	Bethel	310	147	163	50	68	38	62	41	28	18	5
chandpur	Chang-konpang.	411	214	197	88	126	65	49	39	22	22	X
	Seloi	143	80	63	46	44	11	10	23	9	X	X
	Motbung.	199	109	90	25	22	42	26	37	42	5	X
Senapati	Kheng-jung.	209	105	104	42	45	49	45	14	14	X	X
	Gelbung	116	61	55	39	31	19	24	3	X	X	X
Total :		1567	804	763	312	391	269	248	175	119	48	5
Total (M + F) :			1567		703		517		294		53	
Percentage :					44.86 %		32.99%		18.76%		3.38%	

Table 3 :5 reflects literacy level of the people of the eight villages. It is recorded that out of the total of 1567 people in all the age-groups, 703 (Male 312 & Female. 391) i.e. 44.86per cent; are illiterate. Primary level of education during survey was recorded as 517 (Male.269 & Female.248) i.e. 32.99 per cent; higher education in the form of secondary level 294(Male.175 & Female.119) i.e.18.76 per cent and University education recorded 53 persons (Male.48 & Female.5) i.e. 3.38 per cent only. Thus, the total literacy rate at the time of the survey was recorded at 24.76 per cent as against all Manipur general literacy rate of 41.52 per cent and that of India at 36.23 per cent with tribal literacy percentage of 16.35 per cent.

The size of their family is also a very important aspect in demography or population structure. Families have already been categorised on the basis of members constituting into the following:

(i) Small-size family, having upto three members only;

(ii) Medium size family, having four to six members;

(iii) Large-size family, having seven to nine members;

(iv) Very Large-size family, having ten or more members.

TABLE 3.6

Family Size

Village	Small 1-3	Medium 4-6	Large 7-9	Very large 10- Up	Total
1. Songgel	3	6	4	2	15
2. Lhangjol	3	5	2	3	13
3. Bethel	10	26	14	4	54
4. Chiengkonpang	5	18	17	11	51
5. Seloi	5	10	5	5	25
6. Motbung	8	15	7	3	33
7. Khengjang	5	14	8	3	30
8. Gelbung.	3	5	4	3	15
Total	42	99	61	34	236

We can have a population structure of the people (though restricted to eight villages only), which can be taken as a generalised account. But in respect of their involvement in various economic pursuits, we can safely categories the entire population into three divisions. e.g., (1) labour force, (2) non- labour force and (3) working force, i.e. those who are found to be absorbed in various professions and who contribute to the joint income of the family. The labour force indicates persons within the age group of 15 to 60, i.e., those who are physically fit and mentally alert to work. The non-labour force indicates persons who are not supposed to work for economic gains, whereas the working force indicates persons who are actually found working. Involvement of non-labour force into working force indicates people's urgent need for earning or for supplementing their income to strengthen their economic background. Table 3 :7 indicates this aspect of the village life.

TABLE 3 . 7

Labour Force, Non-Labour Force and Working Force

District	Village	Total Population		Non-Labour Force 0-14		Non-Labour Force 61-Up		Labour Force 15-60		Working Force All Age Groups	
		M	F	M	F	M	F	M	F	M	F
1	2	3	4	5	6	7	8	9	10	11	12
	A	48	48	18	21	2	2	28	25	21	18
Chura-	B	48	35	7	20	1	1	32	22	21	11
chandpur	C	167	143	47	68	4	6	96	89	48	12
	D	214	197	93	87	9	6	112	104	69	32
	E	80	63	32	20	8	3	40	40	30	32
	F	109	88	40	30	3	2	66	58	46	44
Senapati	G	105	104	45	25	2	3	58	26	43	45
	H	61	55	15	19	5	3	41	33	31	28
Total:		832	795	297	290	34	26	473	447	309	222

It is a happy sign to see that the older group or the younger group has smaller part to play in economic activities. This indicates, more or less, their stable or self- sufficient economics.

VII

Manipur, as a whole, and the Kukis in particular, in micro-setting are very much influenced by its geophysical impact as well as their historical inevitability. The people here, with their traditional way of life, are adjusting themselves with many distinctive situations that faced them. After independence, changes in the landscape through construction of roadways and establishment of schools etc. have undoubtedly been drawing these traditional hill people towards spectacular changes. The spread of Christianity in its wake has brought more and more of education and all these taken together have been moulding the life-style and the world-view of the people which are found reflected in more than one way.

CHAPTER 4

INSTITUTIONS AND FORMALITIES

I. Introduction

In their society, a Kuki's life veers round three sets of relatives. In Socio-economics, political and religious spheres he moves through these sets of relatives. He is essentially guided by a set-pattern of etiquettes of institutionalised mechanism of social control which manifests itself in a structure from which he cannot deviate. Such relatives are framed on 'reciprocal' basis and 'self-reciprocal' nature. This is possible mainly because of the practice of marriage of mother's brother's daughter by way of preference. Strangely enough, a Kuki may travel far and wide, but he finds the same set of people and establishes himself firmly within the given institutionalised mechanism of relatives by extension of classification of relationship. One set of such relatives is purely the by-product of marriage which is of 'reciprocal' basis, having specific scope and narrow meaning. The persons included in its ambit cannot be taken lightly and ignored. Such relatives are called 'Tucha- Songgao'

When an ego marries the daughter or sister or aunt of a man he earns the relationship of his children and becomes the 'Tute' or 'Tuchas' of his in-laws, i.e.,their 'Pute' or maternal kin. Thus, the 'Pute' becomes automatically the 'Songgao' relatives to the ego and his children. These relationships can be further classified as 'Active' and 'Passive' relatives.

An ego's children and the ego himself are 'Tuchas' to his wife's parents, brother and brother's sons, if it is an MBD marriage. If it is not MBD marriage, an ego's children alone are 'Tuchas' to his wife's parents, brother and brother's sons. Likewise, the in-laws of the ego automatically become the 'Songgao' relatives of the latter. In other words, every man is a 'Tucha' and a 'Songgao' in his relationship with two sets of relatives, one set being that of his mother, wife and daughter- in-law's kin group, if it is MBD marriage and only wife's kin group, if not of MBD marriage and the other set being his own relatives of aunt, sister and daughter. The juxtaposition of an ego in regard to his dual relationship with his wife's brother, in case of non-MBD marriage, and with his mother's brother and sons, in case of MBD marriage, as 'Tucha' of the latter is one of 'Active' relationship on his part, while as 'Songgao' relative in his sister's or aunt's or daughter's husband's house is that of 'Passive' relative. 'Tuchas' are active relatives, in that, they are considered the right-hand men (Khut lekeng) of the ego. They have to do whatever work is there to be performed on behalf of the ego.

It may be noted here that father's sister's husband is not entitled to be in the list of 'Tuchas' though he belongs to the category. He is called 'Mahpa' or 'Makpa' which means brother-in-law. But his sons are the 'Tuchas'. It often happens that a sister's husband is used as a 'Tucha' who can substitute his sons. Whatever be the case, though officially the brother-in- law is not the 'Tucha', he is treated as part of the family and is closely associated in all matters connected with the 'Tuchas'. This is true only in the case of first generation of a MBD marriage. If it is a second generation MBD marriage the brother-in law is also very much a 'Tucha'.

The two sets of people - the 'Tucha' and the 'Songgao' relatives to an ego - are given in the Chart 4 : 1.

GENEALOGICAL CHART 4 : 1

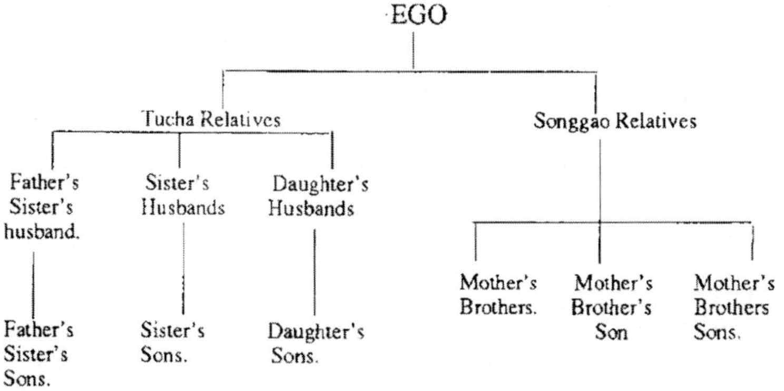

These sets of relatives may not necessarily live together or close by an ego. Under such circumstances, the ego finds out persons who can rêpresent the above sets of relatives and establishes himself within the orbit of such relatives by employing the extended classificatory relationship of 'Tucha' and 'Songgao'. He cannot, however, apply such terminologies at random as he pleases. He should find out a distant clansman of his 'Tucha' relative so that such a man can represent his own 'Tucha' relative in the absence of the latter by extension of the term. In return, the ego becomes 'Songgao' by the same process of extension of the relationship in regard to his new found 'Tucha' relative. Likewise, the ego also finds a person or persons of his 'Songgao' relative who is or are distant clansman or clansmen of his mother's brother, who can represent his own 'Songgao' relative to whom he will be the 'Tucha'. The same principle of extension of classificatory terminology is used here too. This 'Songgao' relative is as much important as it is with the finding out of 'Tucha' relative, in that the ego must have a complete circle of social obligation fulfilled on his part by performing his role of 'Tucha' in relation to his 'Songgao' relative.

As a corollary, the 'Tucha-Songgao' relationship may be well explained in terms of 'Patron-Client' relationship, though the principles of the two relationships are different. While 'Tucha-Songgao' relationship is purely based on blood connections, which expresses loyalty and solidarity of the blood relationship and mutual voluntary obligation, 'Patron-Client' relationship is based on economic consideration. It is also a fact that 'Tuch-Songgao' relationship is based on economic consideration, which is of community nature, but without profit motive, as against the motive of individual consideration in the 'Patron-Client' relationship. 'Tucha-Songgao' relationship is, in fact, a by product of matrimonial alliance and can have no other consideration whatsoever. Unlike this, 'Patron-Client' relationship is purely a product of economic benefit for both the client and the patron for a specific purpose. Thus, while 'Tucha-Songgao' relationship is of permanent and primary importance, manifesting social structure with certain social obligation, the 'Patron-Client' relationship is of temporary and secondary significance which comes to an end as the purpose for which such relationship is formed is accomplished.

There are certain specific duties and obligation assigned to the 'Tucha' relatives which are implied, if a person is in a position of 'Tucha' relation to an ego. In times of weal and woe, the 'Tucha' relative is supposed to stand by his 'Songgao' relative. If an ego has to perform a social, economic, religious or political duty, the 'Tucha' is to be found at his back and call to do all the essential services. Besides his detailed duties, there are certain very common duties of a 'Tucha' relative. If an ego kills an animal in compliance with his social obligation for throwing a feast, his 'Tucha' relative has to dress the meat. Such a duty of the 'Tucha' is called 'Sagil Sah' which term often substitutes the 'Tucha' terminology. The term colloqually means service of food to the guests, running errands, attending to sundry chores, cleaning of the utensils, setting the house in order and a host of other works. He is of course assisted by his wife and other female members of his household. The female 'Tucha' is responsible to draw water, serves Zu to the guests, cooks rice, lays tables for the feast, cleans the utensils and the house as also to assist her husband. The 'Tucha' and his wife are the last persons to leave the house of the ego or their Songgao relative after seeing that everything is in order after the occasion. Thus, a 'Tucha' relative is an 'Active' relative.

But the 'Songgao' relative of an ego is non-functionary and 'Passive'. He has restriction in his movement on an occasion of the ego who is his 'Tucha'. That apart, he gives wise counsel when consulted. He is a man to be served and cared for. He cannot drink and take food inside the house of the ego who is his 'Tucha' relative. His duties are abstract in so far as they relate to the ego. It is assumed that the presence of a 'Songgao' relative on any occasion of an ego, who is his 'Tucha', is associated with his blessings and, therefore, his duties are of notional kind. Normally, a 'Songgao' relative is supposed to be the pillar of dependence for the 'Tucha' relative. He is a man from whom the 'Tucha' relative is at liberty to receive or take anything he desires. The position of a 'Songgao' in relation to his 'Tucha' relative is nothing but to give. He is at the giving end and is a perennial source of supplying to his 'Tucha'. A 'Songgao' relative stands for the mother's brother or mother's brother's son or mother's brother's son's son. In a society where mother's brother's daughter's marriage is preferred, the 'Songgao' relative of an ego occupies a high position. So, it is considered below the dignity of a 'Songgao' relative to take food at the residence of his 'Tucha' on any social occasion. He is served with food, when necessary, outside the house. Though, according to social obligation his presence is necessary, he has no duty to perform. His only duty is to 'give' to his 'Tucha' relative within his means. The 'Songgao' relative thus stands on a unique position of a man who cannot enter into the house of his 'Tucha' relative.

II. Luongman

Coupled with the status accorded to a 'Songgao' relative, a right is also given to him. It is known as 'Luongman', which he can claim from his 'Tucha' relative as the price of the corpse in the event of death of the following :

(1) Mother of the ego ;

(2) Wife of the ego. This is so in the case of mother's brother's daughter's marriage;

(3) The sons of daughters ; and

(4) The sons of sisters.

'Luongman' is claimed in such a way that if the mother of an ego dies, the brother of the former claims the price of his sister's corpse from her son or husband who are his 'Tucha' relatives. This may also be done by the father of the ego's mother or son of the ego's mother's brother. In doing so, he kills a 'Mithun' as a token of expression of his grief, love and solidarity with his 'Tucha' relatives on the demise of his sister or daughter or aunt. This is termed as 'Kosa Na'. It is also called 'Sakeng Khai' or 'Luongman Bet Na'. This implies that the 'Songgao' relative of an ego can claim the corpse price of the latter's mother or wife. When the 'Songgao' relative does the 'Kosa Na', the 'Tucha' relative is bound to give the former one 'Mithun' to the latter as the price of the corpse, called 'Luongman;.

In case a woman does not have a son, the 'Songgao' relative cannot claim 'Luongman' from his 'Tucha' relative. Therefore, 'Luongman' signifies that a woman does great service to the family to which she is given in marriage by giving birth to a son or sons as thereby the genealogy of that family moves on and the generations of the male-line is spread further. In short, the woman saves the family from being extinct in the male line which is called 'Ingam'.

Similarly, on the death of the son of a 'Songgao's aunt or sister or daughter, 'Luongman' is claimed on the ground that the deceased has been given birth to the scions and that the line of the family descent moves on. If a 'Tucha' does not pay the price of the corpse or 'Luongman' to his 'Songgao' relative it is considered as an insult to the latter. It is, therefore, imperative that the 'Luongman' is paid, unless the 'Songgao' relative condones it at his discretion.

The details of duties assigned to the 'Tucha' relative of an ego are numerous. It depends on tne occasion and, as such, can best be described in the context of each such occasion when there are slight variations in his performance of the duties. It is abundantly clear now that one set-pattern of relationshin in a man's life based on reciprocal nature can be termed as 'Active' and 'Passive' relationships of 'Tucha-Songgao' which are further associated with certain rights and privileges in so far as the assigned duties and responsibilities are concerned.

III. Distribution of Meat

The value of food among the Kukis is not only for satisfying the hunger, but also to express their social obligations to their relatives-in-law, their Chiefs and to show their hospitality (Firth 1958 : 64-66) based on the principle of reciprocity.

The rights and privileges of a 'Tucha' cannot be described in detail, but these can best be explained in the context of each occasion. Nevertheless, there are certain common rights and privileges which are enjoyed by a 'Tucha' on all occasions. The Kuki life is hinged on a pattern of community living, sharing almost everything essential pertaining to economic, social, political and the religious life. Therefore, in every aspect of their life their social structure is manifested in various ways. In case a man performs a social occasion in which he has to kill an animal for feast, or even when he kills a wild game, there are certain form of distribution of its flesh by which the different parts of the kill are set apart for certain categories of relatives of the performer. In all such cases, the particular portion to be given to the 'Tucha' relative of a man is earmarked by custom.

The 'Tucha' relative of an ego is always given the waist part of the animal killed on an occasion. It is believed that a man is born out of the waist of the daughter or sister or aunt in the family of the ego. In signifying this fact, and as the 'Tucha' is born of a woman from the family of the ego, the former is always given the waist portion of the slaughtered animal. It is termed as 'Konglo Sa', meaning a reward of the labour of the waist of the woman. It further means that it is the meat of the man who earns the waist of the woman of the family. The Kukis had the custom that if a man wanted to marry a girl, he had to win her hand by working or labouring in the house of the parents of the girl for a period of three to seven years. This is called 'Konglo', i.e., earning the waist of the woman. It may, therefore, be said that earmarking of the waist portion of the animal killed by an ego for his 'Tucha' relative or relatives is in reminiscence of such custom that a man has to labour in order to marry a girl. It may be noted here that this system still prevails among the Kuki tribes of Anal, Moyon, etc.

Usually, a man has many 'Tucha' relatives. For the purpose of social occasion, however, there are only two official 'Tucha' relatives. These two 'Tucha' relatives are the only people who are entitled to get the waist portion of the meat. These two 'Tucha' relatives are again further graded as senior called 'Tuchabul' or 'Tubul' and junior 'Tucha'. The waist portion of the meat is thus divided into two halves, one portion bearing the tail signifies slightly bigger than the other. The bigger portion is given to the 'Tubul', the senior of the two, and the other half goes to the junior 'Tucha'.

Similarly, the neck portion, 'sangong', of the animal killed falls in the share of the mother's brother or mother's father, or mother's brother's son (eldest) who are all 'Songgao' relatives to the ego. It is an expression of recognition of the source of life of the family of the ego. It is believed that because of the woman of the 'Songgao' family, the family of the ego came into being. It is explained much in the same way that just as the neck is the source of survival of an animal due to its joining the body and the head of the animal, the maternal kinsman or mother's brother is considered as the life-giver of the family of the ego because of the woman of the 'Songgao' family. It is therefore, deemed fit and proper that the 'Songgao' being the life-giving source is given the neck portion of the animal. Thus, the manner of distribution of meat to different kinds of relatives is an expression of social structure, and meaningful relationship with the ego.

IV. Becha

As has been stated earlier, the set-pattern of relationship of a man without whom a Kuki is unable to survive, there is another set of relatives complementary to 'Reciprocal' relatives are the 'Self-Reciprocal' relatives of the ego. They are called 'Becha' relatives. This set of relatives of an ego may be termed as representative in nature who have been vested with the full power and authority of an ego. Therefore, the 'Becha' relative stands at a very commanding position of authority, being the spokesman of the ego, and is considered to be the ego himself.

The term 'Becha', in contrast to 'Tucha' and 'Songgao' terms of relationship, is nct necessarily a product of marriage alliance. The term has a wider implication and an elasticity in definition. The 'Becha' relatives are basically exogamous or collateral male relatives of an ego. By extension of the terminology it can include a wide range of people, including good and reliable friends of non-consanguinal relatives. The 'Becha' relatives, therefore, include the following categories of persons:-

(1) Male members of an exogamous relatives ;

(2) Male members of the same clan of the ego, except those of 'Tuchas' and 'Bechas';

(3) Close, reliable and bosom friends of an ego ;

(4) Persons of ability who can efficiently shoulder the respon - sibilities associated with the 'Becha' relatives to act on behalf of the ego.

Thus, the range of being a 'Becha' relative is very elastic. A person whom an ego considers good and who can go along with him and can stand by him in times of joy and sorrow, may be chosen as a 'Becha' relative. Secondly, a man of wisdom, versed in customary laws and traditions, and also expert in interpreting culture and social values, may be so selected. This last relative is to act and speak on behalf of an ego, as if he is the ego himself, and is, therefore, regarded as the representative of the ego when discharging the social, economic, religious or political obligations. The 'Becha' is the spokesman of the ego on a self-reciprocal basis and is the administrator with his full authority to exercise discretion on behalf of the ego. These are, in a nutshell, the duties and powers of a 'Becha' relative. But there cannot be only one 'Becha' relative of an ego. There are several 'Bechas' in the same manner as the 'Tucha' relatives. Customarily, there are only two kinds of 'Bechas' who represent the whole 'Becha' relatives of an ego. Of these two, one is senior, named 'Becha Bul' or 'Bebul' and the other is junior called only 'Becha'.

In addition to the prerogatives enjoyed while officiating as a Becha to an ego, there are certain duties he has to perform. On a social occasion, in happiness or in sorrow, the 'Bechas' are expected to dress the meat of the animal killed. He is also to arrange for the distribution of the meat to different categories of relatives and furnish crockery and utensils. Killing of the animal for the occasion is also done by the Bechas'. A 'Becha' speaks whatever is to be spoken by the ego and deals with delicate matters. He is the de-jure performer of the social obligations.

Along with such duties and responsibilities, certain rights and privileges are associated with the 'Becha' relative. As has been stated earlier, while a 'Tucha' relative is in active involvement, the 'Songgao' relative is in abstract and passive form, and a 'Becha' relative is absolutely committed to a commanding authority with active participation. As in the case of the former two relatives, a 'Becha' relative is also entitled to a portion of the kill for an occasion which reflects his standing in the society.

The rib portion of the kill called 'Anah' is in close physical proximity to the heart. A 'Becha' relative being the replica of the ego is given the 'rib' portion. The ribs and the chest are divided into two chunks and are given to the two official 'Bechas', the right portion being given to the senior 'Becha' called 'Becha Bul' or 'Bebul' and the left portion to the junior 'Becha'. If, however, there are more than two official 'Bechas', the left portion of the 'Anah' is further divided and distributed among all the 'Bechas', junior to the 'Bebul'.

V. Patterned Norms :

The three sets of relatives known as 'Tucha', 'Songgao' and 'Becha' have thus, come to stay in the Kuki society as an indispensable part of their social life in an institutionalised form. Though there are some set-pattern norms for these different sorts of relatives with regard to performing their duties, there are slight variations in the details of such assignments on different occasions. A few examples of such variations are briefly narrated below.

At the time of death of a person in the family of an ego, the 'Tucha' of the family is to act as messanger to inform about the death to all the relatives and well-wishers. On his return, he is to perform an act of 'Kitom', i.e., a show of valour challenging the unseen being supposed to be responsible for the demise of the deceased. In doing so, the 'Tucha' takes a Scythe (Dao) or an axe and cuts a pillar of the house or the frame of the doors etc. by way of challenging the unseen spirit. Likewise, it is the 'Tucha' relative who goes for selection of burial ground with the 'Thiempu'. This is called 'Lhanchan'. Digging of the grave is also not started until the 'Tucha' first digs the ground symbolically. This 'Tucha' cannot enter the house of the deceased until the deceased is buried. The 'Tucha' is in duty bound to cleanse the grave with a torch of fire before the burial.

The act of 'Kitom' on the part of the 'Tucha' who goes to convey the sad news is an act of solidarity, love, affection and loyalty towards the members of the family of the deceased. Such act is supposed to be a substitute for crying. The Kukis consider it below their dignity for a man to cry. Thus, instead of crying, the 'Tucha' does the 'Kitom'. If he does not know how to perform 'Kitom', he is taught how to do so, for it is a compulsory duty of the 'Tucha' relative.

Likewise, the 'Becha' has some variation in his duties on one occasion or another. Generally, a 'Becha' has to slaughter an animal for the occasion of any kind. But in case it is connected with the rites of a religious occasion, the animal is not killed by 'Becha', it is killed by the 'Thiempu', a village priest.

The institutionalisation of Tucha-Songgao relatives as a set-pattern of social behaviour is the manifestation of the degree of importance between the mother's brother and the sister's son. The indispensability of a 'Tucha' in a man's life shows that the sister's son is always the pivotal point of interest and concern for the mother's brother. The 'Tucha-Songgao' relationship may be better understood if a little more detailed discussion of the role of mother's brother is made.

It may so happen that a man lives among the people with whom he has no direct or close connection, but truly they are his 'Tuchas', 'Songgaos' or 'Bechas'. Under such circumstances, the man somehow forges these three sets of relationship by the mechanism of extension of the classificatory terminologies. As stated above, in a man's life these three sets of relatives are intertwined that without them a Kuki is unable to face the reality of life. A Kuki establishes his 'Tucha' relationship with someone whose relatives, near or distant, have married women from his own family or from that of a distant collatoral kinsman. By such relationship, the man or men he thus finds become his 'Tucha' and, in turn , automatically he becomes a 'Songgao' relative of such a 'Tucha'. In the same way, he finds out someone whose female relatives, distant or near, have been taken as wives by some of his distant or near relatives or kinsmen. Such men become his 'Songgao' relatives and he becomes their 'Tucha' reciprocally. In the case of 'Becha' relatives, however, the man need not establish such relationship as it is not necessarily the offshoot of marriage. A man can use anyone on whom he has confidence and close personal good relationship, by the mechanism of extension of the classificatory terminology of 'Becha', which literally stands for any collateral male relatives within the fold of exogamous group. For a better understanding, a genealogical chart of Tucha - Songgao relationship is in Chart 4 :2

GENEALOGICAL CHART 4 : 2

TUCHA-SONGGAO RELATIONSHIP

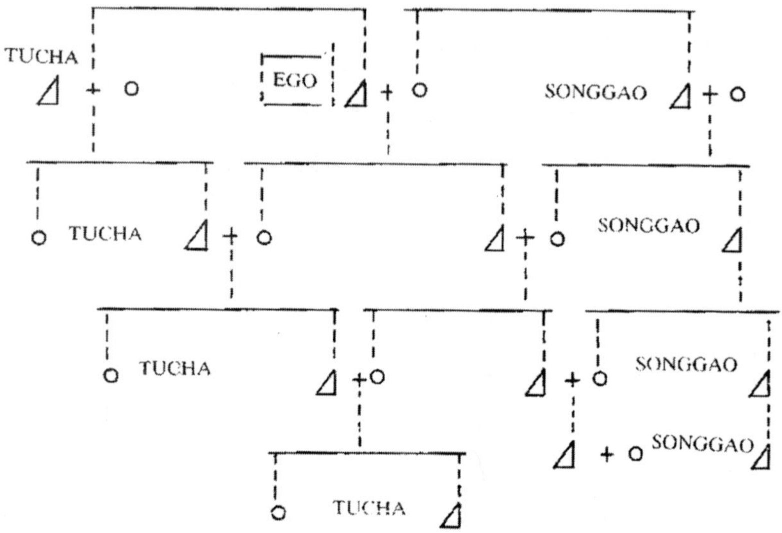

In their work on the African systems of kinship and marriage, Radcliff Brown and Forde (1950 : 62) aptly said :

> ...... that the raison d'etre of an institution or custom is to be found in its social function. The theory is, therefore, that the rules or customs relating to prohibited or preferred marriages have for their social function to preserve, maintain, or continue an existing Kinship structure as a system of institutional relations.

From genealogical chart 4 : 2, it can be clearly seen that all the relatives of an ego, who take wives from him, are 'Tuchas'. Likewise, the set of relations from whom the ego, his sons and grandsons, receive their wives belong to the same family. They are 'Songgao' relatives to the ego and his family. The pattern of genealogical tree and continuity of their relationship with the same set of relatives of 'Tucha' and 'Songgao' are possible due to the prevalence of preferential type of marriage to mother's brother's daughter, who is known as 'Neinu'. However, even in the case of Non-MBD marriage, the two sets of relatives, 'Tucha' and 'Songgao' relationship still exists for a generation or so depending on how long the mother's brother's daughter's marriage is pursued by the family of the ego. With the discontinuance of the system of maternal uncle's daughter's marriage, the 'Songgao' relative of the ego changes. By this it may be assumed that while the father of the ego practised mother's brother's daughter's marriage, the ego has taken his wife elsewhere without continuance of the mother's brother's daughter's marriage. Under the circumstances, the 'Songgao' relatives from his father upto the point of the ego remain the same, for the grandmother and the mother of the ego hail from the same family and that there continues to exist mother's brother and sister's son relationship. Therefore, the 'Tucha-Songgao' relationship of the same set of relatives has to survive so long as the ego lives. After the death of the ego, however, his mother's brother does not have any place in the network of relationship of his sister's son's family. Such relationship is known as 'Tutop' or the end of uterine nephew or grandnephew. The children of the ego will now have their own 'Songgao' relatives different from their father. Thus, it is observed that so long as there is continuity in the relationship of 'Tucha', there are always living 'Songgao' relatives within the ambit of an ego. Such relationship binds the two sets of people very closely to each other. It is mainly focussed on the relationship between the mother's brother and the sister's son whose relationships are based on indulgence, love and affection. Chart 4 : 3 shows changes in 'Songgao' relatives :-

CHART 4 : 3

CHANGE OF SONGGAO RELATIVES DUE TO DEVIATION FROM MOTHER'S BROTHER'S DAUGHTER'S MARRIAGE

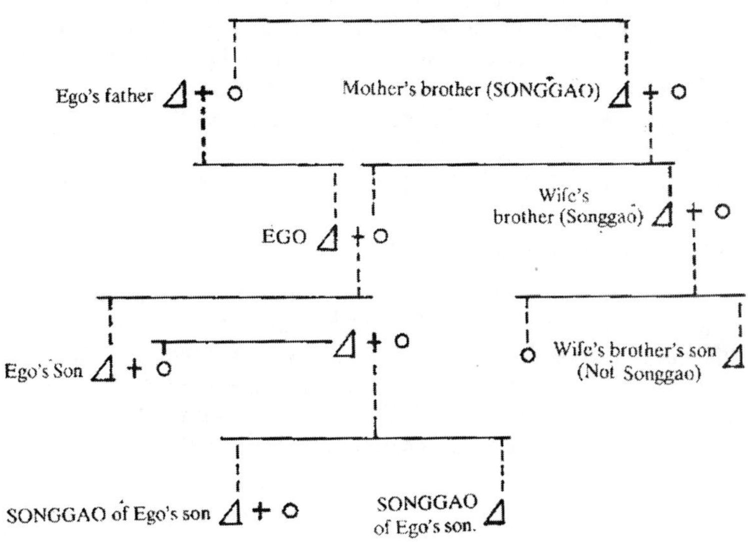

From genealogical chart 4:3, it is observed that so long as the mother's brother's daughter's marriage is adopted, the line of 'Songgao' relative continues to be on a single family.

Till such time as the ego's father follows the rule of mother's brother's daughter's marriage; and the ego follows suit, the 'Songgao' relatives are ego's mother's brother and wife's brother. As the ego's son married outside his 'Songgao' relatives' daughter, the line of 'Songgao' relatives snaps. Since the ego's son is the son of his 'Songgao's sister, the former continues to be the 'Tucha' relatives of his mother's brother and commands usual love and affection as he would have otherwise been bestowed but for his non-MBD marriage due to non-availability of marriageable age-group between the ego's son and his 'NEINU'. The sanguinary relationship between the ego's son and the ego's wife's brother still persists. Marriage deviation only makes continuation of relationship between the children of the ego's son and the grand-children of ego's wife's brother and sister's sons or the ego's wife's brother impossible. But the relationship between the mother's brother and sister's sons or the ego's wife's brother and ego's son continues till the death of the ego's son. It cannot simply be abgroagated because of the marriage deviation. The death of ego's son puts an end to their 'Tucha-Songgao' relationship. With the death of the ego's son, a new set of 'Songgao' relatives comes into the family of the children of the ego.

In this connection, it may be mentioned here that, to a large extent, the mother's brother cares for the well-being and prosperity of his sister's son. The maternal uncle does not eat meat during social occasions inside the house of his sister's son, and does not take cucumber and green pumpkins at the residence of his sister's son. It is said that if he does so, his sister's son will have a bad health. Even after exhibiting so much care, affection and love for his nephew, he subjects himself to greater restrictions or taboos for fear of bringing mischance upon his sister's son.

VI Mother's Brother

Great importance is attached to the relationship of the mother's brother and the sister's son in the Kuki society. This has significance in view of the practice of preferential marriage of mother's brother's daughter. This system gives the sister's son certain special rights over mother's brother's daughter known as his 'Neinu'. The relationship between mother's brother and sister's son may be described as follows :

(1) Sister's son (Uterine nephew) is the object of special attention on the part of his mother's brother (Maternal uncle.)

(2) As a prospective son-in-law, the sister's son is at liberty to do or take anything he likes, including taking food as he pleases in the house of his mother's brother who gives unlimited indulgence to him.

(3) Sister's son has a rightful claim on the daughter of mother's brother, his 'Neinu'.

(4) Mother's brother has an obligation on his sister's son about giving marriage of his daughter to him.

(5) Sister's son is bound by custom to marry mother's brother's daughter. In case he fails to do so, he forfeits all his rightful claims from his mother's brother and all the indulgence he is entitled to. He is then fined to give one 'Mithun' to his mother's brother.

(6) Mother's brother is bound to give his daughter to his sister's son in marriage. If he fails to do so, he forfeits all the respect he commands from his sister's son, but the fine of one 'Mithun' is not imposed, as in the case his sister's son.

To understand the relationship and role of the mother's brother with that of sister's son, it is pertinent to dwell on the position and relationship with the father's sister. An aspect of relationship cannot be studied in isolation. Father's sister, being a relative over all relatives, is the one to be revered and obeyed. But, conversely, the position of mother's brother is diametrically opposite. Of all the relatives, it is from the mother's brother that the greatest indulgence and affection are expected and liberties taken. It may be assumed that division into segments through bilateral kinships is due to relationship through one's father on the one side and mother on the other. The extent of obedience and respect shown to one's father, is also shown to his sister. Similarly, a mother is regarded as the symbol of equal love and affection with unlimited degree of indulgence by her children and is always considered as a refuge to the children. The same kind of relationship is developed towards one's mother's brother. Therefore, mother's brother is a personage who occupies a place of great importance in one's life. Thus, a very high honorific terminology called 'Hepu' is enduringly used for him. In the same way, the fondest of kinship term 'Tu' is employed for any kind of relationship with the grandchildren who are one's sister's sons. Etymologically, the term 'TUCHA' is derived from the kinship term 'TU' meaning thereby, grandchild.

One very glaring example of honour and affection shown to one's mother's brother is manifested in the use not only of the term 'Hepu' to all the members of the family of his relatives, but also to his remotest distant relatives. A tendency to extend certain types of behaviour to all the members of a group, which has its origin in a relationship to one particular member of the group, is also noticeable. For example, if a Gangte-man marries a Sitlhou-woman, the Singson, Haokip, Kipgen etc. who are called together by the name of their progeniter - 'Thadou' along with the Sitlhous are also his 'Songgao' relatives. It may so happen that the Gangte-man and his family lived at one stage among the Thadous in an area predominantly inhabited by the Haokip, Kipgen and Singson, the collateral relatives of the Sitlhou. The man, out of courtesy to the distant relatives of his wife, asks his children to call the Singson, Haokip and Kipgen neighbours as 'Hepu', meaning maternal uncle. In fact, the most emotional part of it is that every one addressed as 'Hepu' by the children of the man, in return, reciprocates with affection and love from them, considering the children as his own 'Tute' or grandchildren. So, the tendency is that the same pattern of behaviour towards one of the mother's family is expected to be shown to all her group, in consideration of the special pattern that manifests itself in the behaviour of a son towards his mother.

In other words, it is mainly from the mother that a son expects care and indulgence. So, he expects to get the same sort of treatment not only from his mother's brother but also from all his maternal kinsmen. As against this, it is to his paternal kins-group that he owes obeisance and respect. Thus, the patterns of relationship which originate from his kinship with his mother and father are generalised and are also extended to the kindred people on both sides.

Mother's brother, who is one's 'Songgao' relative, to the sister's son, plays an important part in a great many ways. The characteristic nature of a 'Passive' relative manifests itself in the 'Songgao' relative. On the other hand, the nature of an 'Active' relative on the part of the 'Tucha' (his sister's son) is commensurate with the type of relationship of the 'Tucha' towards his 'Pute' (Maternal kinsmen), with much liberty and indulgence from the latter.

VII Categories of Relationships :

The terms 'Tucha', 'Songgao' and 'Becha' are not connected with kinships. They are terms by which different categories of relatives are identified and grouped. 'Tucha' is used to denote how a man stands in relationship with his sister's husband and her children as also other close relatives of her husband's kin- group. If a man is a 'Tucha' relative to an ego, it indicates that he has married a woman from the exogamous group of the latter. Through such marriage, the children of a 'Tucha' also are on the same footing with him in relation to the Man's wife's brother and his children. In case it is a mother's brother's daughter's marriage, the 'Tucha' relationship continues till the generation of the grandchildren. This 'Tucha' relationship can be extended to any other relatives of the 'Tucha' by the use of classificatory system of the term in the sense of kinship terminology. The actual kinship term of 'Tucha' relative is 'Hegang', meaning "the man who marries father's sister of the ego". The term 'Hegang' stands peculiarly conspicuous in its usage and implication. It is a term that does not exist by itself. Inasmuch as marriage is a process of changing continuity depending on the persons involved in such marriage, the kinship terminology for the person who marries one's father's sister, 'Hegang', also keeps on changing. There are no set groups who are categorised as 'Hegang' in the same manner as other kinship terminologies are. It is, therefore, said that 'Hegang' is an 'earned' terminology through connubial relationship. The term cannot be extended by classificatory system to denote other close relatives of the man who earns it. Thus, there can be no 'Hegang' kinship without a father's sister, being married to a man. In case of other terminologies, like 'Heno'(Mother), 'Hepa'(father), 'Hao' (elder brother or sister). 'Kanao' (younger brother or sister), 'Hepi' (grandmother), 'Hepu' (grandfather), etc., they can be used by extension of the mechanism of classificatory system.

The term 'Hepa' can be used to denote father's elder brother or younger brother also by suffixing the qualifying words 'lien' for the elder and 'neo' for the younger, as also to any distant relative of one's father's and father's brother's age group, or of the same generation of one's father. It may even be used as a courtesy shown to a non-relative who is of the same age group or generation of one's father. It may further be used to mean a man who has an identical name with one's father. When one says 'Hepa- lien', it signifies that the man is the elder brother of an ego's father, and 'Hepa-neo' means younger brother of the ego's father. The same is true with the term 'Heno'. But this term has a wider scope. It can be used to indicate the elder and the younger brother's wives of one's father. It can also be used for one's mother's brother's daughter with the suffix 'Ngah'. Thus, a combination of mother and virgin-girl is called 'Henongah'. This system of addressing one's mother and mother's brother's daughter by the same terminology, 'Heno' (Heno-Ngah' for mother's niece), is indicative of their social standing. Similar system of using the same terminology for mother and mother's brother's daughter is found among the Ronga, Shona, Nadu, Shangana-Tonga, etc. tribes of Africa (Redcliffe Brown, 1950 :35)

The term 'Heno' stands for mother and 'Ngah' stands for unmarried girl. The combination of 'Heno' and 'Ngah', therefore, makes mother and spinster, an unmarried mother. The spinster is assigned the same status as that of one's mother. None other than the unmarried daughters of one's maternal uncle are entitled to be called as 'Heno-ngah'. This is in contrast with the term used for the son of one's mother's brother who is addressed as 'Hepu'. This is used for one's grandfather and maternal uncle denoting that the person so addressed stands at par in their social order, one stage higher than the daughter of maternal uncle. Therefore, the term 'Hepu' is used for paternal grandfather, maternal grand- father, maternal uncle and mother's brother's son. Likewise, the wives of the above relatives are addressed as 'Hepi'. This signifies that the social status accorded to the men is extended to the women by virtue of their being the wives, and not by virtue of her own merit. The term 'Hegang' however, can only be used for a man marrying one's aunt after his marriage. So, it is an earned terminology. The social status of the woman being lower, the man cannot earn the status higher than 'Hegang', which is at par with 'Heni', the term used for aunt. He is nothing but a 'Tucha' relative to an ego who, in turn, is the 'Songgao' relative to the former.

The term 'Hepu' also means one's grandfather which can be employed by extension to one's maternal grandfather, maternal uncle and maternal uncle's sons. The nature of relationship between the grandfather and the grandchild is one of indulgence, banter and levity based on equality, love and affection. The attitude of the grandson towards his grandfather is free and independent. The same pattern of relationship exists between the maternal uncle and the sister's son, as also with the maternal uncle's wife.

Only by virtue of her being father's mother, or wife or mother's brother or wife of maternal uncle's son, the term 'Hepi' (counterpart of 'Hepu') is used merely as a complementary status. In a Kuki society, the status of a woman is lower than that of a man. In fact, a woman is not regarded as full member of the clan or family. The practice in this society is that a woman assumes the name of somebody's clan or inherit the title of her husband after marriage. This is called 'Miphung luo-ding'. In conformity with this concept, while the son of one's maternal uncle is addressed as 'Hepu' which equates him with the mother's brother, the daughter of the same uncle is addressed as 'Heno' which places her one rung lower than the son in the social ladder but equating her with one's own mother.

There are some set-pattern of social etiquettes by which show of respect and courtesy to older people are obligatory. A person older than an ego must be addressed with a qualifying terminology indicating that the former is shown respect and courtesy to his or her age. An ego, therefore, addresses a person elder than him by extension of the term 'Heo', even though not related, or 'Hepa', 'Heno', 'Hepi' or 'Hepu', depending upon the age. If a person older than an ego is of the age group or generation of one's parents, he or she is addressed by the same term applicable to one's father or mother. The same is true in respect of other terminologies, excepting of course 'Hegang' which cannot in any way be employed to anyone other than the person marrying one's aunt. Therefore, there are three sets of kinship terminologies used for persons elder than an ego, These are :-

I. SET ONE :

(HEPU) (grandfather) stands for	HEPI (Grandmother) stands for
(a) Paternal grandfather,	(a) Paternal grandmother,
(b) Maternal grandfather,	(b) Maternal grandmother
(c) Other's brother	(c) Mother's brother's wife.
(d) Mother's brother's son,	(d) Mother's brother's son's wife
(e) Mother's parallel cousin brother.	(e) Persons of grandmother's generation, or age-group,
(f) Mother's brother's son's parallel cousin brother.	(f) Mother's parallel cousin brother's wife.
(g) Persons of grandfather's generation or, age-group.	(g) Mother's parallel cousin brother's son's wife.
(h) Honorific term used to address person with respect (such as, Sir)	(h) Honorific term employed to denote a lady of repute with respect, (equivalent to Madam).

II. SET TWO :

HEPA (father) stands for :	HENO (mother) stands for :
(a) Father,	(a) Mother.
(b) Father's age-group,	(b) Mother's age-group.
(c) Father's elder brother (with suffix 'Lien')	(c) Mother's elder sister (with suffix 'Lien').
(d) Father's younger brother (with suffix 'Neo')	(d) Mother's younger sister (with suffix 'Neo')
(e) Father's parallel cousin brothers (both younger and elder)	(e) Mother's parallel cousin sisters (younger and elder).

III. SET THREE :

HEGANG (uncle: father's sister's husband)	HENI (aunt : father's sister):
The husband of 'Heni', father's sister. It is applied only to the husband of father's sister and that too, only after marriage. It cannot be used to denote any other person, and is, therefore, limited to the husband of one's father's sister only. It cannot be used as a classificatory terminology, being earned by a man only after his marriage.	Father's sister and by extension to all the clean women of one's exogamous group.

Another term that is being employed to denote both the elder brother and the elder sister is the terminology, 'Heo'. By extension, it is also used for any person who is senior or older in age, but does not have kinship with the ego to show respect to his age. Disrespect shown to one's senior without addressing as 'Heo' is considered unethical and ill-mannered. The term is also used for cousin brother and sister, both parallel and cross. In case there is an MBD marriage for two and more generations in a family, one's 'Hegang', in the non-MBD marriage, is addressed as 'Heo', brother, and not as uncle, 'Hegang'. Similarly, a daughter- in-law in a family where there is MBD marriage for more than two generations addresses her father-in-law and mother-in-law as 'Heo'.

The terminologies, 'Heno-ngah' and 'Hegang', have certain similarities, in that, they imply a limited sense and exclusive meaning. Nevertheless, the basic differences are more glaring and greater. 'Heno-ngah' exists by virtue of birth of a girl in a family which stands necessarily in a juxtaposition of being a 'Tucha' on the one hand and a 'Songgao' on the other in relation to another family. The terminology for one's mother's brother's daughter has been in existence; she, by the rule of preferred marriage of mother's brother's daughter, is one's prospective wife, if she happens to be of his marriageable age group. Such a girl is categoriesed as one's 'Neinu', prospective preferred wife. The term 'Henungah' is, therefore, used only if mother's brother's daughter is older than the father's sister son. Otherwise, the former is the 'Neinu' of the latter if they are of the marriageable age group, i.e., the boy is older than the girl.

But in the case of 'Hegang', the terminology is non- existent so long as there is no marriage of one's father's sister. It exists only when the marriage of one's father's sister takes place. It must, however, be noted that in the case of mother's brother's daughter marriage, the term is no longer applicable. The husband of one's aunt in second generation MBD marriage is addressed as 'heo' and not as 'Hegang'. His position is relegated to one degree lower. He is regarded as a member of the family being a cross cousin, and not an outsider marrying one's aunt. The term has, therefore, limitations and it is static, as it cannot perpetuate for more than one generation in an MBD marriage. While a man in the first generation earns the terminology of 'Hegang', his son, who marries his 'Neinu' in the second generation does not earn the term any more. He is addressed as a cousin brother, 'Heo, and not as the husband of one's 'Heni', called 'Hegang'.

The cousin-brother in MBD marriage in the second generation is relegated to 'Heo' from 'Hegang'. This means that there is MBD marriage for two generations in the same family. On the other hand, the girl who is 'Heno-ngah' to a man is categorised as his 'Neinu' or preferred and prospective bride, if she is of marriageable age-group to him. In short, cross-cousin sister of an ego is his would-be wife who addresses her parents- in-law as 'Heni' (Aunt) and 'Hegang'(uncle) instead of mother-in- law and father-in-law after marriage to her first cross-cousin brother. If it happens in the third generation in MBD marriage, the bride calls her mother-in-law and father-in-law as sister and brother -'Heo'. This is a departure from the general practice of addressing one's parents-in-law as

'Heno' and 'Hepa' in a marriage occurring with a girl not of maternal uncle's. All these terminologies used in addressing different relatives manifest social standing of the different people which conform to their status in the society

Types of Family :

The Kukis practice both joint and nuclear types of family. The permanent type of family among the Kukis is the one in which the eldest son of a man called 'Upa' lives with his parents along with unmarried younger brothers 'Neopa' and sisters compulsorily. Therefore, in every family where there is the eldest married son, the family is composed of the parents, his unmarried brothers and sisters, in addition to his own children. Sometimes, if the grandparents of a married son are still alive, the family is composed of a larger generation. Essentially, the type of family of the eldest married son of a man having three or four generations living together is called a *joint family*. The other type of family is called a *nuclear* family. It is, however, to be noted that such nuclear family ultimately becomes joint family in course of time when the man forming the nuclear family has a married eldest son with his own family and children. Thus, the Kuki family is the smallest social unit of a joint family. This may be said to be a biological growth of nuclear family turned into a joint family one generation later which is called "earned joint family". Basically, therefore, it may be said that every Kuki household is a joint family of two different types - one of the 'Upa', which is the "Inherent permanent joint family", and the other is a family of 'Naopa' being converted into a family of 'Upa' in the second generation called "Earned joint Family". The common characteristic of the two types of joint families among the Kukis are of vertical generation in nature. Two brothers, each having nuclear family, do not live together as per custom. No doubt, there is a short span of time when the younger brother takes shelter with the eldest brother when he is newly married and is yet in the process of building up his own nuclear family. This is only a transition period before the separation from the 'Inherent joint family" to forming a nuclear family. This, however, is not true in the case of the Hmar Kuki where many married brothers live together under one and the same roof, sharing a kitchen, and a granary, under the supreme authority of their father.

VIII Tucha-Songgao-Becha formalities :

The consistency of the institution of family council called 'Tucha-Songgao-Becha' is very clearly expressed when mother's brother's daughter marriage is practised through generations. In such a situation, the three sets of relationship of 'Tucha', 'Becha' and Songgao' can be well channelised in a regular vertical line. An example of such relationship is shown in a genealogical tree, as follows (Chart 4 : 4), in respect of Nguljapao Hangsing, the ego, of Khengjang village.

CHART 4 : 4

TUCHA-SONGGAO RECIPROCAL RELATIONSHIP AS COULD BE SEEN VERTICALLY IN RESPECT OF NGULJAPAO HANGSING FAMILY

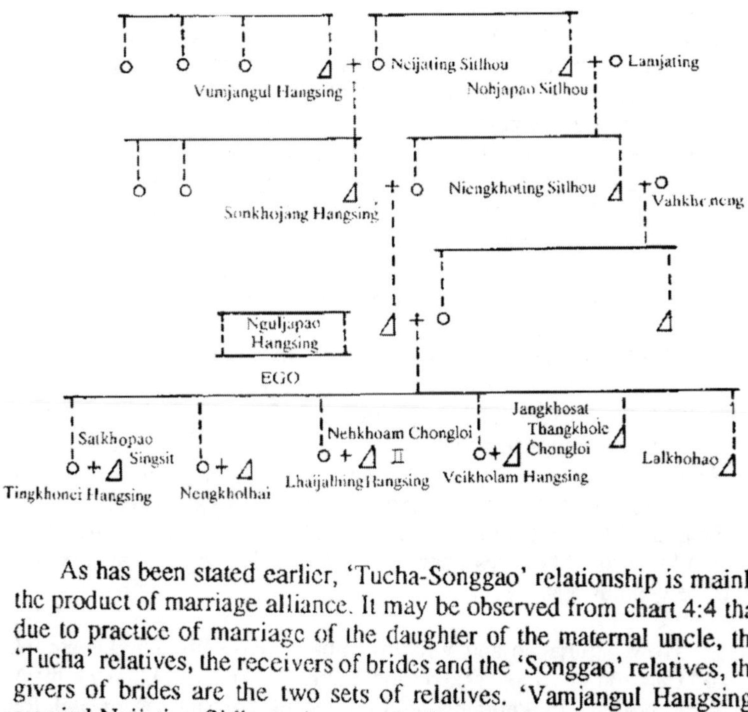

As has been stated earlier, 'Tucha-Songgao' relationship is mainly the product of marriage alliance. It may be observed from chart 4:4 that due to practice of marriage of the daughter of the maternal uncle, the 'Tucha' relatives, the receivers of brides and the 'Songgao' relatives, the givers of brides are the two sets of relatives. 'Vamjangul Hangsing' married Neijating Sitlhou. As a result, Vamjangul's children, of whom Songkhojang is one, have become 'Tucha' relatives to Nohjapao and his sons who, in turn, become'Songgao' relatives to the former. Likewise, Nehkholam(II), Satholpao Singsit and Thandgkholet Chongloi, who marry the sisters of Jangkhosat and Lalkhohao Hangsing become the 'Tucha' relatives of the latter who, along with their sons, become 'Songgao' relatives to those who marry their sisters. On the other hand, Nguljpao Hangsing, the ego also stands on the same footing with his father, to the same group people who are hismother and also his wife's relatives. Both of them have taken wives from the same family through mother's brother's daughter's marriage.

In an extreme case of over-indulgence to the 'Tuchas' by the 'Songgao' relatives, the parents of Nguljapao went to seek the hands of their niece Veikhovah, the 'Neinu' of their son in her tender age. When a 'Tucha' relative asked for such favour taking things for granted, the social etiquette was that such a request from the 'Tucha' was difficult to turn down. After all, the girl, Veikhovah, was the 'Neinu' of Nguljapao under the prevailing preferential marriage system. Even when such a request for the hand of one's 'Neinu' is not sought by the 'Tucha' relative, the custom clearly says that it is nothing but an insult towards the 'Songgao' relatives, and a fine for non- marriage of one's own 'Neinu' is imposed. So, Veikhovah was given in marriage in her childhood to Nguljapao, This is called taking of the bride with her play-things(toys), and is known as 'Akangbawmpumma Kipui'. This is a case of child marriage in MBD. In such a case, bride-price is also not charged. Such a situation is afforded by the practice of mother's brother's daughter marriage which culminated into its extreme nature of overindulgence with particular reference to the relationship between mother's brother and sister's son.

The cross-cousin marriage has come to stay as the foundation of the society on which the family Council of 'Tucha- Songgao' and 'Becha' is built. In the present case Vumngul, Sonkhojang and Nguljapao occupy their social relationship as the grandfather, father and son, respectively. Nguljapao, the son of Sonkhojang and the grandson of Vumjangul, married his mother's brother's daughter Veikhovah. Thus, the wives of the grandfather, the father and the son are from the same family. Here, we find two sets of families stand in 'Tucha' and 'Songgao' relationship for three generations.

Now Nguljapao and Veikhovah have two sons, Jangkhosat (elder) and Lalkhohao(younger) and four daughters, viz., tingkhonei (elder) and Nengkholhai, Veikholam and Lhaijalhing, second, third and fourth, respectively. The two sons are still bachelors. While the elder is making his graduation, the younger is in the Assam Regiment as Havilder. In case there is a marriageable girl among the mother's brother's daughters, the elder son is in bounden duty to marry one of them preferably the elder daughter being his 'Neinu'. The first daughter, Tingkhonei, of Nguljapao and Veikhovah, is married to Satkhopao Singsit and the other two daughters are married to Nehkholam (II) and Thandgkholet respectively. Both the husbands are of Chongloi clan. These married daughters and their families are 'Tuchas' of the Nguljapao family, and the latter's family is 'Songgao' relative to the former.

At every stage of social life of a family, the position of every individual and family is expressed in relationship to each other. Now, Neijating, the grandmother of Nguljapao gave birth to sons, Songkhojang being one of them. This is considered as a matter of pride not only to the family to which she is married, but also a prestige for the family who gives her in marriage. The main consideration of the family to which the woman is married is that a son has been born to the family for continuance of the descent of the family through a male person. It is the wife who makes it possible to propagate the generations of the family without letting it extinct finally. It is called 'Ingam'. In the same way, Nengkhoting, the daughter of Neijating's brother and Veikhovah, the daughter of Neijating's brother's son, are the ones who further propagate generations of the family by giving birth to sons.

In recognition of the contribution of the woman in the propagation of male line of the family of her husband, her father or brother or brother's son is entitled to charge corpse-price called 'Luongman' on the death of the woman. It is, therefore the right of the father or brother or brother's sons to claim corpse- price or 'Luongman' on the death from the husband's family. The husband or sons nave to pay one 'Mithun' each on the death of each of the three women to their 'Songgao' relatives. Had they not given birth to a son or sons, no 'Luongman' was chargeable on their death.

Similarly, the death of every son born out of the three women gives the 'Songgao' relatives the right to charge the 'Luongman'. Worth of each 'Luongman' is a 'Mithun'. The persons who have the corpse-price or 'Luongman' are only the 'Tucha' relatives of the 'Songgao'. In the present instance, apart from the three women who were instrumental to the propagation of the male lineage of the family to which they were married, the death of Songkhojang and his son Nguljapao and the two grandsons, Jangkhosat and Lalkhohao, as also the sons of the two grandsons, would be entitled to charge the corpse-price from their 'Songgao'. This will continue for generations together if MBD marriage continues. But such entitlement does not automatically give the absolute right to demand 'Luongman' by the 'Songgao' relatives. They have to fulfil the social obligations described above. If a' Songgao' does not perform 'Kosana' or 'Sakeng Khai' or 'Luongman Betna', which means asking for the corpse-price by killing a 'Mithun' and offering a feast in expression of his grief, affection and respect, he is not entitled to claim the 'Luongman'. Such claim is expressed in mutual reciprocation basis. It does not come by itself as a matter of course. There are certain duties to be performed by the 'Songgao' and the 'Tucha' relatives. Thus, performance of the 'Sakeng Khai' by the 'Songgao' is the condition precedent to pay the corpse-price or 'Luongman' by the 'Tucha'. As the receiver of wife, 'Tucha' is at the service of the 'Songgao' relative who gives him wife. On the performance of 'Sakeng Khai' of the 'Songgao', the 'Tucha' is bound to give 'Luongman'

As the practice of marrying neice continues in the family of 'Nguljapao', the 'Becha relative also remains constant. The family of 'Becha' is not disturbed in any way by the marriages of the family. This shows that while the 'Tucha-Songgao' relationship is purely a by-product of marriage, 'Becha' relationship stays out of such social intricacies. As stated earlier, the Becha relationship is very flexible or elastic and broad-based in comparison with the 'Tucha-Songgao' relationship which has rigid and narrow implications. 'Becha' relationship can be established and changed circumstantially. The 'Techa' relationship of a family may be converted into a 'Tucha-Songgao' relationship by marriage only. When such a situation arises , the 'Becha' of the family cannot continue in his position any longer. Instead, he becomes either a 'Tucha' or a 'Songgao' relative, as the case may be, to the family where he had hitherto been the 'Becha'. An instance of such a situation can be had from the family of Shongkhokam Gangte of Khengjang village.

Shongkhokam Gangte is the only son of Thongkhosei Gangte, who has eight daughters of whom six are married to the Chongloi husbands, with one each of the Singsit and Kholhou husband. All the daughters having been married, live in the same village of Khengjang with their only brother. Under the circumstances, the families of Chongloi to which the daughters have been married covered almost all the Chonglois living in the village by the 'Tucha-Songgao' relationship through extension of such relationship. Thus, by extension of 'Tucha-Songgao' relationship, all the Chongloi families living in the village are 'Tucha' relatives to the family of Thongkhosei Gangte.

The life-style of a Kuki is such that he has to have necessarily the three sets of relationships called 'Tucha- Songgao-Becha', which can be termed as a Family Council. When a man lives as a neo-immigrant in absence of such relatives, he establishes the above relationships by extension of the said terms. Thus, Thongkhosei Gangte, being the lone Gangte family living amongst the Chongloi and other clans, who are related to him through the marriages of his daughters and grand-daughters, has no collateral relatives who can act on his behalf as his 'Becha'. He has somehow to find out someone to be his 'Becha'. Accordingly, while there are plenty of relatives who are his 'Tucha' for which no search for fresh establishment is necessary, he establishes a 'Becha' relationship with the family of Heljakam Chongloi. By extension of the relationship of 'Tucha- Songgao', Heljapao's family is supposed to become 'Tucha' relative to the family of Thongkhosei Gangte. But their relationship is not bound at this stage by actual marriage between the two families. The 'Becha' relationship between the two families remained till such time Shongkhokem Gangte, the only son of Thongkhosei, married Lamjahoi Chongloi, the niece of Heljepao, the 'Becha' of the former. As a result, the social standing of the two families was disturbed. They could not continue to be 'Becha' to each other. The relationship of the two families took a different turn. Heljapao's place as 'Becha' in the family of Thongkhosei had been replaced by his newly acquired status because of the marriage of his niece. Instead, he became the 'Songgao' relative to the family of Thongkhosi Gangte. In his position as a 'Becha' of the family, he officiated as head of the family in every social obligation performed by Thongkhosi. He became the de-facto head of the family wherein he was the 'Becha'. His activities as a 'Becha' of the family of Thongkhosei were of active and authoritative. With the marriage of his niece in the family where he had been hitherto the 'Becha', his social status with it became a 'Tucha-Songgao' relationship. He could no longer act as a 'Becha' of the family. Thereafter, he had to assume the position of 'Songgao' who is a very passive relative. His position in respect of his relationship to the family where he had hitherto been a 'Becha' now changed from one of active and authoritative to passive and abstract in nature. The genealogical tree of the family of Thongkhosei Gangte will give a clear understanding (Chart 4:5)

CHART 4 : 5 GENEALOGICAL TREE OF THONGKHOSEI GANGTE SHOWING THE CLANS TO WHICH HIS CHILDREN WERE MARRIED TO

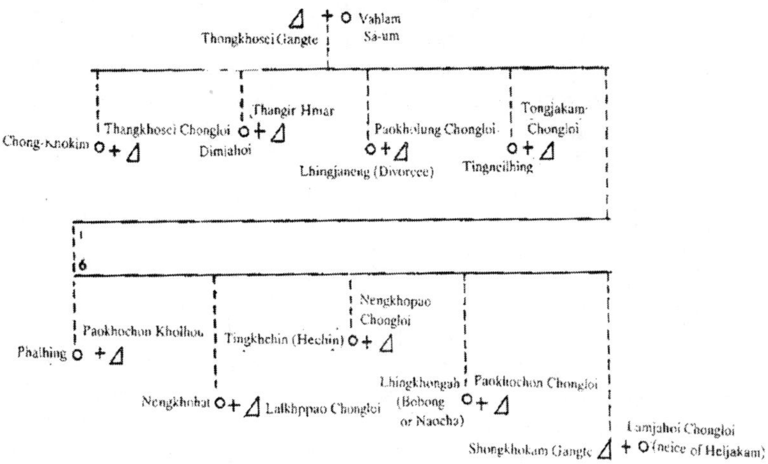

Shongkhokam, the only son of Thongkhosei Gangte, married lamjahoi, the niece of Heljapao Chongloi, the 'Becha' of the former. Children were born to them and Thongkhosei died in 1980. But the 'Becha' of the family had not been substituted as yet. A 'Becha' relative in place of Heijapao had to be established so that he might officiate in any social occasion, in times of weal and woe. Since the family of Thongkhosei Gangte is a female- preponderated one, the marriage of his daughters and the grand- daughters had spread all over the village wherein almost all the families were more or less connected with him as 'Tuchas' to whom his family was 'Songgao'. This made the task of finding the 'Becha' relatively more difficult than anticipated. Despite his becoming automatically the 'Songgao' of the family where he had been the 'Becha' and in the absence of a 'Becha' in his place, Heljapao assumed his duty as a 'Becha' under extraordinary circumstances on the day Thongkhosei died and performed the duty as such. However, very unfortunately, no substitute of the 'Becha' to the family had in the mean time been established. In April, 1986, Vahlam, the wife of Thongkhosei Gangte, died. No 'Becha' was available to perform the duties, while there were too many 'Tucha' relatives. Under the circumstances, the Chief of the village, Thangkhosei Chongloi, who married the eldest daughter of Thongkhosei Gangte, requested Heljapao Chongloi to perform the duties as a 'Becha' of the family for the last time. He agreed to do so because of the fact that Vahlam was the lady-Becha of the family to which he had been the 'Becha.' She was then buried. But this was done only under compelling circumstances and not in terms of the customs. Had he not assumed the role of a 'Becha', the rites of burial of the man and his wife in the family to which he had hitherto been a 'Becha' would have been in jeopardy. This situation manifests the indispensability of the three sets of relatives of a man known as family Council of 'Tucha-Songgao- Becha', reflecting thereby their social relationship and roles.

It is also interesting to note that in the village community of Khengjang where every individual is related somehow to one another through marriages, it is not easy to find a man free to act as the 'Becha' relative of Thangkhosei Gangte's family, the headship of which is now assumed by his only son, Shongkhokam Gangte, who had a wide range of matrimonial alliances through the nuptials of his sisters, their daughters, sons and also of his own marriage to a Chongloi girl. All these by-product of marriages through the sisters and their daughters of Shongkhokam are his 'Tucha' relatives by extension of the relationship of 'Tucha'. Obviously, to find out a person free from any kind of marriage alliance with whom a 'Becha' relationship could be established was no small problem for

Shongkhokam. Traditionally, the office of 'Becha' is held only by collateral male or cognate relatives of a man, as against the 'Tucha' relationship which is connected only through females signifying affinal relationship.

The terms are, therefore, used only in connection with social occasions of a man to categoreis different sets of relatives for clear-cut division of work and expression of their social relationship through which their interaction could manifest in their relationship towards each other.

IX Tucha-Songgao Relationship

Another analogous example of continuation of MBD marriage that strengthens the institution of 'Tucha-Songgao' relationship and the system of 'Luongman' is available in the marriages of the families of Vumkhost Chongloi and Nguljalam Chongloi. The genealogical trees of the two families given in chart 4:6 will give a clear picture of the situation.

CHART 4 : 6

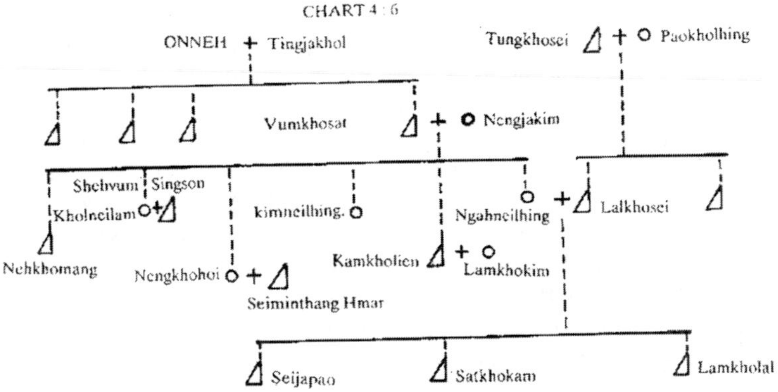

Vumkhosat Chongloi was the second son of Onneh Chongloi, the founder-chief of the village. He was married to Nengjakim, a Chongloi girl from Chaljang village. They had two sons and four daughters. Nehkhomang, the first son, is named after his grandfather, Onneh, while his second son, Kaikholien, is named after the child's maternal grandfather, Otkhokai. Nehkhomang is at the moment serving as a Headmaster of the Junior High School at Ahthibung Headquarters, Nagaland. He is still a bachelor. His younger brother, Kaikholien, is married to Nengjavah, the daughter of Lhunjahao Sa-Um, the second son of Vomiam Sa-Um and born of Lamkhokim, the daughter of Thangir Hmar. Kholneilam, named after her paternal grandmother, Tingjakhol, is the first daughter, and is married to Sehvum Singsit, now employed as a Carpentry Supervisor in the Department of Industries, Government of Nagaland, and is posted at Phanjang near Jaluki. Nengkhohoi, the third daughter, is married to Seiminthang Hmar, the second son of Thangir Hmar.

Ngahneilhing, the second daughter, is married to Lalkhosei Chongloi, the second son of Tungkhosei. The mother of Lalkhosei is Paokholhing. She is the aunt of Vumkhosat. So, by extension of the kinship terminology, the aunt of her father is also the aunt of Ngahneilhing. The marriage of Ngahneilhing to Lalkhosei is, therefore, one of mother's brother's daughter. As per custom, the 'Luongman' of Paokholhing and Ngahneilhing being Vumkhost's aunt and daughter, respectively, should go to one and the same family. Custom permits 'Luongman' to be charged only by the eldest son, if father is dead. So 'Luongman' of Paokholhing is to be received by Thangkhosei, the elder brother of Vumkhosat and the Chief of Khengjang village. Thus, while Paokholhing's 'Luongman' is to be claimed by Thangkhosei, Ngahneilhing's 'Luongman' is to be claimed by Vumkhosat, on his death, by his elder son, Nehkhomang. In case Paokholhing outlives Thangkhosei, her 'Luongman' will be given to Nehkholam, the eldest son of Thangkhosei. Vumkhosat does not have the right, though by age and generation he is senior to his nephew. It is also pertinent to note here that 'Luongman' is claimed only after the death of the person concerned. The 'Luongman' of Lalkhosei and his wife, Ngahneilhing, will go to the same family, because of the marriage being treated as a marriage with the mother's brother's daughter. But Lalkhosei's 'Luongman' cannot be claimed by Vumkhosat though he is entitled to it for his daughter, Ngahneilhing, the wife of Lalkhosei.

The indispensability of mother's brother's daughter marriage is proved not only as a preferred type for the regular maintenance and continuity of 'Tucha-Songgao' relationship, but also as a moral obligation to seek the hand of one's 'Neinu' on the part of a 'Tucha' relative. A glaring example is the marriage between Nguljalam and Hoikhochong Sa-µm as shown in Chart 4 : 7:

CHART 4 : 7

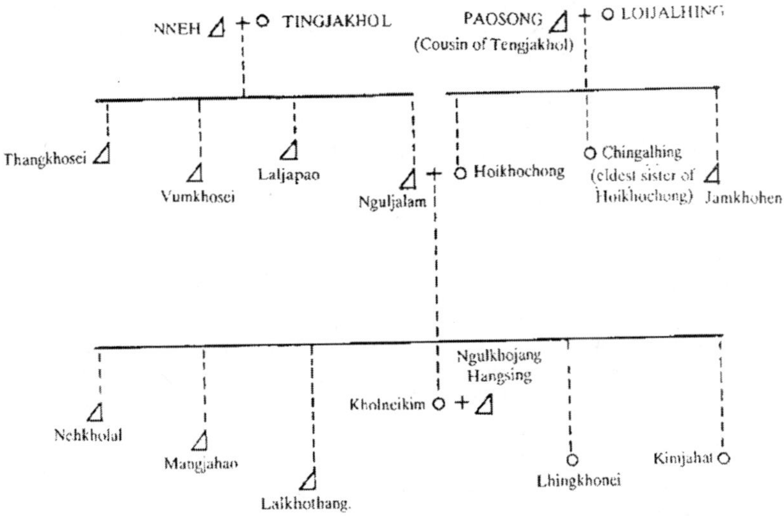

Nguijalam is the third brother of Thangkhosei Chongloi, the Chief of Khengjang village. Nguljalam's mother does not have her own brother. Her only immediate cousin brother is Hoikhochong's father. Nguljalam's wife, Hoikhochong, is his mother's cousin brother's daughter. Thus,Hoikhochong's father is the only next of kin living for Nguljalam's mother. The younger brother of Hoikhochong is Jamkhohen. Hoikhochong's mother's name is Loijalhing, and her father is Paosong. The eldest sister of Hoikhochong is Chingjalhing. As per custom, Thangkhosei, the present Chief of Khengjang village, being the eldest brother of Nguljalam, was supposed to marry his 'Neinu', Chingalhing, being the eldest of the mother's brother's (cousin) daughter. Therefore, the parents of Thangkhosei approached the parents of Chingalhing, seeking the hands of their daughter in marriage to their son. Being the cousin of their daughter for whom she is the 'Neinu', this was agreed. All other formalities having been completed, a 'Mithun' was killed and a feast was hosted by way of a token of this agreement. This was called 'Sum Tan Sa' the occasion when the date for solemnisation of the marriage was fixed. Incidentally, it should be reiterated in this connection that the mother of Thangkhosei, Tingjakhol, and Paosong, Chingalhing's father, were first cousins, their fathers being brothers. As per custom, by extension of the relationship, her only living brothers were her cousin brothers, one of whom was Chingalhing's father. Therefore, by the mechanism of extension of relationship, the daughters of Tingjakhol's cousin brothers, Chingalhing and Hoikholhing, were the 'Neinus' of Thangkhosei and his brothers. The marriage negotiations having been completed, preparations for the actual marriage were afoot, on both sides, Unfortunately, before the appointed day, Chingalhing was eloped by Otkhosei Lhouvum of Ponlien village. There was no way out for them. The marriage proposal between Thangkhosei and Chingalhing had to be cancelled.

After a few years, Thangkhosei's parents looked for another prospective bride for their son. Eventually negotiations were finalised and the proposal was agreed upon by both the parties, both of whom lived at Tamenglong sub-Divisional Headquarters. This time, the agreement was fulfilled and the marriage took place. With the passage of time, the necessity for the marriage of the third brother, Nguljalam, had arisen. The family members considered the situation and decided that with a view to reconciling the strained relationship between the two families, the parents of Nguljalam or Thangkhosei should approach their in- laws again for the hand of Hoikholhing in marriage for their third son.

Accordingly, Thangkhosei, the eldest son, whose marriage with his 'Neinu' was broken was sent along with his wife to open the negotiation. This was done by way of expression of a good gesture and show of loyalty to the maternal-in-laws of the family. The negotiation was happily accepted and it culminated into the matrimonia alliance between Nguljalam and Hoikhochong. The relationship of the two families was once again restored.

As was the case with all other brothers, Nguljalam and Hoikhochong named their first son, Nehkholal, after the paternal grandfather of the child. Thus, came his name from Onneh - Nehkholal. Likewise, the first daughter, Kholneikim, was given the name after the paternal grandmother of the child, Tingjakhol -Kholneikim.

This is another extreme case of indispensability of mother's brother's daughter's marriage among the Kukis to maintain the good relationship between the 'Tucha-Songgao' families so that their social relationship might not be disturbed.

This situation is also a pointer to the indispensability of the existence of 'Luongman' system. Tingjakhol, the mother of Thangkhosei and his three brothers, had no brother of her own. Her only next of kin was her cousin brother, Paosong, the father- in-law and father respectively of Nguljalam and Hoikhochong. In absence of any brother of Tingjakhol, her cousin, Paosong, was entitled to claim the 'Luongman' of his cousin, on her death. In the event of his earlier demise, his eldest son is to claim the 'Luongman'. But, the breach of marriage contract for Thangkhosei and Chingalhing had put the situation in a very awkward position for both the families. Under such circumstances, claiming of 'Luongman' by the maternal kin was indeed a very delicate matter. Somehow, a situation to defuse such an unpleasant episode had to be found out, so that the good relationship was not broken by mere social etiquettes. The entry of marriage alliance between Nguljalam and Hoikhochong had removed the unsavoury memory of the two families and, as a result, all the normal social niceties and obligations could be restored without any prejudice between the two families.

CHAPTER 5

LIFE CYCLE CEREMONIES

I.

Marriage, birth and death are integral parts of one's life and the span of life is ridden with anxiety and tension. As man knows nothing of his future, he either invents or adopts certain manner of rituals or *rite de passages* to palliate his unseen fears which are tinged with ideas that constitute part of his life-style ingressing into his culture and religion that may determine his outlook as well. The Kuki is one of the groups of people who, with their style of life, adjusted themselves with the changing situation since the hoary past, i.e., when they began to migrate from their homeland. In course of this long march, perhaps changes took place and some groups interacted leading to blending and ultimately Christianity made inroads with slow degrees of change of their life-style at varied manner. Modern educational facilities, hospitals and some more present day advantages are open to them and thus the old traditions took new turns.

With all these possibilities, the Kuki life cycle rituals are now in a process of change and a time will come when many of the vibrant traits of their life cycle and rites will fade away. Attempt has been made in this chapter to describe some rituals which are still present in their life, and these are practised by this group of people with some beliefs as part of their cultural traditions.

II Marriage :

Marriage is an important form of institution among the Kukis. There are three types by which a Kuki acquires his mate from amongst their group.

Firstly, marriage by arrangement is the most popular type in the olden days. This type of marriage is sometimes done mainly due to the consideration of a preferential form of Mother's brother's daughter marriage

(MBD). Arranged marriages often take place during childhood of the boy and the girl. When the parents of a boy are determined that their son should marry no other than his Mother's brother's daughter called 'Neinu', the marriage negotiation is initiated by the parents of the boy during the childhood of the boy and the girl. In some extreme cases, when a daughter is born in a family, her father's sister and her husband initiate on her birth the claim that the baby girl being the 'Neinu' of their son, should not be given in marriage to anybody else. She should go to them as their son's wife. Such earmarking is called 'Kikhao Khi', meaning that the girl has been reserved for a particuiar boy and that no one should set his eye on her, either for marriage or for love. In other words, it manifests the pattern of relationship of giver-receiver called 'Pu-Tu' relationship. In this, the 'Pu' relative is always the giver, while the 'Tu' relative is always on the receiving end. When the latter asks something, the former is not supposed to refuse him. As a matter of fact, the initiative taken by the parents of the boy shows that a person is at liberty to take whatever he or she wants from the maternal uncle if the demand is reasonable.

The second type of getting a mate is by mutual consent or love. A boy and a girl may fall in love, ask their parents to give consent to their nuptials. Such a situation often results in formal negotiation of parents and relatives of the boy and the girl. In this kind of love, mother's brother's daughter and father's sister's son are often involved.

The third type of getting a wife is by elopment. When a boy and a girl fall in love and when their parents or either of the parents raise strong objection to union, or when there appears a third person in between the boy and girl, who is likely to stand in their way, because of his being a serious contender to win the hands of the girl in marriage, or when the economic consideration that involves in the event of all formalities of marriage are to be fulfilled in the case of either the boy or the girl being in abject poverty, or even when the girl is impregnated by either of the lovers, in all these cases marriage by elopment is resorted to.

III

In the normal course of marriage, the customary procedures are as follows : The parents of the boy go along with their 'Tucha' and 'Becha' relatives to the parents of the girl to seek the hands of the girl in marriage. In doing so, they take with them one pot of rice-beer, called 'Zubel'. They offer the 'Zu' or beer to the parents of the girl. The parents of the girl inform their family 'Tucha' and 'Becha' to consider the request in the proceedings of which the respective 'Bechas' of the family on both sides would be the spokesman for the boy and the girl. The parents of both have nothing much to offer as their opinion. It depends on the skill of the 'Bechas' of both the sides. The 'Bechas' of both sides, in course of negotiation, interpret various customs and implications and try to convince each other to their point of view. On the first day of such negotiation, the 'Becha' of the boy's side speaks and announces their intention of the visit saying that their boy wants the hands of the girl. This statement is ratified by the parents and the relatives of the boy. If the proposal is accepted, the offer of the 'Zu' is taken and then another date for further negotiation is fixed. This response is not spoken out much in words. But, as per custom, the boy's parents do not, in return, offer back the rice-beer , if the proposal is accepted. They simply try some sort of lame excuses to indicate that they should come again for further negotiation, while the girl's side should consider the case in the meantime. But if the proposal is not acceptable, the 'Becha' of the girl's family speaks some suave and pleasing excuses and offers back a pot of 'Zu', which indicates without much tongue-lashing that the proposal is not acceptable to the girl's parents. The matter ends there.

In the event of acceptance of the proposal, a second visit is agreed upon and a date is fixed. On this second visit, formal agreement from both the sides is openly made known. The girls side informs the boy's parents that the latter has to bring the bride-price after having made known their willingness to the proposal. The bride-price is determined on the customary bride- price of the family of the girl. In case the girl happens to be the eldest in the family, the parents of the girl, if they so desire, charge the price of the mother of the girl in case the mother of the girl happens to be from a clan which charges higher bride-price than the clan to which the girl belongs, or, that of the clan depending on the wishes of the parents of the girl. Thus, the final negotiation having settled, the date for the third visit of the groom's side is decided upon.

During the third visit also they go in the same manner as they had done earlier. They offer rice-beer to the parents of the girl with a request to tell them as to how the former is to come with the bride-price and what is the time fixed for them to take their bride. For this purpose, the boy's parents kill one Mithun in token expression of their thanks and also as witness-meat for the consummation of the marriage negotiation. This is called 'Sum Tan Sa', which means final settlement of the bride-price. All the relatives and other close friends of the girl's parents are invited to join them in the final negotiation of their daughter's marriage proposal. On this day the girl's parents tell the boy's parents, through their respective 'Bechas', that they expect the latter to bring the bride-price on the day fixed when the boy's party would come again to take their bride. In the evening, when the feast for the final settlement of the negotiation is finished by the general public, a special table is laid for the final settlement of the negotiation of the marriage by selected persons as witnesses to the proposed marriage alliance. The persons eligible to participate in such dinner are the following :

1. Two 'Bechas' - one each from both the sides.
2. Two 'Tuchas' - one each from both the sides.

The food for such dinner is called 'Sasa Neh', meaning the witness food, and the meat for such witnesses include the portion of the Mithun as follows :

1. The heart of the Mithun.
2. The liver of the Mithun.

These two portions are considered most valuable parts of the meat representing the life-giving and a source of love and affection. These persons are the witnesses to the marriage negotiations. Therefore, the 'Mithun' killed for the occasion is known as 'Sumtan Sa', meaning final settlement of the negotiation.

During the fourth visit of the boy's party, they have nothing to bring with them, excepting the bride-price and a pot of rice-beer as a token of gratitude and also for showing respect. They have to be fed by the girl's parents. But a big event is to take place on this day. On the arrival day, the boy's party which includes many young boys and girls, apart from the indispensable relatives, 'Tuchas' and 'Bechas' of the boy's family, are challenged by the young men of the village for a wrestling competition, known as 'Lhun Sollah Suontuolkho' saying.

If you are brave enough
To snatch away the girl
From our midst for your wife,
Come and show us your prowess
That you really deserve to be
the man of our beloved girl.

On hearing the challenge, the boy's party comes out accepting the challenge. Before the wrestling commences a circle is formed by spectators which serves as the wrestling arena. Knowing that such a wrestling would take place at the girl's village, the boys party usually brings with them a number of good wrestlers. But unless the issue has become a question of prestige between the two groups of wrestlers, normally the boy's party gives way to the girl's group of wrestlers and allows themselves to be defeated, irrespective of their superiority in strength or dexterity. This is done in the belief that if the girl's party wins, the girl has a bright family life and a happy future with many children . Sometimes it so happens that there occurs some misunderstanding between villages. In such a case, taking advantage of the occasion, the rival Chiefs instigate the wrestlers of their respective villages. So, when the competition takes place with the blessings of their Chiefs, and without giving importance to the welfare of the marriage parties with which the wrestling event is associated, a real show of strength and technique resulting in serious competitions often dominates the occasion.

Wrestling over in the same evening, the whole gathering drink, sing and dance for the whole night. In token reception of the groom's party, rice-beer is offered to them. The groom's party reveals whatever they bring with them as the bride-price. Thus, the bride-price is settled. Nothing is done until the next day when the boy's party is given a feast and a send-off to the girl. On this day also, in the evening,a wrestling bout for the second time commences. That done, when everyone is in a happy mood, all of them are treated to a feast, which is hosted by the parents of the girl in honour of their daughter which, in other words, is a farewell feast to her. This is called 'Chanu Lhahna'. For this purpose, a man may kill one Mithun or more. In such a feast all take part without any eating formality. It may be stated here that the Mithun killed is divided into two halves. The second half comprising the waist portion, including the two hind legs is kept apart, while the first half is cooked for the feast. The portion kept apart is given to the boy's party. This is called 'Chanu Sa', meaning, meat-share of the daughter.

Special System of Marriage :

Every girl is entitled to be married under the system called 'Chongmou Hailam Domma Kipui', fallacious meaning, a 'bride with a gourd in her left hand who walks under the sun', when the girl is compulsorily to leave her natal home before sun-rise. Such a send-off is dependent on the decision of the father of the girl. If he wants to show his love for his daughter and wishes to maintain his prestige and dignity, he announces that he wants to give away his daughter as 'Chongmou Hailam'. He, accordingly, informs the groom's parents. He may also inform the boy's parents that he likes to charge additional bride-price for his daughter which is known as 'Mankang'(Mankang Katuh Ding Ahi). This means that because of his love for his daughter he makes two natal homes for her so that whenever she is in need, she can have two homes called 'Nunglam' to fall back upon. In doing so, he assigns a man close to him, usually a close relative, to receive the additional bride-price, so that by obligation the man thus given the privilege considers the girl as his own daughter. In the same way, the girl also regards the man taking the additional bride-price as her own foster father. Thus, when the bride-price is paid, the boy's father has necessarily to pay two Mithuns instead of one as lead-bride-price, known as 'Man Lamkai'.

Now, that a farewell feast to their daughter has been given, and bride-price settled, the man to receive the 'Mankang' has also received his part of the additional bride-price, the matter is considered to be finally settled. All formalities having been completed, the girl throws a farewell party to her boy and girl friends of the village who make round-the-clock social gathering by singing, dancing and drinking at the residence of the man who takes the 'Mankang' or additional bride-price. Incidentally, it is customary that the boy's party takes the responsibility of ensuring that no untoward incident takes place concerning the girl or the bride. Therefore, right from the twilightdawn they arrive at the girl's village, they keep a sharp vigil on the girl throughout the day and night.

Next afternoon, the boys of the bride's village come to the residence of the girl's parents and start challenging the boys of the groom's party for wrestling. This challenge is in token expression of their uncompromising attitude for winning the hands of the girl of their village, and also as a last attempt to exact revenge for such insult metted to them. Then starts wrestling for the third time. Wrestling over, the villagers along with their guests, drink, sing and dance together the whole night.

The next day is the day of departure. The manner in which the send-off to the girl is given is as follows :

1. The girl is made to dress up with her hair plaited on the left hand side or upside down into three coils ;
2. Her petticoat called 'Ponve' is worn left hand side and is pinned together at the ends by splits of a kind of bamboo called 'Gopi Keh';
3. Her bangles and bracelets are removed as a symbol of the end of her spinsterhood;
4. She leaves her parents' house necessarily before sunrise;
5. The priest gives the last rite of farewell to the girl by letting her sit in the middle of the house where the main pillar of the house stands.

This is called 'Sutlai'. He utters farewell rituals propitiating the gods and goddesses for her health and prosperity, and thereafter lets her drink a cup of 'Zu';

6. As she comes out of her parents,house, she does so holding one gourd in her left hand called 'Hailam Dom'.

7. When she is about to come out of the door of her parents' house, she crosses the door with her left leg first.

The manner of sending off the girl, as stated above, is exactly the same as is done to a women when she dies, thereby equating the girl as dead to the family, which in real sense conveys the significance that hereafter the girl truly belongs to the groom's family for all practical purposes. It also indicates that now the girl has left her natal home, she should not think in terms of coming back through divorce or after quarrelling. She should take her conjugal home as her real home. In other words, she is discouraged to a degree to think that she still belongs to her parents. She should whole-heartedly devote herself to please her husband, parents-in-laws and other relatives of her husband and build up her own home for prosperity without the slightest inkling of divided loyalty. This is called 'Malang Khot'.

As the girl comes out of her natal home, she is taken in a procession in the following manner :

The boy's parents bring with them a girl selected especially for the purpose of receiving the bride-to-be. Such a girl is necessarily a virgin and without any physical blemishes. As the would-be bride comes out of her parents' house, this selected girl accompanies her. She at the same time carries the personal effects of the bride-apparent in a litter-type of basket called 'Beng'. The would-be bride goes ahead, followed by the selected girl, carrying the personal effects of the former. Then follow the parents of the boy, the 'Tucha' of the family, who carries the second-half of the meat given by the girl's parents. After him (in the case of Sitlhous) follow two other persons carrying the waist portion of the Mithun killed for the boy's party, called 'Chanu-Sa' or 'Sa-Haap'. This is done only when the marriage is settled between the children of two Sitlhou Chiefs. The rest go as they please in normal course.

As soon as the would-be bride and her escort party reach the outskirts of the village known as 'Khomol', where a common resting place is usually constructed in every Kuki village, they are greeted by the boy and the girl friends who are her colleagues in the lawn of the village. It is now their turn to send her off by giving a farewell party. On her arrival at the 'Khomol' or resting place , she is offered a seat on a pile of cloth. They filter some rice-beer in a container made of gourd called 'Um'. They then offer the beer to her .As per custom of drinking, whatever cup of beer is offered to her is given back to someone else, without drinking it herslf. Such social nicety is called 'Kedon Ding Donnin' meaning 'please do drink what is supposed to be mine'. Here, the Lawm members of the girl, already knowing well that such offer of rice-beer will not be taken by the girl herself, serve the less intoxicating portion of the brew to her. This process continues till she completes this formality with all her Lawm friends. When this is over, they bring out the strongest portion of the reserved 'Zu', which is not to be offered back to anybody. Since the drinking etiquette is based on reciprocal system, all the friends to whom she had earlier offerd her share of drinks, have the obligation to do the same to her. She has no escape but to drink the whole bout of 'Zu'offered to her. With so much of reciprocal behaviour from every Lawm member whom she had offered 'Zu' earlier, the number of cups given to her in return are obviously beyond her capacity to stand. It goes without saying, therefore, that she becomes tipsy and loses control of herself, which fulfils their avowed purpose of bidding farewell to her. It often so happens that she has to be carried in a palanquine or litter upto the boy's village.

Normally, when the village 'Lawm' has a function, they arrange a campfire which is a traditional custom. The 'Lawm' members, who give her a farewell at 'Khomol', build one campfire, implying that this is the last campfire they have participated together. Apart from this, every 'Lawm' member extends some wedding gifts here in the form of cloths, beads, necklaces, etc. After this, her friends beat a retreat and leave her behind. This is done by beating the drum which creates the finest moment of emotional atmosphere. Her colleagues in the 'Lawm' have now gone with a farewell drum-beating, leaving her behind for her future home. At this stage, she cries to her heart's content to lighten the pangs of separation. This process of biding farewell from her friends may last even the whole day, despite the fact that she left early in the morning her parents' residence and fallaciously walked in the sun. She was earlier not allowed to remain in her natal home till the sunrise.

On such a farewell occasion at 'Khomol', a farewell song composed by the 'Lawm' members is sung, which is as follows :

Miphung Chang Din

Gol jin Bang Lhatange,

Lung Kitohsa,

Dam Dei Jin Bang Tange,

Lung Kitohsa,
Dam Dei Jin Bang Kalhah,
Deija Najot,
Gol Anga Mongin.

Free Translation :

The long friendship that had been established has come to an end as you are prepared to accept the title of someone.

We bid you farewell, love one, like a well known guest. May you be happy with the man whom you have chosen for your life-time company.

On their return to the village, the boys and the girls go back to the place where they had been given a farewell last night by the girl. Usually, the girl keeps ready one jar of rice-beer for her friends for this occasion. The lady of the house, whose husband receives the 'Mankang' for the girl, offers them the said 'Zu' saying that this had been left behind by their friend for them to drink on their return from 'Khomol'.

On their arrival at the boy's village, marriage ceremony is performed the same day, normally in the evening after sunset, by the priest called 'Thiempu'. In the process , the priest lets the boy and the girl sit together in the middle of the house called 'Sutlai', which occupies great significance in social and religious rites. The girl sits on the left side of the boy. They are made to sit on their legs. The priest also sits in the same fashion as the boy and the girl do, facing them with one cock in his hand. At the outset, he smoothens the cock nicely all over its body so that even if some loose feathers are to fall or have already fallen, but remain clinging between the feathers, and are clearly made to fall on the ground. He then begins to tie up each string made of cotton thread of 7 or 14 ply called 'Sa-Aw' separately around their necks with one knot each in the first instance. Thereafter, he takes the ends of both the strings of the boy and the girl and holds them together and starts propitiating in prayerful chanting of certain ritualistic secret words called 'Phuisap' for their health and prosperity. In doing so, he uses ginger. In the propitiation, the most important of the sacred words are :

I have tied the strings called 'Sa-Aw' on their necks along with many sons and daughters.

He then takes a mouthful of rice-beer and then sprays it on the 'Sa-Aws' he holds together. This act of ritual performance is called

'Juphi' which is very common to every rite of a priest. After completion of all propitiations, he ties the second knot separately, one after another, with this, the marriage ceremony is formally closed and by lifting the cock high up he declares them as man and wife. He then observes the cock's legs for a good omen. In doing this, he throttles the cock, which is normally a red one, and lifts it up in between him on the one side, and the bride and the groom on the opposite side. The cock whose respiration has been almost stopped struggles by spreading its wings and legs for escaping. In the course of such struggle if the feathers of the cock fall in a big number, it is considered as a good omen for the couple, who are thought to be blessed with many children. But if the cock passes its excreta, it is considered to be a bad omen, and is believed that the marriage will not be lasting, either the boy or the girl will soon die. After this, the priest allows the boy and the girl to leave the place. The priest then tightly holds the two wings of the cock in one hand, and strangles the neck with the other hand. He controls the tail of the cock putting it under his left foot, holds the wings with his left hand and strangles the neck with his right. He then observes the movement of the legs which struggle vigorously. In the course of struggle, the toes - either of the left or the right leg - of the cock close in sometimes and spread out occasionally. When it spreads it is said to be smiling which is very much liked by the priest as it augurs well for the marriage. The left leg is considered to be in possession of 'Thi- lha', the evil spirit or Satan, while the right one belongs to the couple which signifies a good omen.

In the process, if the left leg spreads slightly, closely followed by the right leg and after a moment's pause of both the legs, the right leg slightly makes movements, it is considered as a good omen. But if it is the left leg that slightly moves last, then it is a bad omen. If the omen is found bad, another observation of omen is preferred with a second cock until the omen shows the good ending. Meanwhile, the cock or cocks thus used are given respiration by blowing wind through its beak (i.e., mouth to mouth respiration revival system) and it is made alive again. Ultimately, the cock which shows good omen is killed and eaten by the bride, the groom and the priest.

On this occasion, several pots of rice-beer are served to all the guests who come to attend the ceremony. But out of the rice-beer served, there are two particular jars which are called 'Jupi' and 'Juthang' that have significance, unlike any other jars of 'Zu' served on the same day for the wedding ceremony. All the other jars of 'Zu' served on that day are sipped by turn in order of precedence of social standing. This is served by the 'Tucha' ladies in the following manner :

The 'Tucha' ladies prepare the 'Zu' by filling water in the jars for each person who sips. They also prepare the measurement level for sipping, which is called 'Leng'. When everything is ready for sipping, the 'Becha' of the family announces that sipping bout of the 'Zu' be started and instructs the 'Tucha-Bul' (seniormost 'Tucha') to fix the sipping measurement-level by which every one who sips is allowed only to the given level. The preparation of the 'Aleng' is called 'Lengsih'. No one is supposed to sip either more or less than the 'Aleng'. When the 'Tucha' finishes the sipping measurement, he announces his doing so. Then the 'Becha' calls the people by turn to sip in order of a set pattern of sipping procedure. The lady-Tucha sits by the side of the jar of 'Zu' and fills the water and regulates the sipping as per measurement.

Normally, the 'Becha' or 'Bechas' going to fetch the girl are called first in order of precedence, followed by the 'Tuchas' or alternately 'Bechas' and 'Tuchas', and youth leaders depending mainly at the discretion of the 'Becha' who does the distribution of sipping turn.

The other jar of 'Zu' called 'Jupi' has to be sipped only when the priest announces for it. The sipping turn which is called 'Kichep-Lhah' is preceded by the preparation of the sipping measurement called 'Alengsih' done by a 'Tucha' as in the case of sipping the general 'Zu' and that of 'Juthang'. In the process of sipping, the turn is as follows :

While every 'Becha' or 'Tucha' or anyone who sips one measurement or 'Leng', the counterpart, who had to be one of the persons who had gone to fetch the girl, is offered double the normal 'Leng'. In case there is an offer of one's share, the return-sip is necessarily double the normal sipping course which is called 'Kito'. Likewise, if a person who has been offered such double sipping still offers back his share for the second time, he still receives in turn one extra sip over and above the double-sipping bout. This is called 'Kale'. Another way of sipping is the offer of one's share to some other person which is called 'Kasih Chep', sipping on one's beheld, which has no reciprocal offer of double-sipping.

Incidentally, while every detail of secular aspect is still observed meticulously as narrated above among the Christians, the ritual aspects, such as, the marriage rites by the priest, the 'Zu' etc. are substituted by the Christian way of marriage in the Church, the marriage rites being performed by the Church Pastor in place of the village priest and tea being served in place of 'Zu'. The same holds true in case of all other occasions where 'Zu' is substituted by 'tea' and village priest called 'Thiempu' is replaced by Church Pastor.

IV After Marriage :

After the marriage is solemnised, the couple assume their role as man and wife in the society. But, if they live with their parents and other unmarried brothers and sisters and the marriage is by arrangement, the couple hardly talk between themselves and are not free in the presence of their elders and other family members, except that they share a bed at night which is also seldom seen by the members of the family. Under such circumstances, the most popular resort for a newly wed-man is to spend his time in the youngmen's dormitory or 'Sawm'. Thus, it is found that among the 'Sawm' members there are some who belong to the category of newly weds. This is mainly because of their attachment to the 'Sawm' atmosphere and to avoid being seen together with their wives in the family by the elders. Sometimes this condition continues till a man has one or two children born.

Likewise, a newly married woman cannot go back to her natal home as and when she pleases, until and unless certain formalities are performed after the expiry of certain period of time. In order to enable the girl to go and have her food and other things at her natal home, the boy's family has to take 'Zu' and seek permission called 'Nungsuleh'. The parents of the girl then formally allow her to enter the house after the priest performs certain rites. Till such time the ritual is completed, the girl cannot take food, nor can she drink even water in her natal home. The completion of this formality is, therefore, a very essential part of the marriage rituals to be performed. This period normally cannot be earlier than six months, preferably after one year, when the girl can adjust herself as one of the members of her husband's family. What the parents of a girl want most for their daughter in marriage is to make her efface herself completely with her natal home and be counted as one of the husband's family. This was the main reason why she was given a send-off in much the same way as a dead woman. Unless this rite is done, the parents or relatives of the girl may take it as an insult to them, for its implication is such that when these rites are not performed, the boy's family impliedly does not wish to establish the good relationship with the family of their bride.

In case of marriage by elopment with a girl, the parents or relatives of the boy immediately go to the house of the girl to inform that their boy is the person who has eloped with their daughter. This helps them to lighten their worries and anxieties about her whereabout. For this they carry a jar of 'Zu' with them. This is called 'Kiphon', meaning self-declaration of the responsibility. A formal negotiation then commences, after begging apology to the girl's parents and with a request to condone the mistake committed by their son and give their daughter in marriage to the boy. If the girl's parents agree, another day is fixed for further negotiations. They also pray to the girl's parents for excusing them for giving a bad name to their daughter. In doing so, the boy's parents bring one jar of 'Zu' along with one Mithun as fine for the misdeed of their son. This Mithun is killed and the negotiation for bride-price and the manner in which the price is to be paid proceeds. This is called 'Sum Tan Khao' feast. A further date is fixed and the boy's parents come with the bride-price. On this day, the boy's parents come with the price and a jar of 'Zu', bringing the girl with them . This is called 'Ki In Lut', meaning apologising and surrendering before the girl's parents for the mistake committed. Until this rite is performed, the girl cannot go back to her parents, nor can she have either food or drink at the latter's place. The boy's parents are fined by one more Mithun over the normal bride-price, if the girl happens to get married by such elopment ahead of her elder sister. This is called 'Unu Dalhah Man', i.e.. the price of leaving the elder sister behind. It is believed that in case the younger sister marries earlier than the elder sister, the latter is stigmatised in society and her prospect of finding a suitable groom is open to all sorts of speculations. Therefore, she has to be compensated.

In all the above types of marriage, the details of rituals, social obligations and other social etiquettes indicate a preference to marrying the 'Neinu', the mother's brother's daughter. Every boy is supposed to seek first his 'Neinu' as his wife. If the boy does not abide by this rule, a fine of one Mithun, which is called 'Hei Chan Man', is inflicted. An example of such an extreme case is given below :

From the above genealogical tree it is found that 'a' and 'b' have two sons and one daughter. Their names are : Thangjakai, the eldest, who is

CHART 5 : 1

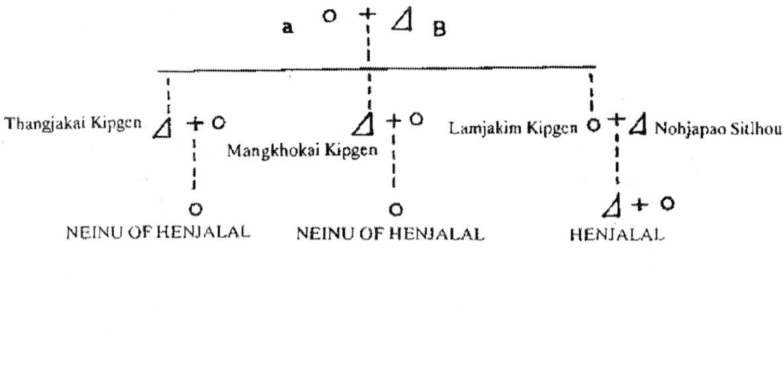

the Chief of Buning, Mangkhokai, the second brother, and Lamjakim, the sister, being the youngest. They are all married. Both the sons of 'b' have daughters, as also a son of their sister. All these offsprings are of marriageable age group. In accordance with the rule of mother's brother's daughter marriage, which is always prefered the daughters of Thangjakai and Mangkhokai are the 'Neinus' of Henjalal, who is supposed to choose any of the two cousin sisters, being mother's brother's daughters, to be his wife before looking for any other girl. Henjalal is the son of Lamjakim, who is the sister of Thangjakai and Mangkhokai. When Henjalal looked for a girl as his wife, instead of looking for either of his two 'Neinus', he chose some other girl and married her.

Since Hanjalal did not marry his mother's brother's daughter as per custom, he is to be fined, which is called 'Nei Chan Man', to the extent of one Mithun. Accordingly, Thangjakai, the elder of the two brothers of Hanjalal's mother felt insulted and considered it to be a disrespect shown to him and his brother: he fined the parents of Henjalal with one Mithun. In doing so, he went all the way from his own village to the village of his sister. Jampi, to announce the imposition of the fine for showing disrespect to her brothers. But since the sister's family could not afford to honour the fine imposed in terms of a Mithun, he was forced to take whatever other valuable article he could lay his hand on. So, he took one big gong called 'Dahpi' from his sister's house in lieu of the Mithun. This custom is to reveal his splean for the disrespect meted out to the maternal uncle by the nephew. The family relationship also become strained thereafter.

Similarly, an instance of the belief that a bride must leave her natal home before sunrise, if she is betrothed under the 'Chongmou Hailam Dom' system, is in regard to the marriage of the daughter of rich man from Sadar Hills, Manipur. This incident took place during the course of field-work. The send-off ceremony of the girl and all other formalities having been completed, it was time for the girl to leave for her conjugal home before sunrise. Knowing about this customary requirement, the boy's parents and relatives demanded that the girl belonged to them, and, as such, it was the duty of the girl's parents to hand over the girl to them, so that she might be taken out of her parents ' home before sunrise. The girl's parents did not allow their daughter to be taken away till late in the afternoon, claiming that having become Christians, such traditional belief must not be observed to interfere with their normal preparation to send-off their daughter commensural with the prestige and riches of the family. Despite this, the boy's party insisted that they should take her out of her natal home before the sunrise or, even if that was not possible, allow them to take her out of their gate and be there across the street before sunrise in a car which had been arranged for her. The request was repeatedly turned down. She was allowed to leave her natal home finally only in the afternoon.

It so happened that not very long after the marriage, the girl eloped with another boy and a very serious situation ensued which wrecked her married life. It was believed that the situation took place due to non-compliance with the customary demand of leaving the natal home before sunrise.

Another instance to the contrary also occurred almost by the same time as mentioned above in which the customary demand of leaving the natal home before sunrise was not ignored. After sending off the girl named Mangnu on the 26th of January, 1986, she was made to leave her natal home the next day in Nagaland. She did not know of such practice or belief, nor her brother who was the performer of the send-off ceremony, in absence of his parents, did know of the custom either. But the elders of both sides knew about it. Nevertheless, both sides took it for granted that she was to leave before sunrise. So, nobody told her about this, nor was her elder brother informed. In the morning, early before sunrise, an old man who was their close relative came to bid her farewell in the belief that she must have been ready for departure from her natal home before the sunrise. But none of the family members of the girl was aware of it, nor was the girl made ready to leave her natal home. On the advice of the old man, the girl was hurriedly dressed and made ready to leave her natal home. Everyone was scared of not complying with the custom. So, the girl left her natal home with bag and baggage before sunrise. Thus, an ugly situation was averted. The belief is that having complied with such traditional requirements despite being educated Christian, the girl who is a doctor is reportedly living happily with her husband who has entered into the Indian Police Service through competitive examination after their marriage.

V Bride-Price :

Origin : Chongthu was the younger brother of Noimangpa, the Chief of the underworld. As per Kuki custom, in the presence of the elder brother called 'Upa', the younger brother called 'Naopa' cannot become a Chief. So, Noimangpa, being the elder, was the Chief. Chongthu also intended to become the Chief. Therefore, he went out in search of a suitable land where he could establish himself separately as a Chief. He found one. On his plan to become a Chief he wanted to go with his own close friends whom he could trust. Thus, he arranged for the marriage of each of his selected men. In doing so, he paid the price of each bride to their parents. In those days, no valuable property or cash was available. All the valuable items that one could think of was a 'Paigen'. This was a belt made of leather and decorated with a kind of beads, called 'Longchang', in seven lines. This was then considered to be a very rare and valuable item of property. This could only be afforded by the Chief alone. So, traditionally it became associated with the sole property, the right of which was vested only in the Chief, and was venerated very much being associated with a certain amount of superstition.

Chongthu being the younger brother of the Chief, Noimangpa, had access to it, and when he arranged for the brides of his friends with whom he planned to go to his newly found land, he paid the 'Paigen' to the parents of the girls as bride-price. It so happened that though the commoners dared not refuse to accept the 'Paigen' when offered to them as bride-price, they could neither dare to keep it with them owing to their superstitions attached to it nor could they dare refuse to give the bride in marriage. Thus, along with the bride, the parents returned the 'Paigen' to Chongthu saying that this being a valuable property associated with the Chief exclusively, they dared not to keep it, lest the wrath of the unseen supernatural power visit them and bring misfortune to them. This process went on and on until Chongthu was able to arrange the marriage of 30 of his best and closest friends with the payment of 'Paigen' time and again as the bride-price.

Hereafter, bride-price of every clan was paid in terms of seven Mithuns based on the seven lines of 'Longchang' on the 'Paigen', with the exception of Sitlhous and Singsons (Singsit) for reasons given below:

Jampi family is the head of all the Sitlhou clans. It so happened that the hand of Jampi Chief's daughter was sought for by the Chief of Aithuh, a junior lineage of the Sitlhou clan, in marriage. As per their custom, the senior man of the clan, and for that matter the senior man, gets the topmost part of the back flesh of the animal killed, called 'Sating'. Now, the Chief of Aithuh, being junior, called 'Naopa', to the Chief of Jampi had so long been paying 'Sating' of animal killed by the former. In the same way, sister's husband or sister's son or daughter's husband or daughter's son are known as 'Tucha'. It was believed that the man was born out of the waist of a woman, and, as such, any man marrying the woman or one's sister or daughter was assigned to receive the waist portion of any animal killed by a man. This signifies that the man who receives it is married to the women of the family.

The Chief of Jampi felt that a man of his junior lineage, who gave him 'Sating', portion of flesh on top of the spinal cord, and with whom he formed an exogamous group, signifying their close relationship, dared ask for the hands of his daughter. By such marriage the normal social relationship would be disturbed. The Chief of Aithuh who was the junior collateral cousin of the Chief of Jampi would now be the 'Tucha' as well. Coupled with the consideration that he could not refuse the request, lest the family relationship be strained and antagonistic over a trifling matter, he was in a problem. Thus, the relationship that was to emerge out of such marriage alliance was one of double relationship . The man who was a collateral parallel cousin was to become, at the same time, a son-in-law. Therefore, it was tantamount to breaking the law of exogamy for which a fine was imposed requiring him to pay double the number of all the leading bride-prices. Since then, the bride-price of the Sitlhous was raised from seven mithuns to ten mithuns. This meant that he was to pay more than what was normally in vogue as is shown below :

Normal Bride-price	**Bride- price with Fine**
1. One Dahpi (Big gong)	1. Two Dahpis.
2. One Khichong (Necklace with rare beads representing precious stones)	2. Two Khichongs.
3. One pair of Khichong (Rare bead used as erring representing precious stones)	3. Two pairs of khichongs.
4. Seven Mithuns.	4. Ten Mithuns.

Among the Kukis, clans are divided and further subdivided, and as such, the rule of exogamy is applicable only to a smaller group of people among the collaterals within three generations beyond which marriage between two members of collateral cousins is permitted though such marriage is not considered desirable. Such was the situation of the above example which prompted the Sitlhous to charge higher rate of bride-price.

There might have been many good reasons for taking the bride-price among the Kukis of which, among other things, the scribe was told that the following were the main considerations :

(1) 'Luong-Kaidoh-Man-Dragging away of a body (meant person):

For this purpose one Mithun is always attached to the bride- price, and is considered to lead the whole lot of bride-price and is called MANLAMKAI.

(2) As a compensation to the economic loss, because of the girls' being taken away from the family who, as is usual among the Kukis, are the main pillars of family economy. The loss of a girl in a family is heavy, for it is only the women who are associated with the welfare of the family economy , means of earning, growth and development of the family.

(3) Being the bearer of children for the propagation of family lines of generation to which she goes.

The bride-price has an underlying social value in that it must by all means be not paid in full. Even if a rich man can afford to pay the bride-price, he is not allowed to do so. A part of it is always kept as due, to be paid in future. By this, it has an implication to the effect that the man should always have obligation, love, respect, etc., for his wife and her relatives thereby enlivened a sense of maintaining constant and good social relationship with his wife and in-laws.

It also has an implicit value on the importance of the wife and her relatives in the family circle of the man. It is said that the components of bride-price, such as, Khichong represents precious stones and ornaments, and Dahpi and Dahbu represent valuable assets which are not within the reach of man's capacity to acquire. In like manner, a man's wife is so valuable that her price is not within the limit of a man's capacity to pay in full. Thus, the unpaid portion or the due part of the bride-price is a constant reminder to the man and his relatives that his wife, and for that matter, her relatives, are as precious and valuable as the priceless precious stones and assets which are yet to be paid in full.

As for the bride-price of the Singsons, it is 30 Mithuns without any other items, such as, Khichong, Khichang, Dahpi, Dahbu, etc., unlike the other clans of the Thadou Kukis. The higher rate of bride-price among the Singsons has no origin. It is said that the Singsons are the direct junior collaterals of the Sitlhous. So, when their senior collateral (Sitlhous) increased the bride-price under the circumstances mentioned above, the Singsons also deemed it proper to follow suit.

VI Pregnancy :

Tribal world is closely associated with certain amount of superstition in much the same way as their day-to-day life which is run by some code or conduct. Thus, every aspect of a Kuki life functions within the ambit of their social system manifested in some form or other. In their habit of drinking , eating, religious and other ceremonial rites, the Kukis move through a certain set pattern of behaviour which reflects their social structure. Such structural functions also regulate their social belief, behaviour and observances of certain restraints in the activities in social, economic, religious and political life.

It is strongly believed that during pregnancy of a man's wife. there are certain things a man is supposed to do and to restrain from, inasmuch as his wife is regulated in her activities. Such socially regulated activities of a man and his wife continue till a baby reaches a point of its age. Such restraint in activities of one's life is the basis of the belief that a man, wife and the child are the subjects of all kinds of misfortune and accident in life during pregnancy and also after child-birth.

It is customary that a man must not quarrel with anybody, nor should he be in polemics during the pregnancy of his wife. It is believed that a man is subject to misfortune and is prone to accidents.

A woman must not take 'Pupa' (Khoinuou) during pregnancy. It is believed that if a pregnant woman takes it, the child shivers like the fluttering wings of the bee when the former grows up.

Eggs are not to be touched by a pregnant woman. The outer cover of an egg called membrane, containing the white liquid of an egg, is believed to have transformed into the membrane of the child in the womb. If, therefore, a woman touches the egg during pregnancy, she experiences problems during child birth. The pregnant woman can, however, eat cooked, boiled or fried eggs.

A snake must not be killed by a woman during pregnancy. It is believed that if a woman kills a snake during pregnancy, the tongue of the child will take after the fang of a snake.

A pregnant woman must not expose her waist to the fire for taking heat-treatment. It is believed that if a woman's waist is exposed to the fire, the womb is pasted to the waist. The womb, therefore, cannot come out easily during child birth and, as such, the woman dies.

It is a taboo to hold a pregnant woman by hair due to anger during a quarrel between the husband and the wife, or for that matter, by anybody. It is believed that if a women's hair is held during pregnancy, the child is born prematurely, or there occurs an abortion.

Rice pounding log or stick, called 'Suh' must not be prepared and cut by the husband of the pregnant woman during the latter's pregnancy. It is generally believed that if a man does so, the child (if it is a boy) is born with circumcised penis. It is also believed that such circumcised person is not liked by serpents (Gulpi) at all.

The husband of a pregnant woman also must not cut the mouth of a bamboo water-container. The Kukis do not have any other type of water container. The only water container of indigeneous product is made of bamboo, which is popularly known as 'Gotui-Thei'. Its mouth is not cut evenly, but slantingly. Therefore, it is believed that if a man, whose wife is pregnant, cuts the mouth of the bamboo water-container, the mouth of the child will be slant, just like that of the container itself.

It is customary among the Kukis that the 'Tucha' of a person who performs some kind of social function, is to clean and dress properly the intestine of the animal killed during such function, which is called 'Sa Gil Sah'. In the social system of relationship a man among the Kukis is either a 'Tucha' or 'Songgao' in relation to someone necessarily through matrimonial alliance. Therefore, the husband of a pregnant woman must not attend to the dressing and cleaning of the intestine of any animal killed, during the pregnancy of his wife. The superstition in this regard is too severe, even to utter about it. It is simply said, " not permitted".This, however, is due to the equation that dressing of intestine of an animal during pregnancy of one's wife represents doing the same to a man's wife. In other words, it is a sign of the death of a man's wife under ugly circumstances.

It is believed that in much the same way as the waist of the mother is open for the birth of the child, everything connected with the acts of opening on the part of the pregnant woman should remain open as the pregnant woman feels the birth-pang for an easy delivery. Therefore, as the labour pain commences,a pregnant woman opens all her boxes, including her cane container or box, and basket type container made of cane, called 'Lel', 'Sinkhup' etc. Normally, from the day a woman knows that she has conceived, she brews one big jar of 'Zu' which becomes as old as nine or ten months. It produces very sweet odour and contain a high degree of intoxicating element. This is to be prepared and offered either for drinking or sipping to those who attend to the woman on the day of delivering a child and also to the guests who come for offering greetings. This act is preceded by the opening of the cover of the jar of 'Zu' which has so far been kept air-tight. She also throws open the gates of her poultry, piggery, cattle- pen, etc.

It is also believed that if a woman fords a stream during her menstruation, misfortune may befall her. Therefore, she is forbidden from crossing a stream.

All these beliefs and taboos are based on practical knowledge and experiences by the elders through ages, which at one time or the other came true in the past. An instance of personal experience can be cited in regard to grabbing the hair of a pregnant woman; during the Second World War, when the Japanese overrun Changoubung village, all the villagers fled from it in fear of danger to life. But a pregnant woman, who was expecting an imminent delivery, could not move out due to her labour pain and when the Japanese gendarmes came into the village, she was in unbearable labour pain. On seeing her condition, and knowing as he did, a Japanese soldier grasped her hair and shook her head, as a result of which she gave birth to a child immediately. The woman concerned told this incident to the scribe herself. Such were the practical experiences and personal knowledge that prompted to lay certain conditions for the pregnant woman and her husband.

VII Child-Birth and After :

As soon as a child is born, a name is given. The moment the sex of the child is determined by the attending persons to the pregnant woman in labour, the child is given a temporary name, which may be changed later, if necessary. It is generally named after one of its grandparents. It is believed that if a child is not given a name immediately, the devils, called 'Thilha Ho', give a name first to the child resulting in the shortness of life of the child. The umbilical cord of the child is cut with a fresh bamboo split, called 'Nat-Go', which is sufficiently sharpened for the purpose. The story of the origin of naming a child immediately after delivery is interesting. It is said that as soon as the child is born, the grandparents or the father or whoever helps in the matter of delivery must say :

> Here do I proclaim that I have cut the naval-cord of my grandchild or child or this child, no one else has the right to cut it.

This naming of the baby is known as 'Nao Min Chu'. Such proclamation stems from the fact that long ago a man went out for hunting when his wife was in an advanced stage of pregnancy. In the forest, it was too late for him to return home. So, the hunter spent the night under a huge tree in the jungle. There was a hollow on the trunk of the tree. He managed to catch a wild hare (Buipi) and carried it. In the hollow of the trunk of the tree there lived a family of devils called 'Thilha'. At the dead of night, when he was asleep, he was awakened by some voices coming towards the trunk of the tree. As the voices reached there, they called out. The family of 'Thinla' living in the hollow of the trunk responded. The voices asked the family that lived in the trunk whether they could join them and go to a nearby village to cut the naval cord of a new-born baby. This invitation was politely refused by the 'Thilhas' on the ground that there was a guest who had a dog with him. This implied that there was a hunter with his cane basket wherein a 'Buipi' was present. Under the circumstances, the devils in the hollow could not join them and the voices should proceed without them.

After a few hours, the voices returned from the village. The family of the devils living in the hollow asked as to the health and condition of the child for whose birth and cutting the naval cord they went. The reply was, "The tiger king had cut the naval cord of the child ahead of us." Then the devil-lady of the trunk inquired further - "What was the time fixed by the tiger king". The reply was :

> The boy becomes a youngman, get married with two wives. The two wives will one day quarrel, while pounding rice using the pounding sticks or legs as battons freely. The boy then would think that the two wives of his ought to have separate rice pounder each. So, he would go to the jungle the next day to prepare one more rice pounder. While he works on the rice pounder, the tiger would have the naval cord of the boy cut.

Now, the hunter suspected that the subject-matter of discussion among the 'Thilhas' must have concerned his own family, for he was fully aware of the fact that he left his wife in her advance stage of pregnancy and whose labour-pain could have started at any time of the day. Being apprehensive, he could no longer sleep the rest of the night. So, before the day-break he started for his home to reach there early. On arrival, when he heard that a son had born to him, he enquired about the timing of his wife's giving birth to the child. He was told that the child was born last night, after midnight. The time, he felt, exactly synchronised with the time the 'Thilhas' were claimed to have been talking about cutting the naval cord of a new-born child.

The hunter kept the episode to himself and did not divulge it to anyone throughout the life-time of his son. He observed the growth and the way of life of his son, keeping in mind the conversations of the 'Thilhas' on that unforgettable night in the jungle. As the boy grew up to manhood, what his father heard years ago came true. His son married two wives and, as was predicted in that fateful night by the 'Thilhas', the two wives quarrelled one day over the rice-pounder. To solve this, their husband thought it better to provide both with one rice pounder each. He, therefore, went to the jungle to prepare one more rice- pounder. His father, knowing what fate awaited his son, followed his son covertly into the jungle in order to protect him against his destined fate, according to the prediction of the 'Thilhas'.

As the son began to cut the wood, a tiger ambushed him for his pray and stood at a vantage point to pounce on the former at the first opportunity. While the tiger was hiding to kill the son, the father was ambushing the tiger to kill him and foil the prediction. As the son fell his axe on the log for cutting the wood, he bent down. Likewise, as he alighted the axe from the wood, he straightened. This movement of bending and straightening made the tiger unable to adjust its target correctly, and as such, it took some time to jump on its pray. At last, as it jumped, the hunter-father also took a head-long plunge into the leeping tiger and killed the big cat with a single shot. All this time the son was unaware of what was happening around him. Having seen a dead tiger and his father, he could sense the happening and was grateful to his father for saving his life. Going to the carcass he cursed the dead tiger saying -

> If my father had not killed you, you would have killed me. It is a petty that you have to be a dead tiger.

As he said this, he unconsciously rubbed the whiskers of the tiger up and down. While doing so, he received a deep cut injury on one of his fingers which brought him death ultimately. He could not be saved despite his father's attempt to do so. The incident proved that what is lotted cannot be blotted. The hunter's son died just the way the 'Thilhas' predicted.

Henceforth, it was believed that the name of the new-born babe should be given as soon as the naval-cord of the child is severed from the mother.

VIII Events During the Post-Birth Period of a Child :

As has been stated above, the cover of the jar of 'Zu' prepared by the expectant mother is to be opened first, distilled for drinking and then offered to the new mother as also to those who nursed her along with those who come to greet the child. This is called 'Nao-Zu' or wine or the child. Indeed, the wine helps the woman to restore her energy and to clear whatever was there to come out with the placenta. The wine is medically salubrious and is prescribed by the Priest of the village who propitiates with his usual rituals for the health of both the child and the mother. Soon after the wine is drunk, the mother feels hungry. By way of a flash-back, as soon as a women feels that she has conceived, she prepares 'Zu' and keeps it shelved for 09/10 months. On the day of delivery, the 'Zu' is uncorked by the pregnant woman herself and taken. On this day also a cock or hen is killed as soon as the child is born. The chicken is then boiled and its soup is taken by the mother of the child. The meat is cooked and boiled well with some rice which is also eaten by the mother. This is believed to give her strength and help her in quick recovery. The meat is also taken by those attending on her. Thus, the wine served on the occasion is continued to be sipped until its intoxicating element is exhausted, which might carry them for the whole night.

As the child grows upto about five years, the head of a girl is shaved, except for a small patch at the back. It remains so till her puberty age. On the other hand, a boy is also shaved clean with a tuft on top of his head which remains as he is grown up. Thereafter he grows his hair long in much the same manner as to that of a girl. This difference in hair cutting during childhood is just to distinguish a boy from a girl.

IX Prohibitive Activities After Child-Birth :

After a child is born, when the mother is able to revert to her daily routine of work at home and field, there are some prohibitions which she is expected to observe. They are as follows :

Whenever the mother goes to the field, she bids farewell to her child saying, "Be at home, my child, while I go to the field." Otherwise, it is believed that the soul of the child may follow her. For fear of the child's soul following her to the field, she is always supposed to say at the time of her returning home thus : "Come my child, let us go home". If this is not said, and if the soul of the child happens to follow her, it cannot come back with its mother. And thus left alone in the field, the child's soul wanders about in the jungle in search of its mother. This results in illness and sufferance of the child. The priest then has to propitiate and call back the child's soul from its wanderings. In the like manner, when the mother of the child arrives home from the field with her load of firewood, in a basket or anything domestically useful, it is not simply thrown down or put down on the ground. It is feared that the soul of the child having followed the mother has come back from the jungle and might be standing or playing around her. If, therefore, the load is suddenly put down without giving prior warning to the soul, the action of the mother might hurt the child accidentally. Therefore, before putting down the heavy load of the mother, it is always said first - "Be away, my child, I am putting down the firewood (or whatever load) on the ground."

Likewise, there are certain things to be observed by the father of the child in the childhood days of his children. If a father is to undertake touring along with a child, burnt-coal or smoked portion of the hearth is painted on the forehead of the child, before the child is taken out of the house. It is believed that such act of painting the child with charred-coal or smoked coal helps ward off the child from all kinds of illness and misfortune. The same procedure is followed during its return journey also. This is to identify that the child is being accompanied by the parents and grandparents, so that 'Thilhas' might not cast their evil spell on it. Similarly, when a child is taken out in the evening after sunset or nightfall, ginger is applied on its forehead to avoid illness.

X Child-Naming System :

The system of naming among the Kukis is peculiar -unique in its system, singularly conspicuous in its reflection to their social structure and manifestly structured social relationships through kinship and marriage. The naming system is so strong that even after generations it still holds way in the Kuki society and can maintain their genealogical tree for generations together without confusion, mainly through the naming system. Of all the social systems among the Kukis that withstands the onslaught of changes brought about by various agencies, such as, Christianity, modern education, developmental schemes, etc., is the naming system of the Kukis. The system is such that the first-born son of a family is necessarily named after his paternal grandfather. Conversely, the first-born daughter of the family is given the name after her grandmother. The third and the fourth children go after the names of the maternal grandparents of the child, or they may as well be named after some other person close to the family. But such naming of the child after someone other than the maternal grand-parents should have sufficiently good reason in doing so. Otherwise, the relationship with the maternal side is likely to be strained. In naming a child after the grand-parents, the method is simple, and this shows a continuity of relationship which can be termed as "Alternate Generation naming System". When a child is named, the last syllable of the grandfather or grandmother or any other persons' name is taken, as the first syllable of the name of the child or grandchild, as the case may be. Since such naming is normally connected with the persons of one generation above the parents, the terminology to be applied to the relationship between the child and the person after whose name the child has been called is one of grandparents and grandchildren. Thus, by extension of the classificatory system of terminology, the person whose name has been given to the child other than one's own grandparents, is called by the latter as 'Hepu' or 'Hepi',i.e.,grand-pa or grand-ma.

Likewise, a person whose name has been given to a child other than the child's own grandfather or grandmother addresses the child as 'Katu', meaning, my grandchild; even if their relationship would have been otherwise. An example of the naming system may be shown in the following manner, from which the genealogical tree of the family could be easily constructed.

Jelhao Sitlhou is one of the progenitors of the seniormost Sitlhou clan, called the family of Jampi or 'Jampi-pa' in Thadou. Jelhao gives birth to Henmang and Goulen; Henmang begets a son, who is named after the grandfather of the child whose name is Jelhao. Thus, from Jelhao the grandson is named as Haokhoton, taking the last syllable from the name Jel-Hao. Hao being the last syllable of the name of the grandfather of the child, the same becomes the first syllable of the name of the grandson. So, the grandson is named as Jel-Hao, Haokhoton. Now, Haokhoton has a son who is named after his grandfather, Henmang. Taking the last syllable of Henmang, the grandson is named Mangtho. Again, Mangtho has a son who is named after his grandfather Haokhoton, thereby taking the name Tonkhothang. Tonkhothang begets a son who has been named as Thosong, being named after the last syllable of his grandfather Mangtho. In continuation, Thosang begets a son who has been named as Thangkhotinmang, being named after the last syllable of his grandfather, Tonkhothang.

It may also happen that a child may be named after the paternal uncle or aunt of the child instead of naming after the grandfather or granduncle in order to show love, respect and affection and to establish better social relationship. Thus, when Thangkhotinmang has a son, instead of naming him after the grandfather, Thosong, of his son, he has been named as Thangchungnung, after the last syllable of his younger brother's name, Jamkhothang, who is the paternal uncle of his son. This is also an act of perpetuating the blood relationship between the paternal uncle and the nephew. The counting of genealogical tree is in no way affected in its continuity. In fact, it helps establishing the relationship between the Senior and the Junior lineages of a family.

From the above statement, a genealogical tree can easily be constructed by induction of the names of alternate generations. It is shown below :

CHART 5 : 2

THE HOUSE OF JAMPI,
JELHAO SITLHOU

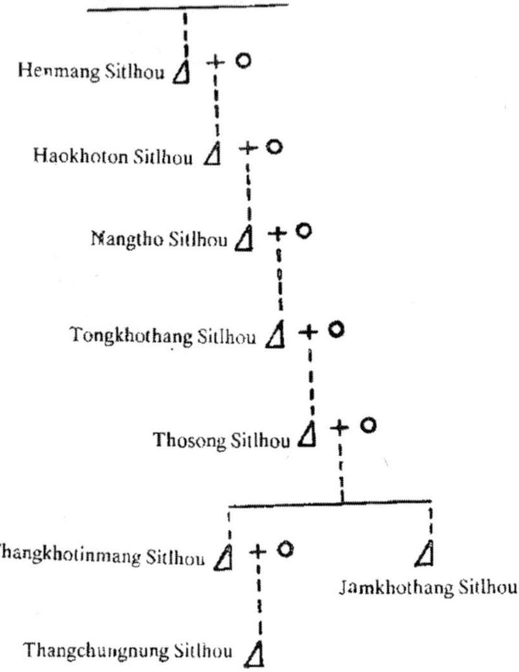

These persons are the descendants of the man called Sitlhou from whose direct line in the genealogical tree Jelhao Sitlhou is the seventh generation in descending order, and counting downwards from the generation of Thangchungnung Sitlhou, the genealogical tree of the family of Sitlhou still continues down to the third generation, the living Sitlhou Chief of Jampi at present being, therefore, Thangkhomang Sitlhou. The same system is followed in the matter of naming the girls who are named after women relatives of the grand daughters. The grandchild and the grandparents have now been treated as on the same footing in such system. Even when a person is not known as to his father's name, by induction from his name, he can be identified as son or grandson of so and so. The relationship of grandchildren with that of their grandparents is therefore, one of friendship and joking, treating each other as equals with tolerance, to the extreme extent.

It may also happen that a child is named after the great-great-great-grandfather or the progenitor of the family with a view to receiving the blessings of such ancient persons. This is resorted to when there occurs many an ill-luck in a family especially to avoid continuation of such ill-health and extinction of male line of the family. Examples of such naming could be provided, such as, naming of Shongkhokam, the only son of Thongkhosei of Khengjang village. After having had five daughters, a son was born to Thongkhosei. In order to receive blessings of the progenitor of the family, Sitshong, he was given the last syllable of Sitshong, Shongkhokam instead of naming after his grandfather, so that ill-luck may not fall on the boy.

In like manner, Jamkithang Sitlhou named his only son, Mangkholien, after the name of the grandfather, Lhunjamang. It is interesting to note that the man did not have a son after five daughters. So, in order that the family is blessed with a son, when the sixth daughter was born she was named after her grandfather which itself is a departure from normal procedure. Normally, a female-child is to take the name of a woman of choice of the parents. This was purposely done to invite the soul of a male-child. Thus she was called Lhungjamang - Mangpinieng.

XI Christening of the Child : or 'Naopui' :

Christening of a Kuki child is called 'Naopui', which is done at the residence of the maternal uncle or of maternal grandparents. When 'Naopui' is done, the parents of the child take along with them the following articles to the maternal uncle/grandparents' house :

1. One jar of rice-beer called 'Zubel'.

2. One cloth called 'Puondum' (among the Thadou speaking clans the colour of the cloth should be black with two lines of white colour on the border, lengthwise.) No other cloth is allowed.

The christening party goes with their 'Bechas' and 'Tuchas', leaving their home early in the morning. The child to be christened is to be carried by lady-Becha of the family, who is not supposed to have moral or physical blemishes. Any lady-Becha who has physical defect or deformity, including squinted eyes and incomplete or extra fingers or toes, forfeit this privilege. A lady whose marriage is not normal, or a divorcee or a widow, is also not eligible to carry the child. Thus, if the lady-Becha is not found qualified to carry the child, any person without defect in any way, including the baby's brother or sister can be given the charge of carrying the child.

On their arrival at the maternal uncle or grandparent's house, the party is not allowed instantly to enter the house. They are stopped at the portico, which is called 'Huongcha' before the main entrance of the house. The Becha of the maternal uncle/grandparents cuts ginger into pieces (called 'Thing Subh Ding') and then the priest or Thiempu performs purification rite, on completion of which they are allowed in the house. This signifies that the child is spotless and pure when they take him or her to the house of the maternal uncle's. All kinds of evil influence and bad things that may be fall the child are then warded off by performance of the purifying rite at the door with ginger.

Then the Thiempu offers them the sliced ginger just prepared. They all take a small piece each and thereafter they are taken into the house. This is immediately followed by the announcement from the 'Becha' of the family of the child, who has come to the house of the maternal uncle, to seek the blessings for the child. The 'Becha' also performs his duty by handing over all the things brought with them for the maternal uncle's family in token of request for their blessings and also as a gratitude for the affection shown to them. The items of articles carried with them, as mentioned above, have great significance and are handed over to the 'Becha' of the family of the maternal uncle of the child by his counterpart in maternal uncle's family. As the articles are received, the maternal uncle's 'Becha' asks their 'Tute', i.e., the grandchildren of the family of their daughter or sister to remain with them for a feast. Now, the 'Zu' brought along with the articles is made ready for sipping, by turn. Such feast is called 'Nao Khuo Del' or giving blessings to the child. A portion of the meat of the animal killed in this connection, which is normally a pig or a Mithun, is cooked and eaten. The rest of the meat, called 'Sa-Hap' is kept apart for giving it to the family of the child. The meat thus saved, includes the hind- leg, half of the waist and tail which is taken to the home of the parents of the child. While the meat is being cooked, the 'Thiempu' performs the blessing rituals to the child, called 'Lha-Lhaw' by presenting a cock which is also taken home with them. The child is given one cloth to boot, called 'Naopuon'. If the maternal uncle is not well-off, he does not kill a pig or a Mithun. But he kills only a cock instead. This does not, however, exempt him from giving another live-cock normally the one used for the 'Lha-Lhaw'.

In performing the 'Lha-Lhaw' rites of propitiation with the cock, the priest ties one string called 'Sa-Aw' around the neck of the child. In the middle of the string, which is made of plaited cotton-thread, are tied some feathers of the cock. The child puts on this string for his or her 'Lha-Lhaw' on the neck as long as he/she wishes. In the process of such propitiation, the priest sits facing the child who is made to sit opposite the priest in the middle of the floor or 'Lhuong-Lai', near the hearth. The required ingredients for this ritual are :

1 A small quantity of a type of solid rice-beer, called 'Anthawm' or 'Vaizu'.

2 The container of the 'Anthawm' or 'Vaizu' which is made of a small gourd, is called 'Vaikawm'.

The priest then takes a mouthful of the beer which he spits out spraying over the child, the act being called 'Phikhum'. This is done before the commencement of the ritual for propitiation. He repeats this act when his propititaion is finished by way of an act of blessing to the child. The grandparents offer one pot of 'Zu' in addition to killing one pig and giving the right hind- leg of the killed animal, which includes the tail, signifies bigger portion of the hind-leg joining the one half of the waist portion which is the portion meant for a 'Tucha' relative.

On their arrival at home, the Thiempu of the family receives the cock brought from the maternal relatives. With the cock the Thiempu performs rites for pacifying omens and portents by observing the movements of the legs of the cock when strangled. Thereafter, the cock is killed, cooked and eaten by the priest and the child. The portion of the meat brought from the maternal uncle is also cooked and eaten by the relatives of the family, including the 'Becha' and the 'Tucha' of the family. The occasion is accompanied with the sipping of 'Zu' arranged by the parents of the child and supplemented by other relatives, who come to take part on the occasion. The jars of 'Zu' brought by the relatives and other invitees are given purely voluntarily and this is called 'Belbing'.

XII Death and Rites Connected with the Funeral :

Deaths are generally attributable to three broad divisions, namely -

(1) Thi-Pha or Natural Death.

(2) Senhut Thi or Childhood Death -Upto the Age of Three.

(3) Thi-Sie or Unnatural Death,

1. Natural Death ('Thi-Pha Thi') :

There are different kinds of natural deaths. The dead bodies of people who meet a natural death are buried in the normal course and in accordance with the rules of the last rites prescribed. When a person dies, messengers are immediately fanned out to inform all the relatives, close friends and others who cared for the dead person. This act is known as 'Thi Jin Kou'.

On their return home, the messengers perform the act of bravery or anger over the death of the person they loved. Such act is called 'Kitom'. In the process, some of them use scythe and some use axe, assuming that the evil spirit that has taken away the life of the deceased is hovering around and watching them, the messengers start cutting the frames of the doors, pillars and wherever the evil spirits are supposed to hide or whatever comes their way. A man having a gun may also use it and shoot a blank fire on the assumption that the unseen evil spirit called 'Thilha' might be killed or injured, so that vengeance is taken against the evil spirit. This also indicates an expression of love and affection shown to the deceased. When such act of 'Kitom' is performed, some of the performers make mention of the names of father, grandfather and great-grandfather of the dead person, eulogising them as well as the deceased and challenge the 'Thilhas' saying that the latter would not be able to have an easy hand-over of the deceased in the land-of-death called 'Mithikho'. The utterances at the time of 'Kitom' run as follows. At the same time, they would be brandishing whatever is in their hand as a weapon, either scythe, gun, axe, etc.

The Utterances During 'Kitom':

I am the son of so and so, who the devil are you to snatch away so and so from our midst? Where are you? Reveal Yourself, I challenge you. If I were able to see you with my naked eyes, I would have done to you like this and like that (Brandishing what is in hand.

Takchepa, keima Hichichu Kahe, Koinahim Kanu, Kapa ahilou leh kau Kanao that na. Muthei hin lang hiti nin nawleing E Kiphuongin.

Thus, the messengers keep on brandishing about their scythe or axe or gun in an act of hurting the unseen killer. Some of them resort to crying, and some whimper uttering poetic language or compose song which is called 'Ka-La'. So, 'Kitom' is obligatory on the part of every messenger on his return from his mission of breaking the sad news of demise to relatives and well-wishers. Even if one does not know how to do a 'Kitom', he is taught how to do it. Otherwise, it is feared that such messenger, who does not perform 'Kitom', will be taken ill.

Generally, when the time comes for digging the grave, the priest goes to select the place for burial. In doing so, he clears the selected spot of trees of bushes, if there be any. This done, the priest will perform a short ritual. The priest is normally accompanied by the highest 'Tucha' called 'Tucha-Bui' of the family. After this, the priest goes back home, leaving behind the 'Tucha-Bui' at the selected site for making the grave. On his arrival home, the priest informs all the young and able bodied men to dig the grave at the site where he left the 'Tucha Bul'. On their arrival at the graveyard, they are not immediately allowed to start digging the grave. The 'Tucha- Bul' whom the priest leaves behind earlier at the selected graveyard, digs first one or two strokes with a spade symbolising the commencement of the work. Then and then only others are allowed to start the digging operation. The first one or two strokes of digging by the 'Tubul' is called 'Lhan-Chan', meaning reservation of the graveyard. After having done this, the particular 'Tucha' is no longer allowed to leave the place and enter the house again until the deceased is buried. A separate pot of 'Zu' exclusively meant for this man is prepared. He sips this 'Zu' near the grave, while others continue to do the work of digging. He may as well invite others for sipping the beer with him. It should be noted here that a graveyard is not allowed to remain vacant overnight. If a graveyard is constructed at all, the same day it is dugged should the deceased be buried. That is why the 'Tucha' who does the 'Lhan-Chan' guarding the graveyard is not allowed to return home until the burial takes place. It is believed that if a graveyard is made to remain open or vacant for an overnight, misfortune takes more of its toll.

When time comes for the burial service, the priest offers a short dedicational rite called 'Phul Sam'. This is followed by cleansing of the grave by the 'Tucha Bul' with a big torch of fire. All the corners of the grave is then well-flamed with the torch. When this is done, once again the priest performs the last rite entering into the mouth of the grave. Having satisfied himself, he goes to the house of the deceased. There he announces that it is time to proceed to the graveyard for the burial service and whoever wishes to cry and perform 'Kitom' for the last time may do so. When everyone does the crying and the 'Kitom' to one's heart's content, the priest himself does his 'Kitom' alone signifying that it is time to pay their last homage to the deceased and the dead body be carried out of the house en-route graveyard. The priest leads the funeral procession and performs the 'Kitom' all the way to the graveyard. As he leads the procession and performs the 'Kitom' rite, he says -

Lam Non, Lam Non,
Kapu That In Lam Non
Kapa That In Lam Non.

Free Translation :

Make way, Make way,
Whoever kills my grandfather, Make way,
Whoever kills my father, Make way.

This last rite in the funeral procession is performed in consideration that the deceased is not stranded or is given trouble on its way to 'Thij-awn-bung', a place before reaching the land of the dead.

As the deceased is brought out of the house, one round of blank- fire in the air is shot to indicate the position of the moving funeral procession towards the cemetery. As the deceased is brought out, the bamboo litter prepared to carry the dead body is also brought out. Everything is cleaned meticulously and it is broken into shreds to be placed in the grave. All the materials used by the deceased while living are buried along with the dead body.

On the day of the burial, if a rich man can afford it, a Mithun or Mithuns are killed to feed all the guests who come to condole or to participate in the funeral rites of the deceased. This is called 'Kosa', an expression of the status and prestige of the deceased and his family. The number of animals killed depend on the ability of the bereaved family to spend. Besides Mithun, all kinds of other domestic animals can be killed for the purpose. The heads of all these animals killed are hoisted above the grave by hanging those on tree trunks to show the status of the deceased. These may also be added in future by any friend or relative who would kill any wild game to express his solidarity, affection and loyalty to the deceased and the bereaved family. If the deceased person is a rich Chief of a clan, his graveyard is to be adorned with the head of a man for which a head- hunting party is organised.

The next day, after the burial of the dead body, tree-trunks are erected with its branches after clearing the bushes and leaves to facilitate hoisting the animal heads killed in commemoration of the deceased or whatever is connected with the deceased. This is done mainly by the 'Tuchas' and the 'Bechas' of the bereaved family. The planted tree-trunks with their branches are called 'Lhan Khuom'.

After the funeral ceremony is over, immediately those concerned in digging the grave, including the 'Tucha-Bul' who takes part in the 'Lhan-Chang' and those who fill the grave take a purifying bath. In taking this purifying bath, some water is prepared in a big brass gong wherein silver and beads are dipped. With such water, the persons concerned take bath symbolically by washing their hands or whatever part of their body they wish to wash. In this process they purify themselves.

If the family of the deceased is very rich, they ogranise a hunting party for killing of animals to get their heads to be hoisted on the graveyard of the deceased person for decoration. This is called 'Kosana'. Such hunting party may kill as many wild games as they can and the heads are hoisted on the graveyard of the deceased. This is the general practice for decoration of the graveyard of the deceased persons. But once it so happened that the Sitlhou clan in order to show their superiority over others used to hunt men for the said purpose, instead of animals or wild games.

2. 'Senhut Thi' or Childhood Death - Upto the Age of Three

This is the case of infant mortality. If a child dies in its infancy, i.e., within the age of its teeth-cutting, the death is considered not as a normal death, but is generally regarded as a sacrifice to God by the family and is, therefore, called 'Senhut'. In such case, the dead body is not buried through normal procedure of burial as it happens in the case of a grown up person. The Kukis, in general, construct their houses with a raised floor, mostly of bamboo split or plank of about three to six feet above the ground level. A dead child is buried under the ground dug beneath the floor almost near the hearth portion of the house. After a pit is dug beneath the floor of the house, it is kept open and the body of the child is dropped in it from inside the house through the floor which is open for the purpose. It is believed that a child dies pure and spotless. The body of the child must not therefore be exposed to sun and rain which may defile the mortal remains.

This kind of burial is practised in the cases of some adults also, depending on the circumstances. It may so happen that death has not touched with its icy hand a particular family. If an elderly man of this family dies, such death of the adult member is not treated as a case of adult-death. It is treated as if the man has died in his childhood and thus it is called a 'Senhut' death. Whatever height of fame he has achieved in the society, he would deserve the burial of a dead child. But there is a little variation in the procedure of the burial. Being an adult person, the burial ground cannot be selected in the same place as earmarked for a child, i.e.

beneath the floor near the hearth. This is due to the fact that the construction of a Kuki house is done always on the slope of a hill, and the ground level where the hearth is usually located is always higher. As such elevation from the ground on that site is closer to the ground. Therefore, burial of an adult at the place fixed for a child is unsuitable for digging and also for health and sanitation of the members of the family. As such, instead of burying an adult in the same place meant for a child, a place beneath the floor at a higher level from the ground called 'Lhuongmuoi' which is located near the eaves of the house is selected. The manner of burial is the same as is in vogue for a child burial.

Below is given a song composed in connection with the burial of adults who are buried under 'Senhut' or childhood death (buried under the floor of the house called 'Huongnuoi') :

Huonna Piguon Hungpengin
Nana Damdei Ken Banjalin Sangnangie

Free Translation

(Be alive again as the vegetables in the garden. I will receive you in my longing arms.)

3. 'Thi-Sie' or Unnatural Death

A person who dies by an accidental fall from a tree or by drawning or is killed/murdered as a consequence of some quarrel, etc. are called unnatural death cases or 'Thise'. The dead body of such a person is not entitled to get proper funeral rites as he would have received if he met a natural death. Such dead bodies are not allowed to be brought inside the village. A man who commits suicide is also included in the list of unnatural death cases, and is treated in the same manner. Such a person, if he is a male person, is not reckoned within the counting of names of male members of the family of the clan he belongs to or of the sub-clan or lineage, despite his fame or importance in the society. Reckoning of all the male line of the particular clan or lineage is called 'Min Lutuo'. A man who murders a person is also not entitled to the formal burial of a naturally dead person along with the funeral rites. An exclusion of persons of importance in the reckoning of genealogical tree of the clan or lineage due to being a murderer is the example of Thalhun in the genealogical tree of the Thadous, because he killed his wife accidentally. He was not entitled to getting the honour of rites in connection with natural death. He was treated as a person with unnatural death, despite his being a great Chief amongst the Thadous. He, in fact, was the progenitor of 'Elmun' (Sitlhou and Sihgson), Haokip and Kipgen, the three famous brothers whose descendants are now known to have numerically preponderated all their collateral brethren within the fold of Thadou speaking people.

XIII Lang Lap Ma Kivui

There is a separate system of funeral rites for thsoe who achieve fame and status in their life-time due to being a good hunter or a wealthy person or being a brave person in war. Such special burial ceremony is called 'Lang Lap Ma Vui'. In such cases, the deceased is not buried immediately after death, as is observed in regard to ordinary persons meeting natural deaths. There are certain elaborate rituals to be performed in connection with their burial, the details of which are given below :

If a man of repute and fame dies, the burial ceremony is entirely different and it is called 'Lang Lap Ma Kivui'. Such burial is given only to a man of highest repute and fame, a person who is rich or brave in war or earns reputation as a good hunter of wild games. Whoever has performed the 'Chon' or given the feast of merit earns the eligibility of getting such a burial which is called 'Langlap'

When a person of fame or Chief dies a natural death, the 'Tuchas' and the 'Bechas' of the deceased person's family prepare one litter with split bamboos upon which the dead body is laid. One end of the litter is put on the rafter of the house called 'Inkam', while the other is placed on the floor. The deadbody is then placed in a reclining position. The hanging end of the litter is split again at one point. In between the litter thus split is hung a live chick by its neck which gradually dies. This is called 'Aah-Lhap'.

Luntong, the Chief of Lhanjang, performed 'Chon' seven times in his life. He married seven times and everytime he married he threw a 'Chon'. Of course, he did not take all the seven wives at one and the same time, but married one after another as the wives died. He could do so only because he was very rich and could stand the huge expenditures required for the 'Chons'. All his wives, however, died issueless. When died, he was without any child to inherit. This is called 'Ingam'. The last man who performed such 'Chon', within the living memory of the people was Thangkhohen, the Chief of Sangnao. When he died, the deceased was not immediately buried like an ordinary man. A man who is entitled to such burial called 'Langlap' is supposed to be preserved for at least seven days after his demise. In the case of Thangkhohen, however, the deadbody was buried after ten days. This was necessary as the Chiefs and other important persons from far and near came to pay their last homage to him. The corpse no doubt got decomposed and foul smell was coming out of it. Any further delay was not possible, the dead body was buried after ten days.

The litter was constructed in such a way that the deceased might be kept on it without touching any other household articles and avoid defilement. The material used for constructing such a palanquine was a kind of bamboo called 'Gopi'. No other material was used. The main props of the palanquine were three solid bamboo poles laid lengthwise. These bamboos were bound together and joined breadthwise with bamboo splits, so that it became a kind of make-shift platform on which the deceased could be laid. On top of it were placed bamboo splits called 'Chipeh', which were made of solid bamboos that were not cut into pieces. One end of the bamboo remained solid, while the whole length of it was cut into several splits, so that when it was spread it served as a plank. The difference in construction of the palanquine called 'Lang' with that of 'Khunsum' is that the main bamboo supports are three in number in the former, while they are only two in the case of the latter. The construction of 'Lang' is made in such a way that whenever the deceased is carried on it for the burial rite it can move to and fro, which is called 'Lap', and an elderly man can take care of the corpse, and the priest, who keeps on brandishing a sword over the body of the deceased in his right hand, can also do his job unhindered. The ends of the solid bamboo are left undisturbed for carrying the palanquine. Thus, while on both sides of the ends of bamboos many youngman and elderly people can take positions carrying the deceased, the elderly man and the priest also carry on their jobs.

The place where the deceased is laid inside the house is the Central pillar of the house which is positioned in the mid-section of the house. The deceased is made to sit in a reclining position on the palanquine. But such act of carrying him from inside the house to the burial ground once in a day consists of seven rounds of in-and-out movement in the house and also to the burial ground. Such act has to be done only once a day which will continue to be done for seven days. Here also, the difference with that of 'Khunsum' burial is that in the case of the former it is seven days, while in the case of the latter it is only three days. In the case of 'Khunsum'burial, it is done for those who performed 'Sa-Ai' or 'Chang-Ai' in their life time. But in the case of 'Langlap' it is done for those who have great fame or repute in warfare, wealth, etc.

Within the seven days of mourning period, it is assumed that during the seven-day mourning period all those who wish to pay their homage have done so. Before the deceased is brought out of the house, one rite called 'Lhaw-lhil' is performed by going round within the house for seven times,as against only three in the case of 'Khuonsuom'. When this is done, the deceased is brought out of the house to be taken to the burial ground. In the process of going out and coming in, the priest who keeps on performing his act of propitiation by constantly spraying the 'Zu' called 'Zuphi' continues brandishing a sword over the corpse of the deceased as an act of protecting him from being harmed by the devils, who are apprehended to be ceaselessly trying to take over the corpse.The Priest will also be giving command to the pall- bearers upon which the priest himself and the elderly man sit. When he commands the palanquine bearers, he uses the word of command for upward lift as 'Chung Leovin'. Similarly, the word of command for lowering the palanquine is 'Nuoi khieh Un' His words of command will be repeated twice.

All other details are the same as that of the 'Khunsum' rites. In case such a person happens to have captured enemies alive and the latter ultimately became his slaves, images of such slaves are made either with bamboo or with woodcurvings and tied to the deadbody with chains, so that the soul of the dead person would take them along with him in his journey to the land of death. They say that on the death of Kuonkhomang Sitlhou, the grandfather of Nungkhothang, his slaves were not shown on his grave symbolising his capture of enemy turned slaves (two), through mistake. He, in consequence, appeared several times in their dreams demanding the slaves. When this mistake was corrected, the soul did not show up again.

With the impact of Christianisation, all the traditional tribal customs, however, are in a process of change and in course of these changing factors many of their cultural aspects are now in the transformational position.

XIV Khunsum Ma kihei - A Kind of Burial Service

A man who has in his life time not killed three Mithuns in celebration of his fame and prestige cannot be accorded this kind of burial service. Even if a man who has not completed killing of Mithuns for three times, but had done so twice, and if his poverty prevented his relatives from killing another but could kill only a goat instead even after his death, he is entitled to be buried under this kind of burial. Among the Kukis, the type of animal killed signifies the importance of the occasion and the person involved therein. So, Mithun has the highest social value and goat is equated with Mithun on social occasion of small scale. Therefore, in this case the Mithun is substituted for a goat. Then comes the pig in order of importance and significance, followed closely by a cock. Other animals have no social values.

When such a deserving man dies, all the able-bodied married male persons congregate at the residence of the deceased. As they assemble there, they start singing a kind of traditional song, called 'Haopnut Lapi' for three rounds. This is preceded by the process of making the deceased sit on a litter called 'Sang', which is prepared by the 'Tucha' of the deceased. The 'Sang' is constructed in such a way that a whole bamboo is split into pieces without letting it entirely separated at the top so that the same still remains as one whole piece at the end. The split portion is widened by separating each split from one another and such splits are intertwined breathwise with pieces of wood or bamboo splits, so that the other end becomes wide wherein the deceased can be made to sit. Prior to this, the deceased is given a clean bath by the lady-Tucha. After this, the deceased is wrapped up with a kind of male attire called 'Delpi'. Such dress is woven by two or three old ladies of the village as soon as the news of death of the deceased is heard, for everyone knows that the deceased was entitled to such a burial. This 'Delpi' is made to be used as a shroud on the dead body, and this is followed by dressing the deceased with a kind of jacket called 'Ponjang'. This dress is not stitched. It is a kind of shawl, the four corner of which are tied together that wraps him from the backside and is again tied together in front, in a quadrangular fashion - the two ends of the cloth are taken from the shoulders, while the other two ends are taken from below the armpit and around the naval cord covering the whole rib portion and the chest of the deceased. Then he is made to lie down on the litter prepared for carrying him. This is made by the lady-Tuchas whose entire responsibility is to construct it. They may be assisted by their respective husbands and other Becha relatives of the deceased, but such assistance is not taken into account. Thereafter, the Thiempu propitiates it with one chick. He puts the legs of the living chick in between two bamboo splits and hangs it on top of the bamboo-litter, the top end of which is tied with the rafter of the building called 'Inkam'. The chick remains alive, struggling for its release from such entanglement. This is called 'Aah-Lhap'. Then the 'Tucha' of the deceased (Tubul) follows the Thiempu by holding an iron implement. The Thiempu takes with him a mug of 'Zu' in the iron pot called 'Vaikhon'. At the portico, both of them sit together - the 'Tucha' being on the left side of the Thiempu. The Priest then propitiates very briefly and then sprays a mouthful of 'Zu'. Thence, both of them proceed further towards the selected site for burial. On reaching there, the Thiempu performs the 'Juphi' rite again. In doing so, he first sprays a mouthful of 'Zu'. In his propititation he utters :

Nuoi Ya Nuimangpa Kadohle
Chunga Pathien Kidoh Tan Eiti e.
Chunga Pathien Kadoh Leh
Naju Lhit Lhah Nalai Tah A
Chun Vuitan Biti i.

Free Translation

When enquired of the king of the underworld, 'Nuoimangpa', the king told me to ask God, pathien, who is in Heaven. When Pathien was asked,he instructed me to bury at the spot where the drops of wine have fallen.

Then the Thiempu digs the earth once to start the work of grave digging. This is followed by a line dug by the 'Tucha' wherein the grave is to be prepared. Then other youngmen of the village continue to dig the grave. Till such time the grave is completed and the deceased is laid to rest, the 'Tucha' who accompanies the Priest, cannot re-visit the house. As the Priest finishes his chanting invocation at the burial ground, he goes back to the house. He asks the 'Becha' of the deceased to arrange for one jar of 'Zu' for the 'Tucha' whom he has left behind at the burial ground. On receipt of the 'Zu' the 'Tucha' begins sipping it. He also offers it to those who dig the grave, by turn, until they complete the work.

On the other hand, at the residence of the deceased, the burial rites are in progress. A stage comes when the singing of one traditional song called 'Haophut Lapi' is sung for three rounds.

The origin of the 'Haophut' song called 'Haophut Lapi' has great significance which runs as follows : Haophut cultivated a land at the confluence of 'Peo' and 'Loh' streams. One day while he was working in the field a kind of animal called Sajo being drawn was brought down floating on a log by the strong currents of the stream. On his arrival back home he found his son dead. He attributed that the 'Sajo' that floated on the log in the stream was an omen. So he composed the song that came to be known as 'Haophut La'. As the log came down floating turning round and round in the midst of the two currents of the two streams, so he did exactly in similar manner in his funeral rite of his son by composing a song :

Peo Le Loh In Bon Luongthing Sajang Alamme

Josa Ahei Lem Lemme.
Khum Lhan Thongte Kalhun Leh
Kavan Sajang Kalamme
Lam Tolla kahei Lem Lemme.
Naopa Ngenten Athat Ne
Keiman Ngente Kathat Ne
Ngente Somsiel Kasom Siel
Ngente Kumpon Kadum Pon

Free Translation

Even the two streams, Peo and Loh float the animal called Sajo in their currents carrying it round and round, so do I the corpse of my son, whom I found dead on my arrival from the field.

My younger brother was killed by the Ngentes,
So did I kill the Ngente.
Thus the wealth and properties of
Ngente were mine
Even the cloths of Ngente were mine.

This song is known as 'Lapi' which is used as funeral-rite- song for those who do not have their own clan funeral-rite-song. This is the last song sung in the funeral rites of man of importance. The other song that is sung common to all those who perform 'Khunsum Ma Kihei' death rite, and known as Khun Sum La is as follows :

Khul A Khulla Kalut,
Dimkhul A Khulla Kalut,
Timta Mei La E.
Kawlni Nou Suo Masanga,
Ngalpa Kakap,
Phung Guol Ngoili Bang Katin,
Timta Mei La E.

Free Translation

As my coffin was lowered in the grave
The grave that had to be filled up,
The pitch-dark grave was brightened

By the flood-light of the firely.
Before sunrise, as I went to the field,
I met a wild-bore which I killed,
So, stopped all others who also went for the field.
Preparing themselves to carry the game that I hunted
Thus the darkness was brightened by the fire Fly

This is a song expressing the fame and glory of the performer of the funeral rites in recognition of his social status which made him deserve to perform the funeral rites called 'Khun Summa Kihei' which had the origin imitating the exact manner of floating of the 'Sajo' animal on a log over the currents of Peo and Loh streams at their confluence. The man called 'Haophut' who saw the Sajo floating on the current of the streams was from the 'Singsuon' clan.

After this, they are to perform an act of mourning. The participants of this act are all married and strong men. These participants take one wood each and slowly move into the house and stop near the deadbody. As they do so, they tramp their right foot in rhytm and strike the stick they hold on the wall and produce a slow and long-drawing sound like 'Ho..o.o'. They repeat this act for three times. This is called 'Lholhil'. After finishing this, when the procession is about to start, they begin the 'Khun Summa Kihei' rite. In doing this, all the able-bodied married men take up two pieces of bamboo sticks called 'Gopi'. On top of the bamboos they place some planks above which they put the corpse of the dead person. They start moving sidewise slowly lifting the corpse on the litter. Before they do so, the priest does his act of propitiation, called 'Juphi' by spraying a mouthful of 'Zu'. The pace of carrying the corpse is accompanied with a long-drawn sound like 'Ho..o..o'. Thus, they proceed towards the grave. On reaching there, the Priest does his propitiation or the 'Juphi' again. Then the corpse is brought back into the house. As the corpse is brought in, the Priest does the same kind of propitiation once again. This process continues for three rounds during which the Priest performs his propitiation six times. On the third round, the corpse is not brought into the house any more. It is kept outside. At this stage, the act of mourning or showing of anger is done. This act is first enacted by the 'Tucha Bul', who cannot enter the house until the burial service is over. Others follow suit. In the process of doing this act, some take hold of a scythe or an axe and cut whatever comes their way. Some also take fire-arms and shot a blank fire. The Thiempu comes last in the line of mourners. Along with this, the tempo of crying and wailing for the deceased among the ladies picks up momentum. They all know that was their last chance of crying in presence of the corpse.

As the corpse is about to be taken out for the 'Khunsum Ma Kihei' rite, the Thiempu removes the chick hanged over the litter and then he, in company of the junior 'Tucha' of the deceased, comes out of the house and proceeds towards the grave, leading the mourning procession. As they reach the site of the grave, the Thiempu chants incantations and hands over the chick to the 'Tucha' relative of the decreased with whom he comes along and then leaves the place to go back to the residence of the deceased. The 'Tucha', who has earlier been left behind near the grave, starts preparing the chick for cooking. When the cooking is done, the meat is packed in a small gourd, which would contain the entire meat of the chick. If the deceased was a man with a family, the pot with which the meat is cooked is smashed and thrown away. But in case of the wife of the person who had in his life performed the 'Sa-Ai', the bottom of the pot is pierced with a hole and it is hung up above the grave of the lady after her burial.

Before the corpse is laid to rest, the Thiempu performs the purification rite at the grave and is immediately followed by the act of cleansing the grave with a torch by the 'Tubul'. In doing so, the 'Tubul' oversees every nook and corner of the grave with the strong light of the torch. Now, as the corpse is lowered in the grave, the chick is cooked near the grave by the Junior 'Tucha' and packed in a small gourd called 'Lhah An' or the food for the soul. It is also buried along with the corpse in the belief that the deceased would take this with him and that on his way to 'Thijon Lamtou', the stiff road to the land of dead, where a lady named 'Kulsamnu' would stand in his way and prevent him from reaching the destination of the world of the dead people called 'Kholmun'. The same would be given to her to appease her hunger. In order to please, the dead person will not only give the cooked chick to her but as also eat himself along with her, so that she might pave his way to proceed towards 'Kholmun'.

To indicate the high social standing and reputation, a man buried with 'Khunsum Ma Kihei' rites, a kind of bamboo called 'Gopi' is erected on the grave the following day. This is called 'Vakoh Kisat'. This is done in such a way that the bamboo is split into four parts, but is not entirely separated. One end of it still clings to the bamboo. In between the splits, pieces of kind of tree called 'Khongma' which is made flat into small pieces, are sandwitched. The number of such small pieces of 'Khongma' should tally with the number of sticks called 'Samol' placed near the caves at the residence of the deceased. In case only one bamboo cannot accommodate the number of 'Samol', more such bamboos can be added. The bamboos thus decorated with the pieces of 'Khongma' are pitched into the ground and erected over the grave. The 'Khongma' pieces which should tally with the number of 'Samol' signifying the number of wild games hunted during the life time of the deceased are inserted into the bamboo split in such a way that the pieces should cross each other, one layer after another. On the same day, a kind of tree called 'Se' is erected with its small branches sharpened and pointed like spikes. This is called 'Lhan Khom'. It may be noted here that when such a famous person dies, one Mithun, a pig, a goat and a dog must be killed in honour of the deceased which act is called 'Kosa Na', on the day he is buried. The heads of such animals killed are hoisted the next day by the 'Tucha' relatives of the deceased on top of the spike-like branches of 'Se' tree erected over the grave of the deceased. If he was a warrior who killed his enemies in battles, the heads of as many enemies as he killed are curved in wood and hoisted on the grave. Such skull-like wood curvings of the vanquished enemies should be hung with rope on their necks, believing or symbolising that such enemies are dragged with rope by the deceased as his prisoners and slaves. If he has killed a tiger in his life time, another kind of tree called 'Lheh' is erected. This is called 'Thing Gel'. The tree should have a trunk and two branches in 'V' shape. At the base of the two branches, where they meet the trunk, is curved the picture of the sun, while the branches are curved like arrows on both sides of the edges. Another pole near the 'Lheh' is pitched, which bends towards the 'Lheh' just above the base of the two branches being supported by one post. At the end of the pole a string is tied and at the other a gourd is hung, the main body of which is cut into two halves providing a lamp-shade. Beneath it and through the hole made at the thin handle-like side of the gourd where the string is hung, a lizard-shaped wood curving is tied. It is believed that the tigers come to see the grave of such men knowing fully well that the deceased had killed tigers in his life time. With a view to taking revenge on the tigers killed by the deceased, the tiger counts as to how many arrows are there in the curvings on V-shaped branches of the trunk erected. It may so happen that as the tiger is about to finish the counting of the curvings, the lizard-shaped wood curving hanging over the V-shaped branches may peeve the tiger. As a consequence, it cannot finish the countings. It has to start counting anew. This process is repeated time and again. Ultimately, it cannot complete the counting of the curvings. Along with the lizard-shaped wood curvings are hung over the oval shaped gourd three strings at an equi-distant point on which three sticks each are placed. When the wind blows and as the gourd moves about, the sticks around, it make some sound. This may also add to the diversion of the attention of the tiger.

The use of lizard has an interesting story behind it. It runs as follows:

There was a time when a man could communicate with animals and insects. On the day when a man called Dapa performed his 'Chon', a ceremony proclaiming one's success and reputation in life, the lizard called 'Thangkip' was also invited. As per custom, all the invitees were given share of meat on such an occasion. The lizard, as per its nature, was able to change its colour as and when it wished. So, when such a share of the mean was distributed on the day of Dapa's 'chon' the lizard changed its colour seven times and took share of the meat on as many occasions. Likewise, the lizard should change its colour whenever the tiger comes to count the arrow-shaped curvings, so that ultimately it might confuse and threaten the tiger which would disturb its attention in counting. This would make the tiger run away without completing the counting.

CHAPTER 6

POLITICAL ORGANISATION

I. The traditional political life of the Kukis as a separate institution cannot be studied in isolation. The institution is closely intertwined with other institutions, such as, social, religious, economic, etc. A superficial knowledge on the Kuki society will reveal that the institutions of political, social, economic and religious are overlapping with one another, and one may draw the conclusion that there is no political institution at all among the Kukis.

Political system or institution among the Kukis as also among other primitive societies is based on kinship relation (Schapera, 1963 :1). Mains (London, 1972 : 76) observed that :

> All ancient societies regarded themselves as having proceeded from one original stock, and even laboured under an incapacity for comprehending any reason, except this, for their holding together in political Union. The history of political idea begins, in fact, with the assumption that kinship in blood is the sole possible ground of community in political functions, nor is there any of those subconscious or feeling, which we term emphatically revolutions, so startling and so complete as the change which is accomplished when some other principle - such as that, for instance, of local contiguity - established itself for the first time as the basis of common political action. The idea that a number of persons should exercise political rights in common simply because they happen to live within the same topographical limits was utterly strange and monstrous to primitive antiquity.

Such a system of political institution, based on kinship relation is termed as a mere "Social Organisation", which is distinguished from "Political Organisation" of the civilized communities (Morgan, L.H.,

1877 : 6766). Similar views were also expressed by Durkheim, Hobbouse, Vinogradoff, etc.

MacIver (New York, 1965 : 119) however said :

> In the primary sense a tribe is community organised on the basis of kinship... and usually claiming to be descended from a common ancestor. Tribal Government is characteristic of simple society and is then equivalent to Primitive Government.

Yet, another anthropologist (Malinawski, B, 1947 : 263-66) whose authority on the primitive people was undisputed, said :

> The primitive State is not tyrranical to its subjects because, first and formost, we know that a primitive tribe is always a body of people related by bonds of kinship and relationship, by clanship and age-grade; and he also speaks of the tribe as a group where practically everybody is related, really or factitiously, to everybody else.

The one focal point that has to be highlighted is Chieftainship and the concept of territory among the Kukis. The village is the highest political unit among the Kukis, and Chief of the villages and his Council of Ministers which function within a territorial jurisdiction (Gangte, 1982 : 55) weilding its political authority and prerogatives over the villagers in absolute terms are the supreme political power. Schapera (1963 : 14-15) said :

> Each tribe claims exclusive rights to the land it occupies. All people living there are subjects to the Chief, as head of the local Government, and only by moving away can they escape his control. Outsiders may not settle in its territory without his permission; and he places them where he wishes. Henceforth they are his subjects, and if they disobey him they may be expelled. He also regulates the distribution and use of the land.

II. Chieftainship among the Kukis is associated with the 'Upa' or senior man. The term 'Upa' is conferred on a person by way of reverence, and a great deal of veneration is attached to it. 'Upas' are the only persons who can become Chiefs. Thus, Chiefs are synonymous with 'Upas'.

The term 'Naopa' stands for the junior man. 'Naopa' cannot in the normal course of the customary law become the Chief. He can become so only with the full consent of the Chief, who is his 'Upa', as also with the concurrence of the Council of Ministers of the Chief, which is known as 'Semang-Upa' or 'Pachong' collectively. Before a 'Naopa' can become the Chief, certain formalities and obligations are to be gone through.

Under the circumstances, there is limited room for growth of political leadership among the 'Upas' alone. Unless specifically desired by the 'Upa' to develop and groom his 'Naopa' (literally younger brother) for leadership, there is no chance for the 'Naopa' to become the leader or Chief.

Leadership manifests, therefore, in the rights and privileges handed down to the 'Upas' and these prerogatives are institutionalised in Village Organisation and the customary law, through the system of Chieftainship called 'Haosa' and its Council of Ministers called 'Semang Upa' or Pachong'. Thus, the Chieftainship has come to stay as an institution which is the perennial source of customary laws, and the mechanism by which such laws are interpreted in the soical system that makes them a living force enabling to maintain their separate identity inheriting a rich cultural heritage.

III. A village is an independent political unit among the kukis, and the Chief of the village and his Council of Ministers are the political leaders. Administration of justice, enforcement of executive function, maintenance of social practices and customary law, including religious performances are the areas of the village administration under the Chieftainship and his Council of Ministers. Thus, a Kuki village is an important administrative unit.

A Kuki village has inevitably got a Chief, which post is not elective but hereditary. The Chief is assisted in his administration by a team of persons, collectively called 'Semang -Upa' or 'Pachong' which is similar to the Council of Ministers in modern times. The office of the Chief is hereditary, and is passed on from father to his eldest son, who otherwise is known as 'Upa'. The office of Chieftainship is called 'Haosa' which is vested with so much of power and authority over his subjects that a person in that capacity is often prone to abuse his power and thus turn himself into a despot.

The structure of the village political organisation is given below :-

CHART 6 : 1
ADMINISTRATIVE STRUCTURE
OF KUKI
CHIEFTAINSHIP

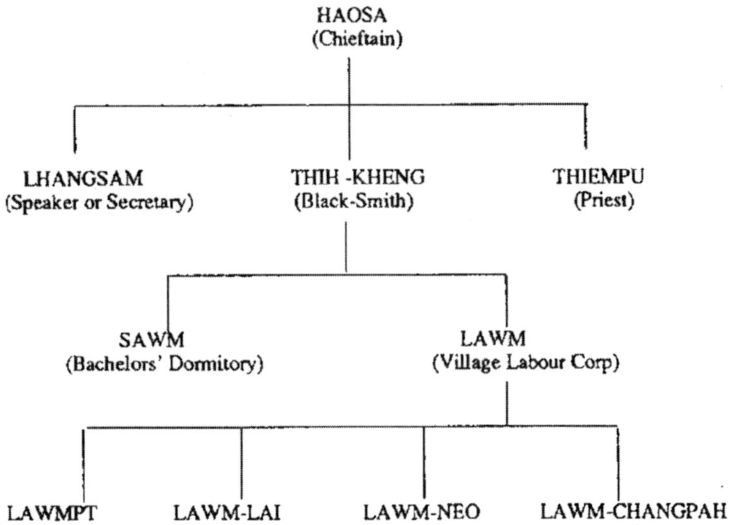

'Haosa' (Chief):

'Haosa' is the office of the Village Chief. It is hereditary, passing from father to the son. The office is occupied only by the 'Upas' except among the Lushai Kukis which goes from father to youngest son. Among the Kukis, and unlike the Nagas, 'Haosa' has the absolute right of ownership over the entire land of the village. The villagers have no right over the land whatsoever. Even if a villager, who is generally a 'Naopa' wishes to establish a new village, he can do so only with the permission of the 'Haosa'. The 'Haosa', however, absolute his right over the land might be, normally allows, in consultation with his Council of Ministers, the villagers to cultivate and utilise as per their requirements. But the villagers have to pay to the 'Haosa' in return for such privileges in the shape of tributes called 'Changseo', even of the part of hunted games called 'Saleng'. 'Changseo', is payable annually after harvest. The 'Haosa' is also entitled to free labour of each villager once in a year called 'Khuo-Tha'.

Together with such rights, the 'Haosa' has certain obligations over the villagers. In return to the services rendered by the villagers, free of cost and the tributes paid as token of loyalty, recognition, obedience and solidarity, the 'Haosa' has to protect their interests by providing security socially, politically and economically. It is also the bounden duty of the 'Haosa' to see that every villager is protected from external aggression and danger.

The 'Haosa' system is very similar to the Social Contract Theory of Hobbes who enunciates that rights imply duties. By this system both the villagers on the one hand and the 'Haosa' on the other, are in duty bound to fulfil their rights and obligations towards each other.

The 'Haosa' wields a great deal of authority over the villagers who are mostly his kin group and junior to him by descent. He is assisted in his day-to-day administration by a Council. In short, he is the head of a big famiy in times of war and peace. Although he is the legal owner of the land, the 'Haosa' owns little and he administers the village according to the advice given by the elders of the Council.

Many writers having a superficial knowledge about the men and affairs try to draw a similarity between the 'Haosas' and the 'Zemindars' and often jump to a conclusion that the system of a 'Haosa' is despotic. Of course, there is sufficient room for a 'Haosa' to become a despot and tyrranical, but such things are of very rare happenings. Despite such possibility of being so dreaded by the villagers, there are thousand and one ways by which such a situation can be averted due to interaction of forces within the system. The villagers are at liberty to leave the village and migrate elsewhere in case the 'Haosa' is found failing in his duty to protect the interest of the villagers. This happens to be the main factor that contributes to the nomadism of the Kukis.

The 'Haosa'system is indeed very firmly entrenched among the Kukis. Notwithstanding the inherent defects associated with the 'Haosa' system which the kukis cannot do away with, there are some merits also in this system to set-off the evils in it. The 'Haosa' system has come to stay as a perennial source of custom and tradition, in that, in spite of the onslaught of modernism and advancement in all walks of life, they are able to inherit a rich cultural and traditional heritage. The Haosa system, be it on matters relating to economical, political, religious, judiciary, etc., has its bases on the proper interpretation of the customary law and tradition.

Unlike the Naga tribes of Manipur, who have no permanent and strongly established secular head of a village, the office of which is usually held by an elected man called 'Gaonbura' for a specified term, and also the Nuer tribes of Africa, who do not have a permanent Chief of the village other than the Leopard-skin clad Chief (Evans-Pritchard, 1940:163), who, though wields a great deal of influence and acts as a go-between to settle disputes, the Kukis have a very solidly established institution of Chieftainship who, being the 'Upa' of a particular clan or lineage or sub-lineage, is considered to be the fountain-head of all customs and retainer of tradition. Like the African Nuer (Evan Pritchard, 1940 : 6), the Kuki political structure

> . . . . is segmented into lineages which are diverging branches of descent from a common ancestor.

Thus, the nomenclature of every clan, lineage or sub- lineage, bears the name of each founding father and thereby the members claiming blood relationship of a common ancestor.

On this very kinship genealogy is built the political structure of the Kukis which has been institutionalised in 'Haosa'. This is the main reason why the system of 'Haosa' could not be given a go-by, despite varied changes all around. The political structure of the Kukis is, therefore, based on kinship hierarchical order of the clan. The Kuki political system has a peculiar way of effective functioning to meet external aggression by expressing kinship solidarity and loyalty despite their inter- clan rivalry and feud.

IV.

With reference to the Thadou speaking Kukis, it can be said that they are the descendents of a common ancestor, called Thadou, who had one elder brothers named, Doungel, and two younger brothers, named, Chongloi and Hangsing. Out of these four, the descendants of Thadou became numerically preponderant over others. Thadou had a son, Thalhun, who had three sons, named Blmun, Haokip and Kipgen. The descendants of the three sons were further segmented. All the descendants of Thadou still call themselves as Thadou, while they maintain their separate identities all the same. These Thadous are spread over all the hill areas of Manipur, apart from their being in Assam, Burma, Bangladesh, Nagaland, Tripura, etc. The Doungels are dominant in the North East, bordering Nagaland, with the seniormost 'Upa', Doungel Chief, living at Aishan village by which name he is better recognised. In other words, the 'Upa' of the Doungels is better known as 'Aishanpa', the Chief of Aishan. Similarly, the Sitlhou Thadous are dominant in the North West, bordering the Nagaland, contiguous to the Khonoma Angami Nagas. The 'Upa of the Sitlhou Thadou lives in Jampi village and is known as 'Jampi-pa', Chief of Jampi. The same holds good for the Naokip Thadous who are dominant in the East, bordering Burma, though they are scattered in the South-East,South-West and western part of Manipur hill areas. The 'Upa' of the Haokip Thadou lives in Chahsad village, and is known as 'Chahsad-Pa', meaning thereby Chief of Chahsad. These three examples identifying the Chiefs by the name of their villages signify their hierarchical order in the political system. These Chiefs were not without internal dissensions which at times surfaced in serious inter-clan rivalries. Tension and hostility often dominate in place of peace and tranquility in their internal relationships. However, in times of external attack they bury their hatchet and stand united to fight the common enemy, mainly by expression of their kinship solidarity, loyalty and identification as could be seen during the Anglo-Kuki war of Independence in 1917 - 19.

The Kuki Chiefs resisted the expansionist colonial design of the British India Government,and thereby opposed when the Maharaja of Manipur first extended invitation to the British in Manipur. The necessity of fighting the British openly arose when the Kuki Chiefs refused to assist the British during the First World War in their war efforts.

Despite their scattered nature of living, the British authorities were surprised to find how the Kuki Chiefs could mobilise their strength and unity at a very short notice to face a far superior power of the British Government.

Higgins, the then Political Agent of Manipur, while fighting against the kuki Chiefs, expressed surprise at his opponents' alacrity and complete unity against the British India Government which took three long years to suppress them despite their waging a full-fledged military operation, treating it as a part of the World War I. He apologised for the mistake he had made in underestimating the ability of the Kuki Chiefs and observed that the reason behind the solidarity of the Kuki Chiefs was kinship ties that bound them together through their age-old culture of 'Sajam-Lha' which signified a decision to wage war unto death.

It was a fact that the Chief of Aishan killed a Mithun and sent pieces of the flesh far and wide so as to reach his other collateral Chiefs, such as, the Chiefs of Jampi, Chahsad, etc. signifying that he had to fight against the British and at the same time appealing to them to join hands with him as brethren in blood. As per custom, when such an appeal comes, refusal is difficult, for such action amounts to social antagonism and ostracism reducing the person refusing it to a total outcast. This might even result in physical annihilation altogether. The Chiefs of Jampi and Chahsad responded the same by performing similar 'Sajam-Lha' among their respective tributory or junior Chiefs who also responded favourably mainly in an expression of kinship, solidarity and loyalty shown to their 'Upas'. Thus, we find how the institution of 'Haosa' as a political system works on kinship which has an overtone of hierarchical orders.

V.

The institution of 'Haosa' does not, and cannot function in isolation. In other words, the institution of 'Haosa' presupposes the existence of 'Semang Fachong' Council. It has to work through the Council which assists him in his day-to-day administration. This Council is composed of persons of wisdom, integrity, knowledge of customary law etc. and are nominated by the 'Haosa'. Special representation is always given from the minorities and the poor villagers in the Council. The Council members assemble and make deliberations. They remain in office as long as the 'Haosa' is pleased. Social, political, economic, judicial matters etc. are dealt with by the Council.

The main mechanism through which the Council exercises its administration is the interpretation of the customary laws. The 'Haosa' as the Chairman or Head of this Council presides over the meetings. The members of the Council are exempted from payment of all kinds of tributes levied on the common villagers in token recognition of their services.

The components of the Council are given below :

Khawsam or Lhangsam Pa

He is the spokesman (Convenor or Secretary) of the Council. Literally speaking he is the councillor incharge of Information and Broadcasting. In actual fact he holds a far wider scope of responsibility than the designation indicates. He convenes meeting of the Council, conveys decisions of the Council to the general public, and enforces or implements the decisions of the Council. The task given to him is not specific. He may be asked to act in any capacity, such as, emissary, negotiator, mediator, depending upon his personal talent.

Thiempu (or Village Priest)

'Thiempu' is the office of the village Priest or medicine man. Literally speaking, he is the councillor-in-charge of public health in the truest sense of the term. Persons for this office are chosen from among those who know the 'Thiem-Thu' (the secret words of medicine). This office is very often regarded as hereditary, because the secrets of the medicines are not revealed to each and every person. Thiempus generally prefer to teach their sons and grandsons the secrets of the words. Moreover, to learn this secret costs a lot of money and time. Therefore, very few persons bother to learn this knowledge.

The 'Thiempu' will attend to all the villagers in times of sickness and he officiates on social and religious occasions. The 'Thiempu' is so important in the life of the Kukis that for an ordinary observer he seems to be the head of the village, because on every occasion - temporal and religious - he takes precedence over the 'Haosa'. For example, wine (Zu) is very important in the life of the Kukis. Therefore, on every occasion wine is served in order of social position and seniority in age. Irrespective of the fact that he is junior or lower in status, the 'Thiempu' will be served the wine first on social and religious occasions.

The office of the 'Thiempu', more or less, enjoys autonomy from that of 'Haosa' and his Council. He treats all the ailing villagers, free of cost. In return, he is allowed to collect his 'Changseo', i.e.., a bucket of paddy paid as a tribute to the 'Haosa' and the 'Thiempu', annually. This is paid in acknowledgement of his services for the welfare of the village community. But the rate of 'Changseo' he receives annually is lower than that of the Chief. 'Thiempu' is also entitled to a share of the wild game hunted and brought by the villagers. This share is called 'Thiem-Sha' (Meat-share of the secret word). This share is not the same as the 'Haosa' receives by way of 'Samal' or 'Saleng'. It is connected with the religious belief.

Thih-Kheng (Black-Smith) Pa

'Thin-Kheng' is the office of the village Black-smith. This office goes to the person who has the highest dexterity in black-smithy. He is the authorised black-smith of the village. He does not charge for what he makes for individual villagers. Everything is done free of cost. He makes agricultural implements, such as, hoes, axes, spades etc., and manufactures weapons, like swords, arrows, guns, bullets, etc. In recognition of his services, he is given 'Changseo' by all the villagers annually, but the rate will be lower than that is received by the 'Haosa'. Just as the 'Thiem-Sha' is given to the Thiempu, 'Thih-Kheng' is also given 'Thih-Kheng-Sha' (Meat-share of the Black-smith) by every hunter. This is a symbolic payment to the 'Thih-Kheng' for having manufactured the bullet for the hunters.

Lawm (Village Labour Corps)

The functions of 'Lawm' are concerned mainly with the economic life of the village. All the able-bodied men and women of the village join this organisation, irrespective of age and sex. Any household of the village can requisition the services of the Lawm. All the villagers, therefore, are to join the Lawm. The number of work, other than his own, attended to by a 'Lawm' member will be credited to his name and the same number of work he thus earns will be repaid to him by other members with labour. In this way, the 'Lawm' members reciprocate in helping each other and keeping the village, as far as practicable, self-sufficient in the matter of physical labour. Sometimes their 'Lawm' can be hired by any villager or Chief. In return, they are given food and drink. But this entertainment need not be instantaneous. It may be on a later day when the person who engages the 'Lawm' is in a position to repay. It is an organisation in which training for leadership is given to the young people of the village. It is also an organisation in which the young ones learn a sense of duty and dignity of labour. This organisation is in a way connected with the 'Thih-Kheng' office, because the success or failure of the organisation depends upon the ability of the 'Thih-Kheng' to produce and to provide implements.

The word 'Lawm' means an informal labour organisation in a simple and corporate village life of the Kukis, wherein all the able- bodied young boys and girls are members. There are four types of 'Lawm' among the Kukis. The basis of this division is the age- group of the members and are as follows :

1. Lawmpi

Its members are mainly grown up boys and girls. Sometimes newly married male members continue for a while after marriage, for they feel misfit to remain outside the 'Lawm' organisation. So, till such time they are used to outside 'Lawm', they continue to remain as 'Lawm' members. Any minor boy or girl in whose family there is no grown up member to join the said 'Lawm', such a boy or girl is allowed to join the organisation mainly with a view to extending the services of the organisation to him or her. This is the biggest among the 'Lawm' organisations.

2. Lawm-Lai

Lawm-Lai is an organisation whose members are junior unmarried boys and girls whose elder brothers and sisters are in the Lawmpi organisation.

3. Lawm-Neo

Lawm-Neo is a group where the third brother and sister of a family and other teenagers are the members.

4. Lawm-Changpah

Lawm-Changpah is a group whose services at home are not very much required and they are in need of some sort of training in cultivation work. This is mainly a training group.

Sawm (Bachelors' or Village Youths'Dormitory)

'Sawm' among the Kukis is the name of the other youth organisation which concerns only able-bodied young boys of the village. It is a bachelor's dormitory in which all the young boys of the village sleep together at night. The nature of hostility and practice of tribal raids necessitate the existence of this organisation, so that in times of emergency the services of all the able-bodied men might be available at short notice. They have to offer their free and compulsory services to the village. Although the main purpose of this organisation is to defend the village from external dangers, in times of peace they render every possible service to the village community whenever required. Moreover, it is an organisation for recreation of the young boys. In the 'Sawm', younger boys are taught all sorts of things, from cutting jokes to taking responsibilities. Stories are told by the elder members and sometimes topics ranging from girls to war become the subject matters of great interests. This organisation is also connected with the 'Thih-Kheng' office, becasue the efficient mobilisation of the village youths for defence depends mainly upon the ability of the 'Thin-Kheng' to produce weapons.

This organisation may be likened with that of Defence and Home Department of modern administration.

The Kuki society is such that during the days when inter- tribal feuds were a part of their way of life, every able-bodied youth of a village slept together so that they might be readily available for deployment in times of emergency. This place is also considered a place of learning. There stays boys of different age-groups who are assigned various jobs and other sundry chores. The boys of younger age-groups learn the things from the older groups. They also learn social customs and manners. It serves as an institution of learning, discipline and other essential characters necessary for a man in future life. It has thus been considered as a very essential part of the village administration among the Kukis. This is an organisation responsible for mobilisation of the services of the youngmen to meet the exigencies of the society. In this connection Roy (1918:218) describes the bachelor's organisation as :

> .....archaic form of economic, social and religious organisation. It must have been its times and effective economic organisation for purposes of food quest, a useful seminary for training youngmen in their social and other duties, and an institution for magico-religious observances calculated for magic-religious observances calculated to secure success in hunting and to augment the preventive power of the youngmen so as to increase the number of hunters in the tribe.

Thus, the young boys of the village are concentrated at a place for emergency service. In this connection a story is current, which runs as follows :

There was a time when every tribe was scared of the Pawis because of their ferocity in warfare. But the Sitlhou Chief of Jampi village, the head of all the Sitlhou clan of the Thadous, arranged things in such a way that he and his collateral brothers must not move out from their place for fear of the Pawis. He asked his younger two junior collateral Chieftains of Lhungtin and Aiyang villages belonging to the Hangsing and Chongloi clans to remain in their present villages on condition that he as a senior collateral cousin would remain together with them. So, the three villages forming a confederacy remained in union where they were based. Now, having stood their ground unitedly, Lhungtin and Aiyang villages acting as buffers between the Pawis and the Jampi village, became the thorn in the flesh to the Pawis, who could not any longer stand in the face of such combined force of the three confederate villages. In order to relent the situation and with a view to living side by side in peace and amity, the Pawis sought for the concurrence of the Jampi Chief to pacify his junior collateral two cousins of Lhungtin and Aiyang Chiefs. As a token of peace and amity of the proposed pact, the Pawi Chief came to him pleading that the Pawis were no longer able to live in peace because of fear for "Your brethren Singhangs (Hangsings). Please be kind and pacify them and ask them not to trouble us any more, so that we all might live in peace as good neighbours." In proposing such a peace pact with the three collateral brethren Chiefs, the Pawis brought two shields to be used in front and back-'Lum Le Phaw' - one big type bead, called 'Khi-chang', one spear, known as 'Tiengcha', one belt which has seven lines of one rare kind of beads, called 'Paigen', to the Chief of Jampi. It was obvious, when one comes with such a peace and goodwill mission that the proposal was difficult to be turned down. Therefore, accepting the proposal of the Pawis in good faith, the Chief of Lhungtin and Aiyang villages relaxed and were at peace with the Pawis. Obedience and veneration to the senior Chief were the mode of life in those days. Thus, when a senior collateral Chief advised them to stand down, there was nothing but to abide by his wishes, which they thought to be in their best interest. Accordingly, the Pawis also ceased their hostility against the three villages. But this was a lull before the storm and it lasted only for the first year. Believing in what superficially appeared as being reality of the situation with complete cessation of arms hostility on the part of the Pawis, the three collateral cousin Chiefs became complacent with over- relaxation.

On the other hand, the Pawis had been surreptitiously planning to attack the Lhungtin village by surprise. It so happened that one night, when all the able-bodied youngmen of Lhungtin village slept in their dormiroty, the Pawis stealthily came and butchered them, killing instantaneously as many as eighty able- bodied youngmen. As a result, the Hangsings were scattered and fled in different directions. Most of them were found to have settled down among the Paites. The one that gave a serious impact besides all other repercussions was that the institution of 'Sawm' which was centralised took the character of a scattered form due to defensive strategy. Such a different form of 'Sawm', though it still continues, exists on a small scale at different houses where there are girls.

VI In recognition of the services rendered to the villagers, in gratification for allowing to enjoy the amenities of the village life and as a mark of respect to him, all the villagers are supposed to contribute to the welfare of the Chief. In doing so, certain tributes are paid by the villagers. But these tributes vary from clan to clan. However, some common types of tributes are mentioned below :

Saleng (Semal):

This tribute is given to the Chief by a hunter. It is paid in the shape of the right hind-leg of the killed game brought into the village by the villager. This payment is made in token gratification of having given the opportunity to hunt in the jungle of the village. The hunter would not have been able to go a hunting wild games and make sports had he not been allowed by the Chief to hunt in the jungle which falls within the jurisdiction of the village.

Salu (Head of the Killed Game)

The head of the animal killed is given to the Chief. This is not exactly the payment made exclusively to the Chief alone. It is a payment in token acknowledgement of Chief who is the head of the village and, as such, the preserver of wellbeing of the villagers. The head of the animal thus given to the Chief is cooked and eaten by the Chief in the company of the village elders, and its skull thereafter is kept hanging on the front wall of the Chief's house. This is particularly true with the Haokip Chiefs. In case of other clans the head of the hunted game is given to the sub- clan 'Upa' of the hunter. If the Chief happens to be the 'Upa' of the hunter, he gives the head to the former, if not, it is not compulsory that the head should be given to him.

Changseo

This is a kind of annual payment to the Chief by the villagers. This tribute is levied on all the villagers with the exception of village councellors and near relatives of the Chief. By the term 'Changseo' it means that every villager would pay a fixed basket- ful of paddy annually to the Chief. But the Chief can exempt a villager who cannot pay it on account of his poverty or poor harvesting. A villager exempted from such payment is to give a fowl or a jar of 'Zu' (rice-beer), instead, on the day of 'Changseo-Juneh-Ni', which means the day of payment of 'Changseo'. On this day, all the exempted villagers and other relatives of the Chief, who do not pay 'Chengseo', will bring one 'Jubel' (a jar of rice-beer) each which will be given to those who bring the 'Changseo' along with the 'Jubel' given by the Chief himself. Matters relating to the cultivation of field and the area of cultivation for the next year are discussed on this day.

Khuotha

This term signifies that it is the labour of the villagers which the Chief as well as the villagers can requistition when necessary. The person who engages the 'Khuotha' will have to give 'Zu' at the field or place of work. He will also entertain the 'Khuotha' with supper in the afternoon. If any villager engaging the 'Khuotha' cannot afford to entertain them with 'Zu' and supper on the day they are engaged, he will have to give them on a later date when he is in a position to do so.

The Chief can engage the 'Khuotha' in place of 'Changsco'. In such cases, the Chief need not entertain the 'Khuotha' with 'Zu' and supper. They are supposed to come with their own victual.

VII Khuomuol

This is a very important place for a Kuki village. This is built near the entrance of the village from the main road. It is important becasue it is used for all political, religious and social occasions. A resting place as it is, the skins of hunted tigers are kept here. It is considered undesirable to bring in the corpse of the hunted tigers inside the village - a superstition mainly because it is inedible. To kill a tiger is also considered a sin, as it is said that it does not harm anyone unless it is provoked. The Kukis are by nature headhunters and, as such, the 'Khuomuol' is used for keeping the head of their killed enemies. It has, therefore, a political significance. A 'Khuomuol' is also a place for performing all sorts of rites, like 'Kithoi' (appeasement of the evil spirit), and a place for welcoming the guests or a point upto which guests or persons leaving the village on tours are seen off.

'Khuomuol' is very important in the village life of the Kukis in view of the political, social, economic, religious, significance being attached to it.

VIII Khuojeh

It is a measure taken to fight an epidemic in the village. When an epidemic breaks out in a neighbouring village, 'Khuojeh' is enforced in order to prevent its spread in the village. In doing 'Khuojeh', 'Ai' or wild termaric is twisted and cut into pieces and spread all over the households of the village. At the main gate or 'Khuomuol', a tube made of bamboo, called 'Guobong', is placed. It contains the liquid form of 'Ai' plant. Along with the 'Guobong' are hung many other wild plants including a wild creeper called 'Kang-Gui', which are cut into pieces at the end for using it as brush for application of the 'Ai-Tui' or liquid form of 'Ai'. Any villager going out of the village for business, like touring, cultivation, hunting etc., has to touch that 'Guobong' at the 'Khuomuol' and sprinkle to himself with the liquid of the 'Ai' plant inside the Guobong'. The sprinkling of the 'Ai-Tui' is to be done all over the body. It is generally believed that a person having duly sprinkled with the 'Ai-Tui' can neither contact the disease, nor can he be accompanied by the epidemic into the village.

In addition, if there occurs any disease, such as, diarrhoea, flue, etc. in a village, 'Buchunlham' is performed, in order to stop further spread of the ailment in the village.

Umnit

This means observance of confinement at home on a particular day. On this day, nobody in the village is allowed to be away from the village. The Chief announces the date. It is usually done only for a day. This observance occurs when there is (i) unnatural death, like 'Thinga-Lha' (death from the fall of a tree), 'Tui-a-Thi'(death from drawning), 'Hiem-ma-Thi' (death from accidental gun fire) 'Nao-nei-na-a-Thi' (death during childbirth), 'Sa-Tha' (killed by wild animals), 'Tuolthi' (Homicide) etc., and (ii) 'Inka' (house on fire). If occurrence of these incidents is heard 'Umnit' is observed. It is considered bad if any person does not observe it. It is associated with the belief that any one who breaks this observance may suffer himself in the same way for which the 'Umnit' is observed.

Khuothiensuo

When the year comes to an end, this is observed. Generally, there is one particular drum belonging to the whole village. This drum cannot be beaten in the village, except on a particular occasion. During the forbidden period the drum is kept hanging on the rafter in the centre of the house of the Chief near the ceiling, called 'Inting' and it will remain so until the season for 'Khuothiensuo' comes. On the day of 'Khuothiensuo', the drum can be beaten, as this day happens to be the day for collection of the villagers' tribute of paddy-tax, called 'Changseo', and a party called 'Changseo-Junch-Ni' is held in which the drum is beaten.

On this day, the whole of the work for the New Year is discussed. If any 'Semang-Pachong' is to be changed or added, it is considered on this day. It is also discussed which side of the forest will be tilled by the whole village for the next season. Then the area of cultivation is decided and the villagers choose their own plots for cultivation by putting signs. Such a sign or marking is called 'Chemtah' which bears the plus-sign of marking. A place marked with such a sign is not encroached upon by anybody else.

IX Changes

Since the time of Pax-Brittanic, the feudal system of 'Haosa' and its prerogatives have lost their fervour considerably. Consequent upon the developmental schemes taken up during the post- independence days of the country, the institution of 'Haosa' has shown further changes, the importance of it has greatly declined, and the effectiveness of the institution and its authority waned.

With the introduction of the Village Authority Act. 1956 in Manipur, the village organisation under the leadership of the 'Haosa' has changed in its structure and function. According to this Act, the 'Haosa' is the ex-officio Chairman of the village authorities. The members are no longer nominated by the 'Haosa', but are elected by the villagers themselves, through ballot system. This system has given birth to different parties within a village and, therefore, the village as a single unit could not be cohesive. The solidarity of the whole village which used to be the backbone of the political system is utterly shattered.

Villagers are no longer governed by their customary laws, but are administered by the village Authority Act. The Act says that the villagers have direct participation in the Village Government and the villagers are the persons who run the machinery of the Government. This new system indeed sounds very well and the people are enthusiastic about giving a fair trial to it.

Moreover, with the infiltration of a number of Christians, the Kukis are now more inclined to make a departure from their traditional social norms of life. This trend has further been accelerated by the spread of education, and mobility of the rural population to the urban areas for enjoying greater amenities of life available there.

The village Chief cannot officially or openly enjoy its age-old prerogatives, such as, tributes of 'Saleng'(Samal), 'Salu' 'Changseo', 'Khuotha', etc. now. Unless the village Authorities so decide that the 'Haosa' be given the annual traditional tributes, the 'Haosa' has to manage without such prerogatives. As for 'Khuomuol' and its importance, it still holds good. While 'Khuojeh', 'Unmit', etc., rites to ward off epidemics and other village cleansing ceremonies are no longer in vogue, as Christianity has supplanted them all, the same are still practised in non-Christian villages.

CHAPTER 7

SOCIAL CELEBRATIONS

I.

The humming activities of year round tribal life among the Kukis revolve within the ambit of earning bread for survival without consideration for future growth and development on an agro-based economic system which has no place for saving, consumption being conspicuous and community bias. Such a life of routine nature becomes obviously monotonous which must find expression in various forms of soical celebrations to give vent to their longing for a life away from sacrosanct. In doing so, their structural functions of life are made often manifest in more than one way as illustrated below :

SAWM KIVAH or SAWM JUNEH

Under the present system of Sawm, some boys sleep together in different houses, where there are girls who are at the back and call of the boys. They live so closely with the family of the girls that they become almost identified as being members of the family of the girls. The boys of one particular 'Sawm'help the family of the girl in all possible way, even in the matter of cultivation when the family members of the girl fail to complete it in time. When there occurs a feast of the Lawm of the village, the girl and the boys of her 'Sawm' go together taking care of each other during the feast. Sometimes it so happens that the girl becomes inebriated by over-drinking of rice-beer. In such a situation, all the boys of the 'Sawm' take special care for her and bring her home safely. Likewise, the girl also take care of the boys. Even the parents and other members of the family regard the boys as part of their family.

With the passage of time, a stage came when most of the 'Sawm' members grew up. Some of them pursued diverse interests. Some had grown enough to fall in love with some other girls. Even the 'Sawm' girl had fallen in love either with a boy other than her own 'Sawm' members or with one of the 'Sawm' members. They felt that time had come to part company and that the 'Sawm' be disbanded. Under such circumstances, they considered that it was best to have a farewell party provided the parents of the girl gave consent to the proposal. When such a situation arose, the question of 'Sawm Kivah', meaning thereby a feast of the 'Sawm' cropped up for consideration. When such a 'Sawm Kivah' is proposed, the members of one particular 'Sawm', the number of which varies between ten and twelve, discuss the proposal with the parents of a 'Sawm' girl. If they agree, a date for it is decided upon and preparations start for the same. Normally, the young boys buy a small pig which is kept under the charge of the parents of the girl. As the day for such 'Sawm Kivah' approaches, the girl of the 'Sawm' also requests her close friends to prepare a few pots of 'Zu' by way of helping her for the occasion. Those girls will, in their turn, ask their friends to help them. Thus, a chain of help for preparation of 'Zu' for the 'Sawm Kivah' is sought. Ultimately almost all the girls of the village are involved in this function. The same is true in the case of the boys of the 'Sawm'. Each of the 'Sawm' member asks his close friends to join him on the occasion. Ultimately, boys of the whole village are covered. In accepting such invitations each of the boy friend invited contributes one pot of 'Zu' on the day. Finally, it becomes usually the affairs of the whole village, though it is initially thought to be an affair only for a small group of ten or twelve boys. Of course, the particular boy members of the 'Sawm' bear the bulk of the expenditure for the occasion.

In the previous evening of the night before the 'Sawm' Kivah', the members of the 'Sawm' serve one pot of 'Zu' to the parents of the girl wherein the Chief of the village along with his Council of Ministers, the Priest, the 'Tucha' and 'Becha' relatives of the parents of the girl are invited. The 'Sawm' members will request them all to join them in the feast and to extend all possible help to make the occasion a success.

Early, the next morning, the 'Tucha' and the 'Becha' relatives of the girls' parents do all the needful. They take up the entire responsibility for the function. As the meat is cooked, all the invitees are asked to have it to their heart's content. But the Chief and his Council of Ministers, the Priest and the father of the girl or, in his place, his 'Becha Bul' will take the 'Sapang' or the head portion of the pig. In addition to this group of people, another group of the members of the 'Sawm', which hosts the feast and their 'Sawm-Nu', the girl of the 'Sawm', are given a portion of the meat kept apart by the 'Becha' of the girls' parents. The rest of the people take the feast at random, as normal feasting is done, without any formality.

On this day, the drinking method of the 'Zu' is such that apart from all other pots of 'Zu' served on the day, two particuarlr pots are separately kept and these are served at a special place. One of them is the pot contributed by the boys of the 'Sawm', who host the feast. The other is the pot contributed by the parents of the girl. The 'Zu' contributed by the boys of the 'Sawm' is first sipped by the Chief, followed by the Priest and then the father of the girl. Sometimes the mother of the girl is also included in this sipping spree. The style of sipping is that one full bottle of water is the measuring level called 'Aleng'. The bottle of water is poured to the pot of 'Zu' without ceasing, and whoever sips the 'Zu' is made to do so without ceasing until his level of sipping is finished. The level of sipping for the above VIPs is made double of the normal level. The same is done to the other pot of 'Zu' offered by the girl's parents, which is given to the boys of the 'Sawm'. The order of sipping among the 'Sawm' members is that the leader of the 'Sawm', called 'Sawm Upat', sips first. He is followed by others in order of seniority. While the 'Sawm' members sip, they are tied with a rope on their waist and bound to a place upon the rafter of the building, so that they do not run away being unable to do justice to the level of sipping fixed for them. Thus, the 'Zu' contributed by the parents of the girl is sipped by the boys of the 'Sawm' and the girl, while the pot of 'Zu' contributed by the boys is sipped by the Chief and his Council of Ministers, the Priest, the father of the girl or his 'Becha' simultaneously. All the other pots of 'Zu'prepared on that day is served for drinking only and not for sipping.

The next day is meant for the Chief and his Council of Ministers, the Priest and the 'Tucha' and the 'Becha' relatives of the girl's father. A feast is arranged for them only and the pride of place is given to them by offering the head portion of the slaughtered pig. In doing so, each of those who had the privilege of eating the 'Sapang' brings one jar of 'Zu' each. On the other hand, the boys of the 'Sawm' who host the feast provide the meat for the day. They may buy another pig or some of their friends may make a gift of some cocks for the purpose. These are flayed, cooked and eaten along with the leaders who are offered the meat with 'Zu' on the day. After the feast, the elders retire. With the approach of the evening, the young boys and girls collect themselves at one place with a view to passing the night in singing and dancing.

On the stipulated third day of the feast, the young boys and girls, belonging to some other 'Sawm' would come with gifts of 'Zu' and other eatables to help their friends who hosted the feast. In this way, they continue the feast for the third day. On this day, however, the elders do not take part in the feast or in the drinking bout. At the close of this day's feasting and drinking, the 'Sawm Kivah' comes to an end.

Thus, the beginning of gradual dissolution of the old members of the 'Sawm', which has hosted the feast, is initiated. On this occasion some of the boy members get betrothed or marry a girl. In case there is a younger sister of the disbanded Sawm girl, the sister continues to care for the remaining junior 'Sawm' members who may like to continue in the same 'Sawm' where they have so long been junior members, instead of joining some other 'Sawm'.

It is, therefore, in an entirely different situation that the 'Sawm' institution survives today. In view of the fact that the society is changing, most of the boys and girls have started looking for greener pastures of social mobility in the urban areas of the country. Despite this, the old system of 'Sawm' in somewhat decentralised form still survives.

LAWM-SIEL-KAI Celebration :

'Lawm-Siel-Kai' meaning thereby, fatching of the Mithun for the Lawm festival which is used to denote the festival itself, is decided by the members of the 'Lawm' for the purpose of having a feast of all the members in a year. When such a decision is taken, one jar of 'Zu' (Rice-beer) is offered to the Chief of the village by way of putting up an application for permission or approval. Every member who engages the 'Lawm' in his or her field offers one jar of 'Zu' to the members in the evening at his or her residence. When the turn of the senior member, called 'Lawm- Upa', comes to do so, instead of giving the 'Zu' to its members at his house in the evening, it is taken to the house of the Chief. The senior boy and the girl members accompany the 'Lawm- Upa' to the Chief's house. The Chief then enquires from them if such a costly affair could be undertaken in view of the prevailing economic condition. The 'Lawm-members' having considered the economic condition earlier say that there is justification for holding the feast which is called 'Lawm-Kivah' or 'Lawm-Siel-Kai'. After the matter is approved by the 'Semang-Pachong', Council of Ministers, in a meeting, the Chief gives his consent. For the meeting, the Council of Ministers are given a jar of 'Zu'.

Then the 'Lawm' members go again with one jar of 'Zu' called 'Zubel', to the house of the Chief to formally place their request for allowing the Thiempu (Priest) to officiate in the cleansing rites of the village and dedicating himself to the proposed festival. This done, the 'Thiempu' is given a full cup or 'Umkhat' of wine. He takes the same and goes round all the lanes and byelanes of the village covering all the places.

Prior to this, the 'Thiempu' performs divination by cutting the leg of a chicken which is kept covered with a kind of grass-turf called 'Phoipi'. The act of practising divination is to know the future of the village and is called 'Phoitan'. Some do this with eggs also and this is known as 'Ahtuisaan'. If the proceeding is found good, the cleansing rite of the village is considered to have been gone through properly. After all these formalities, the boys and girls of the 'Lawm' start preparations for the festival.

The 'Lawm', in doing so, first decide the amount or quantity to be contributed by every member of the 'Lawm'. They also allot some work to the girls for preparation of 'Zu' and also for pounding of rice every evening for the feast. They then decide whether the 'Mithun' for the feast called 'Lawm-Siel' belonging to a particular person of village or elsewhere has to be brought in cash or kind. The 'Mithun' for the feast is also brought and kept ready for slaughtering.

As per custom, the young boys of the Lawm hunt rats for presentation in the festival. Symbolically, 3 to 5 rats are counted for each girl member of the Lawm. In order to fulfil this obligation on their part, the young boy-members go in for rat hunting called 'Lawm Zuvai'. Whatever is caught by every boy is kept smokedried. In case of any shortage, they lengthen their period of hunting of rats until the required number is caught. On completion, they pool together all the rats and hand them over to the leaders fof 'Lawm' who sort out the rats and tie together in three or five in a bundle called 'Zulom'.

An evening, preferably in the month of November, is fixed for the Lawm members to decide the date of the feast. This meeting is generally held in the house of the Chief. Coupled with this, the 'Lawm' leaders find out partners of a boy and a girl from amongst the Lawm members. For that meeting, five to six jars of 'Zu' prepared before-hand are served. When the proceedings of the meeting are in progress, the leaders who confidentially hand- picked the pair of boy and girl partners earlier, announce by surprise about the different pairs of junior 'Lawm' members, much to their embarrassment. The purpose of such declaration of the couples is to drink, dance, dine and work together during the feast. Such arranged partners are called in pairs and are made to drink wine together that evening in the meeting from two Mithun- horns, the ends of which are tied together by a string as a token of an official announcement of the pairs being accepted as partners for the feast. Drinking of wine from the two Mithun- horns bound together signifies their obedience, loyalty and devotion to the orders of the leaders. After drinking, the boy is asked to present the rat bundle called 'Julom' bound in threes or fives to his girl partners, thereby putting their seal of willingness to drink, dine, dance and work together during the Lawm feast. With the announcement of partners, the real atmosphere of the festival is created.

The 'Julom' (a bundle of rats) need not necessarily be rats. It may be substituted by any flesh of dried meat called 'Sagop' and cock or hen, depending on the availability and capacity of the 'Lawm' boy-member for presentation to his girl partner.

Paddy for the occasion is contributed only by the boy members of the Lawm for brewing rice-beer called 'Zu'. Such paddy is collected and put together at a place which is called 'Chang- Hai'. The place of collection and storage may be selected anywhere. Every evening, the girl members will pound some quantity of the paddy for preparation of the occasion. The boys good humourly and in a jovial company help the girls in pounding the paddy. The paddy thus pounded is distributed among the girls for preparation of beer for the 'Lawm-Kivah' (Lawm feast). Rice for the feast is contributed exclusively by the Chief or his nominee in whose house the 'Lawm-Kivah' is to be held. Otherwise, normally the feast is held only at the residence of the Chief. Such contribution on the part of the performer or the Chief of the village is, in the like manner, pounded by the young boys and girls of his 'Tuchas' and 'Bechas'.

The 'Mithun' to be slaughtered for the occasion is called 'Lawm Siel'. This has to be purchased only from the contributions made by the young boy members of the 'Lawm'. The 'Mithun' may be from the village itself or from any other neighbouring villages, answering the right size and weight. A group of young boys is sent out to find a suitable 'Mithun' for the occasion. In the meantime, every girl of each pair contributes rice about one pot each for preparing beer which is known as 'Ah-Zu' and a jar of 'Siel-Zu'. Thus, contribution for the occasion is divided among the boys and girls in two parts - the boys contribute paddy for the beer called 'Chang-Hai' and the price of the 'Mithun' called 'Lawm Siel Man' and the girls contribute only the beer known as 'Ah-Zu' and 'Siel-Zu'.

The boys and girls of the 'Lawm' fix a day or days for collection of firewood for the occasion. On such day or days, they go beating drum, gong and Mithun-horn while proceeding to the jungle for collection of fuel. On arrival, they settle down and start cutting and collecting the firewood. The collection of sufficient quantity of firewood over, they start homeward carrying the bundles. Before proceeding towards home, they dance and sing for three rounds, in accompaniment of drum, gong and blowing of 'Mithun-horn'. The leader of the firewood-collection team is called 'Lawm-Upa'. The song for such dance runs as follows :

> Incidentally, the group is divided into two who sing in responsive style to each other.

First group :

Thing gapou te,
Gol ge nuto chonthing
Gapou te.

Free Translation :

Let us go to fetch fire-wood,
Let all the members of the Lawm
Who are bosom friends, fetch the Fire-wood for the occasion.

Second group :

Chon thing pohna,
responding: Gol ge nu,
in Chorus: : Dai cham lah a, lengval ye.

Free Translation : The Lawm members are extremely busy gathering the fire-wood for the occasion of the festival.

(This song is sung on occasions of great festivals, such as, 'Lawm-Siel-Kai', 'Chon', etc.)

While singing this song two girls and one boy, selected for the dance, are to dance in the midst of the whole group who encircle them. After this, they prepare themselves to go back home in a procession. Such procession is led by a virgin girl who has no blemish in her body, which means that she does not have any defect in her person. On returning home, they form a circle without alighting their loads. Thus, the two girls and one boy who would dance in the jungle unburden themselves while others carry their load and thus commence dancing as the rest of the boys and girls start singing. They do the same thing for three rounds while others continue to sing with their load. After doing this for three times, the whole 'Lawm' alight their loads simultaneously with an exclamation - 'ho,ho,ho'. As they exclaim for three times, they also go to the jungle for the firewood for three times. They are welcomed on return with rice-beer by a set of people called 'Lawm Tucha'. These Lawm Tuchas are selected from amongst the Lawm members by the Lawm leaders. Likewise, there are 'Lawm Becha' and 'Lawm Tungvah'. Such persons are selected by the leaders of 'Lawm' in consideration of their efficiency in performing the task assigned to the custommary social people whose set of duties are already fixed as per custom. After collection of fire-wood, if the rice-beer called 'Change Hai Zu' is found ready for consumption, the young boys of the 'Lawm' prepare themselves to go in search of a 'Mithun' for the 'Lawm Kivah'. Finding the right type of 'Mithun' for the purpose, they bring the same home. They will be welcomed by the girl members of 'Lawm' and also other people in general. The welcome song is as follows, which is sung after they are offered rice-beer by the girl members :

Siel lo hung veo vin,
kholen kho siello hungveo vin,
kholen kho siel abei leh eima kho ah
Leng siel tam nante.

Free Translation :

Come, see the Mithun,
Come, see the Mithun of big village,
If the Mithun of big village is not available,
There are plenty of our Mithun village-Royal.

While singing the above song, the selected boys and girls for dance continue to dance until they do so three rounds. After this, the whole crowd proceed towards the site of the Lawm feast. That night all the Lawm members sit drinking and dancing. The next day, all the Lawm girl members who prepare 'Ah-Zu' and 'Siel Zu' start distilling their respective 'Zu' for the festival which is to start from the following day. This is called 'Zu Lhoh'. The leaders of the 'Lawm' go on around to every house to check the taste of the beer on invitation of each girl. While doing this, the leaders often get drunk. The tempo for the festival is thus created. The following day, the Lawm leaders go to inform the Chief and his Council of Ministers that everything is set for the festival. On receipt of this information, the Council of Ministers formally announce among the villagers to the effect that 'Lawm Kivah' festival is going to be held from the following day, and that no one should go out of the village. In case a person is found absent in the festival, the devils called 'Thilhas' consider him or her not as a villager. This may make the absentee fall an easy prey of the 'Thilhas' resulting in his/her ill health. The day is called 'Ah Zu Hom Ni'. In the early hours of the festival day, the village priest will propitiate with his 'Juphi' or spraying of 'Zu' inside the building where the festival is to be held. He will also do the same in the front and the rear portions of the house. That done, all the girl-members of the 'Lawm' will bring their own 'Zu' together to the house where the festival is to take place. All the villagers sit together at the place fixed and the leaders of the 'Lawm' once again call the rolls and enquire if there is any person left out in the gathering. This precedes the distribution of 'Ah Zu Hom'. The distribution of the beer is done in the following manner :

> The leaders of Lawm select one girl from amongst the Lawm members. Such girl has no blemish, which means that such girl must not have any defect in her body, nor has she have character- defamation nor is she morally loose and has lost her virginity.

The girl thus selected leads all other girls in the distribution of beer to the public. Each girl is supplied with bamboo cups prepared by her boy partner. So, being led by the selected girl, each girl offers her own brewed beer to all in her bamboo cup. While drinking, most of the villagers normally get drunk before the round is completed by all the girls. Often it is found that distribution of the beer by the girls continues till late at night.

The next day is the 'Siel Juneh Hi' meaning, the day of the beer being served for the 'Mithun'. The procedures is the same as above. The village priest does his propitiation and is soon followed with the announcement by the leaders demanding the presence of each and every villager. Before public assemblage, the Lawm boys and girls bring the tree with which the 'Mithun' is to be tied up and killed. This is called 'Lawm Siel Khuom'. They bring the 'Siel Khuom' and, on their arrival at the place, they erect the same at a spot which is earlier sanctified by the village priest. This is followed by the distribution of wine in exactly the same manner as the 'Ah Zu Neh' had been done the preceding day. The selected girl again leads other girls for the distribution of wine, while other girls distribute their respective wine to each and every one in small bamboo cups provided by their male partners. In this connection, it may be mentioned here that after completing the carrying of firewood for consecutively three days, on the fourth day, the boy members go to out 'Lawm Siel Khuom', i.e. the post for the 'Mithun'. The cutting of 'Lawm Siel Khoum' is, therefore, done in between the collection of firewood and the 'Lawm Siel Zu Neh'. The kind of tree for the 'Siel Khuom' is the type of tree called

'Sething', 'Sahi'is Manipuri. The beautiful bushes with straight trunks are selected and cleaned while keeping the bushes at the end of each branch, including the tompost bush of the main trunk.

On the erection of the 'Siel Khuom' the same day, all the girls and boys perform a dance in a circle mixing themselves alternately, and standing slightly bending forward. They do this dancing for three rounds. As they finish it, they sing in a doggeral as 'Li, Li, Li, Li, Li' and 'Ha, Ha, Ha, Ha, Ha'. Then they stand erect and again slightly bend forward on their waist, clap in quick succession as they move sidewise in rhythm with clapping, to the right first producing at the same time a sound 'Bru...U'. This is done three times. All the boys join hands on their shoulders leaving the girls in between them with their feet apart. As they are in such a pose, they bend thrice on the right side first and then, as they do so each time, they slightly move their body towards the left also three times. While doing so, they produce a sound 'He.....E'. After doing this, they straighten themselves and produce the sound 'Li, Li,Li, Li,Li' and 'Ha,Ha, Ha, Ha, Ha'. The old and the young are to take their position on a platform usually erected in every Kuki house which is called 'Kem'. The boy members of the Lawm then bring out the 'Mithun' kept underneath the floor in an enclosure fenced with planks called 'Hongnoi'. As they bring the 'Mithun' out, they tie the same and the village priest propitiates it by saying -"This is friendly fun. Do not be offended with humiliation. Accept it sportively, and do not harm the youth with anger". Thus, the priest symbolically appeases the 'Mithun'. This is called 'Siel Lhai Na'. After this, the young boys of the village wrestle with the 'Mithun'. This is called 'Siel Bot'. The young boys are necessarily to wrestle it at least three times. If by that time it is not tamed, they continue the wrestling for two more times. It is believed that the Mithun should not be wrestled six times. It has to be necessarily three or five or seven times. Thus, when it is found sufficiently yielding, the Mithun is made to stand erect for high jump competition by the young boys and other strong married men who know the skill of high-jump. This is called 'Siel-Kal-Kitet'. He who jumps the highest is praised and recognised. He is offered with more 'Zu', specially by the old and married ladies, for generally girls feel shy to offer anything to the boys for their victory. This programme usually takes almost the whole day.

After this, the boys and the girls take the Mithun to a place earmarked for the procession to honour the man or men for their capabilities in different fields. This act of honouring a man or men is called 'Pah'. As they take the Mithun round the village towards the place of the 'Pah', they sing all the way as follows :

Siel Kakai ye,
Changsiel len len (Some says alien lien),
Kakai Ye.
Changsiel lenguikhao vo tange,
Gol to nitnin Kanomme.
Gol to nithin kanomme,
Gol to tangkho Kalamme.
Kasiel patchon kaba peh e,
Sijol apah vil velle.
Sijol banna phungchong pah e,
kadongma toh te ngon ne.

Free Translation :

Mithun is being harnessed,
A big Mithun is harnessed.
The big Mithun is tightly roped,
The occasion is being spent with exceeding joy.

The occasion is being observed with exceeding joy with friends
Dancing ceaselessly with friends on the occasion.

The Cotton earings of the Mithun looks magnificient, Glittering as
Glittering as the field of Cotton flowering called 'Sijol'

Seeing the beauty of the Mithun with earings of cotton
I cannot but compare it with my fiancee.

As they sing this song, the girls offer the Mithun all kinds of decorations. Many girls volunteer to remove their copper bangles and put them on the horns of the Mithun. Sometimes, they put cotton wool in the ear of the Mithun as earings. At this stage, the Mithun becomes fully tamed and the boys and the girls consider it as one of the members of the Lawm. Likewise, the Mithun appears to understand their treatment. This endears it to the members of the Lawm. For this emotional attachment, often many Lawm girls cry when the Mithun is killed for the feast.

On arrival at the scene of the 'Pah', all the boys and girls start singing and dancing. Some of the boys and girls, however, prepare the 'Zu" brought along with them and offer the same to the man and his wife who have been asked to sit in the middle of the group forming a circle in front of the house called 'Leituol'. The man refuses the offer saying that unless his 'Tucha' and 'Becha' are with him, he cannot either entertain them nor can be keep their request. So, the Lawm leaders are forced to fetch his 'Tuchas' and 'Bechas'. On arrival of the 'Tucha' and 'Becha', they all are made to sit in the following order:

> The man of the house sits on the extreme right, on whose left side his wife sits, parallel to them the Becha of the man sits near the man while the wife of the 'Becha' sits on the left side of the wife of the man. The 'Tuchas' of the man sit behind them as they wish to sit.

They are now offered rice beer which the man accepts. As they start sipping the beer, the members of the Lawm begin singing in praise of the man. The song of the occasion is :

> Nang Kipah e, Inpipu (whoever is the man is to be mentioned)
> Nang Kapah e.
> Inpipu na sing sungah
> Zu le sa beimo e.

Free Translation:

> We honour you, owner of the house,
> We honour you.
> The owner of the house,
> May meat and 'Zu' flow
> In plenty in your house.

While singing this song, they keep on dancing to show the happiness and joy of the Lawm. It is now the turn of the man to tell them what he intends to do for them for what they have honoured him. But, his 'Becha' officiates for him. His Becha speaks his words. It is usually the promise to offer a feast to the Lawm for such an act of honour, normally he kills a pig for them. They sing, dance and drink for the whole night in praise of the man whom they have honoured. Such celebration continues for two to three days at different places giving honour to different persons. At last, when honouring of the individual persons of fame or riches is over, they come back to the site of the festival. Before leaving the place, however, after performing the 'Pah', a farewell song is sung. It is as follows :-

Chun in Junbang Neilhao Vin,
Senna Colho Chetange,
Senna Golho Chetange,
Khumlhan Lam Bang Jontange.

Free Translation :

Lady of the man, 'Chun' (Mother)
Bid us farewell so that we, your children (members of the Lawm) may depart happily.

Bid us farewell,
So that we might depart for our homes.

This song is composed by the leader of the Lawm. With the song in their lips and joy in their heart, they proceed towards their place where they will start their festival. On arriving the festival place in the morning for the big feast, the killing of the Mithun takes place. Before killing, the village priest performs his propitiation called 'Ganlhaa Lhai'. In doing this, the priest sprays a mouthful of wine on the Mithun and then pours the whole wine contained in a gourd, starting from its head to tail, followng the line of its ridge. This process is called 'Gan-Lha-Lhai', meaning thereby appeasing the soul of the Mithun. The killing of the Mithun is done by the 'Becha' of the family in whose house the feast is held. The method of killing is by piercing a bamboo-spike beneath the left fore-leg and through the heart, so that the animal dies instantaneously. This act is a called 'Sa-Sut' or 'Sa-Dawt'. In the case of 'Sa-Ai' and 'Chang Ai', the killing of the Mithun is done by the senior man called 'Upa' of the performer (elder-brother). On that day, the feast is meant for the whole village, irrespective of age, sex, caste, creed, etc. A special category of meat is set apart, which is composed mainly of the head portion of the animal. It is called 'Sapang'. This meat can only be partaken or eaten by some selected people who are normally aged, including the Chief and his selected Council of Ministers called 'Haosa' and his 'Semang Upa'. The persons entitled to eat this meat are normally selected on behalf of the Lawm. In such selection the Chief usually makes it a point to include persons belonging to different clans and lineages living in the village, besides the indispensable village elders and the 'Semang Pachong', Council of Ministers. The village priest, the family 'Becha' and the village Chief are compulsory persons to be included in this category of persons.

The next day is the day of gradual recession of the festive mood. On this day the rice beer prepared by the Lawm girls called 'Siel Zu Hawm Ni' is taken. The procedure of taking the beer is exactly in the same manner as had been done earlier. A girl having no black spots morally or physically is selected for the purpose and she leads other girls for distribution of the beer to the whole community without anybody being deprived. For such occasion, an announcement is once again given by the leader of the Lawm. Drinking of the 'Zu' is done in the same procedure as followed in the case of 'Ah Ju Neh Ni'.

The next day of 'Siel Ju Neh Ni', is the third phase of the festival counting from the day of 'Ah Ju Neh Ni'. On this day, all the persons who are entitled to 'Sapang' meat bring one jar of 'Zu' each, which is called 'Jubel'. They are accompanied by their respective 'Tuchas' and 'Bechas' to officiate for the man and to help him serve the people in offering the 'Zu'. This day is called 'Sapang Suoni', which means the day of those who have been privileged to take the special meat called 'Sapang'. The method of taking the 'Zu' is at random. No formalities or procedures are observed in this sort of drinking.

The following day is called 'Innei Suoni', the day of the family in whose house the festival has been held. The family offers to the Lawm members one big jar of 'Zu' prepared for this purpose and reserved strictly for the occasion. On this day, while the 'Zu' of the family is sipped from the pot of 'Zubel' through a bamboo pipe called 'Dawn', all other pots of 'Zu', specially the 'Zu' prepared by the Lawm girls, for the occasion are distilled and drunk from bamboo cups. The particular way of sipping through a pipe called 'Dawn' signifies the importance of the occasion and the offer of 'Zu'. The procedure of taking the rice-beer is as follows :

The 'Tucha' and the 'Becha' of the family prepare the 'Zu' and insert in it one piece of stick as the measuring rod called 'Leng' for the level to be sipped by an individual invitee. This is called 'Aleng Si'. Everyone sipping the 'Zu' will do so only upto the measurement level marked on the rod. The 'Becha' of the family distributes and supervises the sipping-turn of the Lawm members, while the 'Tucha' sees to it that everyone invited does so neither more nor less of 'Aleng', or, the 'Tucha' regulates the sipping level as per 'Aleng'. At the beginning, the 'Becha' calls upon the leader of the Lawm called 'Lawm Upa' to do the sipping first. This particular pot of 'Zu' is served only near the central pillar of the house. This place occupies importance and signifies its status. When the Lawm leader reaches the place, a rope is tied to the rafters of the house. The other end of the rope is hung downwards to the floor. This end is tied round the waist of the leader of the Lawm as he is about to start sipping the 'Zu' upto the measuring level. As a rule, he is to take double the general level meant for others. He must not go away or run away from the place till he can finish his level or 'Zu- Leng'. The next man in the Lawm heirarchy is 'Lawm Tangva'. There are usually two persons for this office. They are called 'Lawm Tangva' and 'Lawm Upa'. Then comes one male-Tucha of the Lawm and two Lawm girl-Tuchas, who are below the Lawm 'Nungah Upa'. The office of the Lawm Nungah Upa' is held only by one girl and is in between the 'Lawm Tangva' and Lawm Tucha' in the organisational set up. These seven persons are supposed to take double the normal level. No other person, including the Chief and his Council of Ministers and the man of the family, is given any importance on this day, as is shown from the way of sipping or drinking the 'Zu'. The Chief and his Council of Ministers, the man of the family and the priest of the village drink the 'Zu' in cups along with the general public. The Lawm girls, in the meantime, also offer 'Zu' for the general public which is prepared by each Lawm girl for the occasion. From every 'Jubel' (pot of beer) given from such preparation, one gourd called 'Umkhat' is kept apart. Thus, as the preparation of 'Zu' continues one after another, the number usually goes up very high at the end of the day.

On the next day, the Lawm boys and girls specially invite all the old and the young men of the village for taking a drink. They offer them the 'Zu' saved from the previous night and one gourd each from every 'Jubel' is offered to the public. Again, they invite all the village old people also separately. In this function, the pots of 'Zu' saved are only the best portion from every pot of 'Zu' which is served on this day. Such portion of 'Zu' is called 'Zu Chih Chah', i.e., the most valued and highly intoxicating portion of the wine. The formalities of serving the 'Zu' on this day is as follows :

The Chief and his Council of Ministers, including the Thiempu or priest, are made to sit on a guddi made of traditional cloths called 'Puonmongvom' or 'Thangnang' or 'Saipikhup' which is spread over on the ground. The Chief sits on the extreme right- hand side, the village priest on his left and the Council of Ministers sit next according to their official heirarchical order. In this connection, it may be mentioned that a man always lets his wife go or sit on his left-hand side, either on formal occasion or informal occasion. Then each girl selected from amongst the senior Lawm members brings out one bottle or gourd of 'Zu' and gives the same to those who are made to sit on the guddi. This kind of forced drinking continues till they gulp it down to the dregs. No other person can drink or touch the beer until these people's drinking is over. This is in reciprocation of the manner in which the senior Lawm leaders have been made to sip on the previous occasion. This is done by the man of the family called 'Innei' Soni'. When the Chief and other village elders have finished their share of drink, the general public are allowed to start drinking which continues for the whole night. Thus, on the next day comes the end of the 'Lawm Siel Kai'. The enthusiasm, spontaneity and joy associated with it for all during the Lawm festival are great. The festival over, a girl feels lonely and recollects the happenigs of the festival in her mind. She composes a song to give vent to her emotion in the following song :

> Goltoh Changang Kikhennin,
> Vai Lou Konning,
> Kiseil Lavao Gamjanga Tang Lamme.
> Kisiel Lavao Gamjanga Atang Lap,
> Lenchom Levao Kajah Lonlhi Longe.

Free Translation :

> After the Lawm festival, When I went to the paddy-field, the beauty of the Mithun horn in the festival kept flashing back in my mind.
>
> In as much as the beauty of the Mithun horn kept flashing back in my mind, it also kept ringing in my ear the drum-beat sound of the festival which made me cry recalling the exceeding memory of the occasion.

II. Voicha Kih :

This occasion has originated from amongst the members of the 'Lawm' in the village. As there are very few social occasions through which the monotomy of the day-to-day life can be broken, some plea is forged for organising a social occasion for the young boys and girls of the 'Lawm'. In the present case, the 'Lawm' members try to find out a well-to-do villager to organise a social occasion for them by working in his field in more efficient manner. In doing so, the boys and girls of the 'Lawm' decide that they would go to the field of the selected man for the 'Voicha Kih'. Then they would all go to work in the field of the man chosen. While working in the field, they would suddenly stop the work and return home before time. They would then inform the owner that they have stopped work. Being asked, they would inform the field owner that they prefer to work in the field on some other day in an organised way and in a happier mood. When he agrees to organise the 'Voicha Kih', a day is fixed. On such a day, they all go to the field as on the previous occasion to work in the field of the man. On this day, every member of the Lawm would carry with him one lunch packet each without curry. The rice thus brought by the members is pooled together for tiffin during the day.

The owner of the field, on his part, prepares curry for the entertainment of the group. In doing so, he kills a pig which is dressed and cooked by the 'Tucha' and the 'Becha' of the man. After the meat is cooked, the 'Tucha' and the 'Becha' of the owner of the field bring it to the field to be offered to the young workers. On this day, they really work hard with an aim to compensate for the loss they have incurred on the previous day. They are offered a sumptuous mid-day-meal. The man also remains present in the field to encourage the boys and the girls in their work. In the evening, when the day's work is done, they prepare themselves to return home. In doing so, they carry the man on whose field they work in a 'Litter' which is prepared earlier for him on that day. On their return to the village, they enter it with much gaity and applause, singing and dancing while carrying the man in the 'Litter'. This is called 'Pal Lhun'. This is usually done from the outskirt of the village. On return, they are offered with 'Zu' at the residence of the man on whose field the work was done and they continue to sing and dance the whole night.

On the following morning, the boys of the 'Lawm' arrange to get a pig at their expense, while the girls contribute 'Zu' for the occasion and they feast together at the residence of the man on the excuse of harvesting or sowing. On this day, all the elders of the village, the Chief and his Council of Ministers as also the Priest are invited. The usual way of sharing the meat by the elders, the Chief and his Council of Ministers is followed. The Priest performs the propititation cermony of 'Kaolhai', which means pleasing the devils responsible for casting a spell of ill-health on the congregation. In doing this he takes one piece of liver, sprinkles a mouthful of 'Zu' on it after a short invocation and then throws it away in a symbolic act of offering the same to the devils.

The 'Sapang' or the head portion of the slaughtered animal for the occasion is offered to the Chief and his Council of Ministers, the Priest, the owner of the house and some other selected elders of the village. No other person is entitled to this portion of the meat. In addition, another portion of the meat called 'Sachan' is given to the lady of the house, the 'Tucha' and the 'Becha' relatives of the family as special shares. The rest of the meat is cooked and eaten by the general invitees and the young boys and girls. On this day, the 'Zu' offered by the boys and girls is the only rice-beer offered to the invitees. All the drinks served are only done by sipping from the Zu-pitcher or pot.

From all this, it is seen that their agricultural life is punctuated with the social life of feasting and merry-making.

The next day is marked by the contribution of 'Zu' by 'Tuchas' and 'Bechas' of the man in whose house the festival takes place and by those who had been given the privilege of having 'Sapang' and 'Sachan'. The 'Zu' brought by the Chief and those who had been given the privilege of having 'Sapang' is called 'Sapang- Zu'. Likewise, it is 'Becha-Zu', 'Tucha-Zu', etc. The lady of the house also offers a pitcher or pot of 'Zu' and it is called as 'Innei Zu'. There is no formality of drinking the 'Zu' on this occasion.

III. Puon Kaap

This is an occasion for merry-making and fun spinning for the members of Lawm boys and girls. The girls attempt at ridiculing the boys so much so that the boys could not go on hunting, as they are painted as unfit for the shooting expedition. Even the petticoat or 'Lungi' of a girl is made the butt of ridicule by the boys. Such jokes and banalities in the matter sometimes take a serious turn on the part of the boys. Ultimately, the boys snatch away one of the petticoats of the girls and spread it over at a place as the target of their shooting competition. At times it so happens that best shot boys fail to show their shooting skill. Everyone present becomes surprised and then it is ascribed to a certain superstition. It is believed that if the petticoat is removed by the girls from their thighs through their private parts, the same is very difficult to hit as a target. The older generation interviewed confirm this. Likewise, a boy or a man known as a shooting expert fails to hit the target, but an unworthy hit it better. Such an instance is that of Paokhuochuon, who has been, then, in his mid-teens, with no experience in shooting.

When the Lawm members decide to hold the 'Puon Kaap' competition, the Lawm leaders approach the village Chief to permit them to organise such a competition. They submit their prayer along with a pot of 'Zu'. This formality is a must, for the Chief is supposed to know everything that happens around him. He is consultation with his Council of ministers and the village Priest normally gives consent to this. On receipt of the permission, the Lawm members start organising the other details of the competition. Meanwhile, they contact a person in whose paddy field they would go for the work on the day the shooting competition is organised in the midst of their work in the field. They also make preparations for offering one pot of 'Zu' to each by the girls, while the boys contribute for rearing up a pig for the feast. The cost of the 'Zu' for the occasion is shared by the boys and the girls and this is called 'Changhai'.

On the day of the competition in the field of the man already selected, the Lawm members come prepared with their lunch packet. All the girl members of the Lawm also come prepared with 'Zu'. On the part of the man in whose paddy field they will be working also come prepared to feed the Lawm members by killing a pig or whatever he can afford along with 'Zu'. In doing this, his 'Tucha' and 'Becha' relatives take the most active part in all works connected with the occasion. Thus, he asks the village Chief, his Council of Ministers and the Priest to join him at his field on the occasion.

On their arrival at the field, the Lawm members start working in the field as is done on any normal working day. They continue to do the work throughout the afternoon, i.e., till their mid-day meal is served by the man of the day. That done, they become busy in preparing for the shooting competition. When everything is ready, the Priest does the ritual invocation for the welfare of the family on whose field the shooting competition is organised. The ladies' 'Lungi', known as 'Pon Lhai', required for the competition are arranged. Formalities, like drinking, eating, etc. are not observed during the competition in the field while they work, and also after the competition. When the competition is over, some of the Lawm members, who in the meantime, prepared one 'Litter' for the owner of the field in whose farm or field the competition is held. He is made to get into it. When they proceed towards his home, the owner of the field is carried all the way in the Litter upto his house by the boys of the Lawm. On returning home from the outskirts of the village, the Lawm members keep themselves in a befitting joyous mood by singing and dancing and making all sorts of sound. This is called 'Pal Lhun', i.e., arrival in jubilition with ovation to the owner of the house. Thus, on their arrival at his residence, the man offers them one pot of 'Zu' by way of expression of thanks. On the next day, the Lawm members kill the pig they kept ready for the occasion and feast together at the residence of the man on whose farm they had the shooting competition the previous day. In the feast, the Chief, his Council of Ministers, the Priest and 'Tucha' and 'Becha' relatives of the man of the day are invited. The Lawm girls and boys busy themselves in preparing other things, including serving 'Zu' to the guests. In the meantime, 'Tucha' and 'Becha' relatives of the owner of the house become engaged in preparing the meat and cooking the food-stuffs and meat. The pig slaughtered for the occasion is done by the 'Becha' of the man. While the meat is cooked and consumed by the public , the Lawm members and other guests, some portions of the killed animal are kept apart for different categories of people in the following manner :

'Sapang':

This is the head portion of the animal killed. This is meant exclusively for the Chief and his Council of Ministers, the man of the house and the village Priest. No other person is entitled to eat this meat.

'Sachan':

This particular piece of meat is meant for 'Tucha' and 'Becha' relatives of the man. In normal course of distribution of the meat, these categories of relatives would have been given the waist and the rib portions, respectively, if the occasion is actually organised by the person whose house is used by the Lawm members. But this being the occasion of the Lawm, 'Tucha' and 'Becha' relatives of the man are not entitled to get their due share. It may be noted that since the man of the house is involved in such affeirs of the Lawm, by virtue of their relationship, which is based on mutual respect and involvement, 'Tucha' and 'Becha' of the man take active part on the occasion. In the 'Sachan' includes the pieces of the best portion of the meat.

Although it is the day of the boys and the girls, they are not entitled to have any special privilege in the eating formalities, nor in the distribution of the meat. They all are to eat in the company of the general public. Everyone eats at random, but those who are entitled to take 'Sapang' have some eating formalities. They are to eat in the inmost recesses of the house called 'Intom'. There, they distribute food in the manner of the age-old tradition. Regarding those who are entitled to 'Sachan', the 'Becha' of the family arranges things in such a way that the share of each person is already kept earmarked and when they eat the particular share of meat is served to them.

The people who are entitled to eat 'Sapang' and 'Sachan' sit together in a camera and decide that each of such man should offer one jar of 'Zu' to the Lawm members the next day. On this day, the 'Zu' prepared by the Lawm girls are served for drinking. It is customary that any kind of 'Zu' offered by the Lawm boys and girls is served in cups for drinking and not for sipping. This is indicative of the importance given to them and less importance put on others during the occasion, as per custom. The occasion being organised mainly by the boys and the girls, the jar of 'Zu' offered by each person entitled to 'Sapang' and 'Sachan' is served only in cups. Thus, the offer of 'Zu' by such persons comes only on the following day of the feast with the pork arranged by the Lawm members. Such counter entertainment on the part of the elders to the boys and the girls takes one more day. Then comes the end of the 'Puon Kaap' competition festival.

CHAPTER 8

SUPERNATURALS : RITUALS AND CEREMONIES

I To many primitive people, their world was full of play and counter-play of mystic powers which supposedly influenced the shape and destiny of men. It is true that some groups of people, being confronted with problems and having failed to grapple with them, try to attribute the cause of these problems to some unknown and unseen forces. These mysterious powers are generally called supernaturals. Nanda (1984 : 196) describes:

> Supernatural refers to those powers, events and experiences that are beyond ordinary human control and the laws of nature and outside reality as normally experienced. Every society has some set beliefs and practices that enter into the relationship of the humans to the supernaturals.

Tylor (1874 : 425-47) also gives the definition of 'religion' as the belief in supernaturals. However, each society or a group of people has traditional method of controlling these powers or to subordinate them through certain actions of occultism or esoteric practices, rites, rituals and ceremonies or celebrations in accompaniment with offerings, prayers or sacrifices so as to appease, placate or propitiate in order to enjoy a trouble-free life, having no anxiety or tension. This, in course of time, gradually take the shape of an institutionalised system of beliefs, rituals, rules, procedures, etc. through cults or systematised celebrated rituals or manifestations. With the passage of time, these are handed down from generation to generation and are entrenched into the thickly woven fabric or culture. Durkheim (1915 : 10), therefore, propounded the concept of religion as having grown out of the social experience of man.

Probably, the Kuki groups of people from the hoary past adopted themselves with the ecology and environment, and thereby fashioned their life-style. Interactions with varied situations might have weathered or attuned the cultural core through their migrations from time immemorial. Series of rolling ridges with disproportionate undulations, forest clad mountains of variable intensities and the gorging rivers might have influenced their cognitive system or cosmology. Seasonal variations and distinctive action patterns for survival strategies have perhaps contributed to the understanding about themselves. The transforming world with some concept of hitherto unseen forces, considered as supernaturals, also could be discenible to them. Thus, supernaturalism has variations and distinctive categories.

It is the concept of *Chung Pathien* or the source of 'All Creations' that is considered to be the Highest benovolent God who lives in heaven or sky. Such concept of religion, according to Andrew Lang (1887:327), manifests in the belief in High Gods. He is believed to have created the universe and all the living beings. All people firmly believe that everything concerned with prosperity, growth and strength in life is nothing but the free gift of *Chung Pathien.* He is considered omnipotent and also omniscient. Thus, he is all powerful but he does not want any propitiation or worship or appeasment through sacrifices and offerings. He does good to all and sundry.

The concept of *Chung Pathien* is abstract and thus it has no anthropomorphic form or a permanent place or residence. The nomenclature of *Chung Pathien* signifies an honorific term used for addressing a male person with respect and veneration. Dichotomy prevails while conceptualising *Chung Pathien,* viz., the benevolent with also evil or bad power having the forces of destruction, and all other forms of evil activities. He is supposed to live in the underworld and is called 'Noimangpa'. He is believed to have been sent by *Chung Pathien* from the heaven or the sky to dwell at 'Kholmun' where all living beings are found.

Therefore, the world of supernaturals reigns supreme among the Kukis, while the other entities are related to evil and are susceptible of being appeased or placated through performance of elaborate rituals and sacrifices which constitute prayers of 'Phuisap' by the Priest called 'Thiempu', who officiates the ceremony among the Kukis. Some evil spirits are :

(i) 'Gamhoise' devil of the jungle and 'Inmunse', devil of the house, meaning thereby 'accursed place' by a combination of the two words. Souls of the persons meeting unnatural death become this type of dangerous spirits. They are supposed to create trouble to the people according to their own sweet will, at the places where such unnatural deaths occur. In otherwords, the place is haunted by the soul of the person.

(ii) 'Joumi' is a dangerous male spirit. It frightens people and people may die out of shock and fear. It is active during night and its form is said to be elastic though mostly it is seen very tall. It is said that it usually stands at the same height of any tree nearby which it happens to appear. The 'Joumi' is reportedly very fond of chicken. It kills mostly cocks and hen by throtling the neck and sucking its blood.

(iii) 'Kulsamnu' is considered to be a female spirit which is in- charge of keeping the souls of the individuals. After the death of a person it has to take away the soul and keep the same in a permanent resting place, known as 'Van'.

(iv) 'Chomnu' is another female spirit, but it rarely causes any trouble to mankind. It is considered to be a harmless spirit.

(v) 'Gamlahlen' is yet another male spirit who causes disease or sickness to the peop e. It resides in the jungle and to appease it, effigy of a buffalo made of clay is offered along with 'Zu' cock and unboiled rice.

(vi) 'Gamkao' is an evil spirit of a particular place of a jungle which can cause serious illness to the preson who meets such spirit.

(vii) 'Kaomei' is an evil spirit which flies at night like a fire- fly in a much bigger volume of fire-ball.

(viii) 'Kaosie' is a greedy spirit. It can enter in a person and convert such person into a different personality, changing the voice, the behaviour and strength. Such spirit can be released only when it is appeased with what it wants.

II Ritual formalities :

Herskovits (1955 : 223) observed :

> The ways in which men seek to bring themselves into harmony with the powers of the universe are many. They may be intensely personal, or require participation by the entire group. They may be pulic or

private. They may involve highly keyed emotional improvisation, or demand precision of movement, set by an ancient tradition. They may call for the recitation of elaborate formulas, or may be wordless. They may utilise special objects, carefully made and of intricate form or they may be restricted to non-material expresseion in word or song or dance. Any of these, moreover, may be found alone or in combination with others. And any of them, or all, may be used to petition or compel action by powers whose resources transcend those of the human being who invokes them.

Prayer is one of the principal categories of worship. It may be defined as the use of words to bring about the favourable intervention of the powers of the universe in the affairs of men. It can vary from casual address to formalised plea, and may be specific or general in its reference.

Rituals or ceremonies are the pivots round which some thoughts about supernatural rotate. Myths, lores or some incantations are there and these are woven in esoteric words which express gratitude and promises for future, vis-a-vis prayer for protection, help and security against rainy days. It is chanted in their own broken doggeral language which is known as 'Phuisam' meaning thereby utterances of words of magic called 'Doithu'. These are impregnated with magical potentialities and are believed to have tremendous impact on the spirit.

The sacred complex (Vidyarthi : 1962) as found elsewhere is not pronounced in the life of the Kukis, while dealing with the supernaturals. The idea of a sancturay is absent among them. As we find elsewhere, certain specific sites, either fixed traditionally or finalised by the people, is conspicuous by their absence. It is done or finalised by the priest, 'Thiempu'. His post is hereditary and practically he has to hold his position by his capabilities and social image. Then there are elaborate rituals, sometimes with offerings and sacrifices, as there is no anthropomorphic form of the deity and only one God is present. Their religion therefore, is not based on pantheon but on monotheism, though some evil spirits are named which have specific activities, and manifestations.

The Thiempu has to do every-thing through oneirology which he gets during night while sleeping. Through dreams and visions, he gets all directions as to what he should do, when and with what materials or ingredients, what incantations are to be used are also indicated as his guidelines by the spirit who appears in dream to the Priest. Theoretically, the priest is the only professional specialist in the trade in the Kuki society in the interpretation of dreams, visions, stars, omen, etc. He is the only individual who has to maintain communion in the form of sorcery or magic with the supernatural elements and the human beings. And some in the profession had acquired so much of knowledge that they can even counter any spell cast by evil witchcraft. Naturally, therefore, his position in the society is highly esteemed as the 'Thiempu' who is the Priest of whatever religious form of belief they attribute.

Hills, forests and rivers are conceived as having some potentialities and the people have to interact with them all the time for their existence and perpetuations. The bounty of nature is reflected through these natural phenomena. As such, the veneration and respect for these are unquestionable.

Therefore, some formalities are maintained by the Priest on the following causes :

In the case of forest and sylvan spirit, locally called 'Gamlah Vei', pig is sacrificed as an important item. Besides pig, a little 'Kolbu Kanpoh' (Pop-corn), 'Chang Kanpoh'(Pop-rice) and 'Nakena' (a kind of leaf, the tree of which is called 'Nake'. One side of the leaf is white, while the other is green). The 'Phelex', which is made of thin bamboo split, is normally used in building construction for fixing up the joints. This is also called 'Nang' which is coloured with white, black and red colours. It is quadrangular in shape. On top of it, another 'Nang', thinned further, constitutes the decorative part. Generally, all these ingredients are placed on a small cane-built platform which is normally used as a contraption for dining table, usually about six inches above the ground. It is known as 'Ankong Lui Na'. This is also called 'Maicham' - the holy platform. All the above ingredients are spread over the 'Maicham' on which blood of the sacrificed animal is sprinkled. The meat of the sacrificed animal is also placed on it in the following manner :

(a) A small portion of meat taken from the end of the mouth.
(b) Toes (the tips),
(c) Uppermost part of the ear, and
(d) End of the tail.

But, in the case of ceremonies associated with water-spirit living in the lake, stream or brook, known as 'Tui Thilha', a goat is sacrificed instead of a pig.

All the evil spirits required different kinds of animal as sacrifices.

There are village rituals and these are performed during the spread of epidemic diseases, like cholera, etc. which spread very fast and are of contagious nature.

Excepting these festivities and elaborate rituals, there are familial worships or rituals which are done as per vows. It has been stated earlier that there is no specific date or place for performing the rituals associated with a particualr spirit; meticulous directions are received by the 'Thiempu' in dreams. As is the prime duty of a physician in any society, amongst the Kukis also it is the responsibility of the Priest called 'Thiempu' to find out causation (Herskovitch, 1955-221). Causation of disease and the nature of divination are to counter the evil spirit. As calamities/diseases/misfortunes are considered to be the handiwork of some evil spirits, the kukis have a clear idea of the seasonal variations and the whole year has been grouped into 12 months, which have great influence in the propitiation of the priest.

It is also of great curiosity and interest to note as to how the Kukis evolved naming of 12 months according to changes in nature and positions of the moon in the sky. Table 7:1 below shows months both in English and in Thadou and the meanings thereof:

Darkheim (1915 : 10-11) observed :

The divisions into days, weeks, months, years, etc., correspond to the periodical recurrence of rites, feasts and public ceremonies. A calendar expresses the rhythm of the collective activities, while at the same time its function is to assure their regularity.

TABLE 7 : 1

Months with English Equivalence

Sl.	No.Months	with English Equivalence
1.	Tolbol (There is much dust due to dry season)	January
2.	Bulte (The time for 'Thuom' and 'Bul' to bloom. 'Thuom' is a flowering tree while 'Bul'is fruit-bearing tree. It is the time when jungles are slashed for jhum cultivation).	February
3.	Lhakao (It is the month when a small insect called 'KAO-JANG' comes out in menacing number. It enters even in the clothes which makes great discomfort to wear, when people spend their days and nights in the field in hut or make-shift called 'Lou-buh'. This is the time when the trees that have been slashed are dried.)	March

4.	Lhatun.(It is time for sowing. 'Tun' means 'to sow'. It is the time when a kind of bird which chirps as 'Muchi-tun-tun', indicating that sowing seed should commence. people start sowing seeds.)	April
5.	Lhaphul. ('Phul' stands for 'Sproud'. It is the time when herbs, trees and all other greenery sproud and germinate)	May
6.	Lha-dou (This is the time when bamboo-sooths come up in plenty. It is also a time when a kind of wild temeric called 'Aidou' blooms in plenty all over places and when people go to work enduring all hardships including the rain. Such endurance and bearing of harship is called 'dou'.)	June
7.	Lha-mul.(This is the time when grasses grow in plenty. The ground becomes woolly which is called 'Mul' with such plenty of growth.)	July
8.	Lhajing. (This is the time when all herbs, grasses,trees and other greeneries grow to their full height resulting in the darkening of the jungles, roads, etc. The moonlit also faintest, if not darkest. The sky is also always cloudy and moonlit is seldom seen. 'Jing',therefore, stands for darkness. So nights are darkest during this month.)	August
9.	Lhalam. (This is the time when sky becomes clearest. Clouds have receded. Harvesting commences which is called 'Changlam'. It is the time when moonlit is brightest when girls can pass thread through the eye of their needle under the moonlit.	September.
10.	El-lha. (This is the time when winter sets in. People start having better health which makes them more jovial, elatic, and fun and frolic loving which is called as 'El'. This is the best time of the year round.	October
11.	Phal-Lha. (This is the time when paddy had been collected after harvesting which is called 'Changphal'. This is the gathering time.	November.
12.	Awl-lha.(This is the time when people take respite from their hard labour and toiling of the year which is called 'Awl', meaning thereby leisure.)	December.

Counting of month-days is not based on a certain number of fixed days for a particular month. It is purely based from new moon to new moon. There are stages of marking the moon as follows (1) Lha-thah, (2) Achol-ke (oval shaped-moon), (3) Avom-lu-tai (like breast-head, almost fullmoon), (4) Alihtai (full moon), (5) Aheh suh tai (waning commences), (6) Avom-lu-tai (waning Ist stage), (7) Acholketai (half-waning), (8) Nisa-to-kilhon-tai (goes along with the sun).

As regards naming of the week-days, the Kukis do not have them in the traditional form. But after becoming Christians, the first Christian among the Kukis, Ngulhao Thuomsong, in his Thadou primary book published in 1927 gave the names based on Biblical creation-week as given below which was furnished by Thanggoumang, then Chief of Sangnao and Ex-member electoral College, Manipur :

	In Thadou	English Equivalence
1.	Dempatni (Beginning of creation-day)	Sunday.
2.	Leisiemni (Creation-day of the Earth).	Monday.
3.	Vah-Channi (Day of award of light)	Tuesday.
4.	Vah-hawm ni (Distribution-day of light)	Wednesday.
5.	Gan siem ni (Creation-day of birds, animals)	Thursday.
6.	Mi siem ni (Creation-day of man)	Friday.
7.	Chawlduo ni (Resting day)	Saturday.

III. Tuolsuo Rituals :

Anyone wishing to perform 'Chang-Ai' or 'Sa-Ai' cannot do it as and when one wishes to do so. The intending person has to go through a hard and elaborate test to make himself eligible for either of them. He has to undergo very vigorous self-abstinance and social restraint through an elaborate and lengthy performance of different rites. Such a person is called 'Tuolsuo Ding Kiguot.

When a family has for some consecutive years harvested rich paddy, the credit is given to the house-wife of the family, for the agricultural work is done mostly by the woman. Thus, the ceremony named 'Chang-Ai' is associated withe the woman of the family. In point of fact, in terms of division of labour among the Kukis, a man is primarily concerned with hunting wild games or to go to war etc. When a man considers himself that he has hunted sufficient number of wild games, he becomes eligible to perform 'Sa-Ai'. But not all the wild games are counted. The ferocious animals, like tiger, wild-boar, 'Thoche', 'Vengke' etc. and among the birds 'Muvanlai' (Vulture) etc. are the essential types of fauna that will entitle him to perform 'Sa-Ai'.

When such intention of performing 'Sa-Ai' or 'Chang-Ai' is expressed, the husband and the wife discuss it with their 'Becha' and 'Tucha'. Then a formal announcement, which is called 'Tuolsuo-Ding-

Kiguo', is made. With this, the man and his wife have to undergo a vigorous test of self-abstinance, social restraint, personal purification etc. Fulfilment of such ritual obligations alone transcends the man to the stage of actual performer of the proposed ceremony. To pass through these lengthy and elaborate rituals, a man has to attain the ritual status of purification by stages of ritual performances as enumerated below :

The First Stage :

Having formally announced for 'Tuolsuo-Ding-Kiguo' as above, a separate hearth called 'Tap-Kuong' at the inner portion of the house, close to and behind the main pillar of the house known as 'Sutpi', is constructed. On this, three elongated stones in a triangular form, called 'Lungthu' or an oven, are erected. Then the 'Becha' of the family informs the 'Thiempu' or Priest in the evening to perform the rites connected with the proposed ceremony. The 'Thiempu' in his turn instructs the 'Becha' to arrange for the following things :

(1) A spotlessly white cock.

(2) A new and unused jar of rice-beer.

Accordingly, the performer arranges the above items through his 'Becha'. Then the Priest comes in the evening to the house of the prospective performer of the ceremony. On arrival, a jar of 'Zu', other than the wine in a pure jar is served to the priest. The place where the jar of 'Zu' is located has a special significance. It is kept at the outer portion of the house where it is sipped, in turn, by the Priest, the 'Becha' and the 'Tucha' of the family. This particular 'Zu' is called 'Thiemphit Zu' which means the propitation 'Zu' given in the name or honour of the village Priest. By this time, the Priest performs the rituals by reading the signs from the white cock, ultimately killing the same in the process of muttering incantations called 'Phui' for the rich harvest, more wild games and all the riches for the family of the performer of the ceremony. The priest performs this act of propitiation in front of the man and his wife, both of whom now enter the inner portion of the house where a hearth with the elongated stones for the oven have earlier been fixed. None other than the man, his wife and the priest can enter this portion of the house. The Priest instructs the man and his wife to cook the meat of the sacrificed cock after dressing it properly. He also bids the wife to cook it in such a way that the flesh and the bones can be separated. The man alone is entitled to eat the meat thus cooked and he is forbidden from taking the slightest portion of the bones. Even when the bones are separated from the flesh, the same must on no account be broken, except at the joints. The wife will only cook the meat, but cannot take it herself. She may, however, join the rest of the members of the family for having her food.

In course of propitiation, the Priest utters all the secret words in desibels and performs rites seeking the blessings of a rich harvest, begging of more wild games and overall prosperity and welfare for the family. These rituals are called 'Chang Lha', 'Sum-Lha' and 'Sel-Lha-Kuo'. Thus, all the sacred words of invocation for such blessings are repeated within the hearing of the man, called 'Tuolsuo kiguo' or a prospective performer of 'Sa-Ai'. Ultimately, when the rituals are over, the prospective performer of the ceremony also is fully conversant with the knowledge of a Priest's work. As a result, he also becomes eligible to become a celebrated Priest by dint of his proficiency in uttering the words known as 'Thiem Thu'. Such sacred rites are called 'Doi Thu' of the Priest.

In the meantime, the jar of wine, especially procured for use in connection with the 'Tuolsuo Kiguo' rituals, must not be allowed to be defiled in any way by the persons who eat the flesh of monkey. Widow (Meithai)/widower (Pagong), murderer (Tolthat), etc. are also forbidden from touching it. If anybody of the above category of persons defiles the jar by using it, the same has to be replaced by a new one. As the rites begin, the couple is confined to the inner portion of the house. Such initial confinement is to last for one day only. They are completely segregated or isolated from other people. But the wife has freedom of movement within the house and meeting people. She cannot, however, go out of the premises. She is also not allowed to touch the ground during such ritual of abstinance. It may be pretinent to mention that the house of a Kuki is usually constructed on a slope or on a levelled ground with a raised floor which sometimes is as high as seven feet and above. The flooring is made either by planks or by split bamboo. So even when the wife moves about within the house, she cannot go beyond the floor area of the house and come directly in contact with the earth.

The first phase of this ritual followed by absinance comes to an end at the dawn of the next morning. The same process is repeated three times in gradually larger scale. Such phases, however, need not necessarily be performed continuously. A man can do these within one week, or one month, or even after one year, depending on the convenience and capability of the prospective performer. But these should be taken up without the least possible delay. It is believed that if any misfortune befalls the family within the intervening period, the effort goes in vain and the intending performer of the rite is no longer eligible to proceed with the proposed ceremony of either 'Chang-Ai' or 'Sa-Ai' festival.

Second Stage:

In the second stage, the 'Becha' of the family informs the 'Thiempu' of their intention to proceed with the self- purification rites to attain purity - physically, mentally and spiritually. The Thiempu then advises the 'Becha' to arrange one spotlessly white cock and one growing pig (Voh-Gol) for the occasion, which are readily arranged. As was done earlier, the cock is killed in the same process. When it is cooked, no salt and chilly are mixed with it and it is boiled with water only. As regards the pig, it is pierced right underneath the left foreleg armpit in order to puncture the heart, so that the pig dies instantaneously. This killing of the cock and the pig is done at the inner portion of the house where the prospective performer of the ceremony is kept confined. The 'Zu' meant for the man and his wife is served from the same jar of 'Zu' kept pure and clean.

The outer portion of the house is kept in charge of the 'Becha' and the 'Tucha' of the family. They prepare a big jar of 'Zu', called 'Belpi Zu', which is sipped by all present. A portion of it is, however, distilled through a bamboo pipe or 'Donkai' into as many gourds as there are maternal uncles of the performer, who are known as 'Mipu Te' (Songgao to the performer). When the gourds are filled, 'Tuchas' and 'Bechas' of the family take them to the maternal uncles. The former offer the drinks to the latter and join with them in drinking. This offer of 'Zu' to the maternal uncles ('Songgao' relations to the performer) is in token help sought from them. The maternal uncles in response to such request contribute in the form of chicken, dry fish, dry meat etc., whichever is available at their immediate disposal. All such contributions are brought together to the house of the performer by the maternal uncles along with a jar of 'Zu' each and they eat together at the residence of their 'Tu Te', i.e., the performer of the ceremony, who is their nephew or son-in-law, the next day following the day of the request made by the 'Tucha' and the 'Bechas' of the performer. When they eat and drink together, the meat and 'Zu' brought along with in the form of contribution, at the outer portion of the house of the performer, they do not bother to meet the man and his wife. It must be recalled here that as per custom, the 'Song-gao' relatives of a man are not to partake anything at the residence of their 'Tucha', and, as such, the maternal relatives of the performer of the 'Tuolsuo Kiguo', do not eat and drinl inside the house though as per ritualistic norms they come together for the purposse mentioned above.

In the inner portion of the house, the man and his wife cook the sacrificial cock without breaking the body and after cleaning the intestinal portions which are thrown away, keeping only the heart and the liver. They also dress the pig for cooking. But, in the case of the pig, the bones are broken and mixed with the flesh. The man and his wife are then joined at this stage by their eldest son. All of them eat the pork together. The chicken, however, is eaten only by the father. The chicken is cooked with water, without spices, salt or chilly. The bones are carefully separated from the flesh and are not broken, except at the joints.

As was done during the first stage of his confinement, the performer remains in seclusion for three days during the second stage of consecration and personal purification. While the father remains in isolation, the mother moves freely within the house and the son has no restriction on his movement. The son can enter the inner sanctuary where his father is in sacred seclusion and he can mix with others outside the house. On the expiry of the third day, the 'Tucha' and the 'Becha' of the family will come and offer a jar of 'Zu', called 'Belbing'. They will also invite the Priest who declares the consecration period of three days as closed with a dedication which is known as 'Thien So'. Then he declares the performer as purified.

Third Stage :

As in the cases of the first two stages, there is no such time fixed as to the date of performing the third stage. It depends on the convenience and wish of the performer. If he wants to hold it early, he can do so. If not, there is no harm in delaying it. But it is to be borne in mind that the sooner such self-abstinence and the period of sufference can be got rid of the better.

The third stage of self-denial of the performer is known as 'Sekon-Tun'. On this day, the same procedure of inviting the 'Thiempu' is followed. The Priest, the 'Tucha' and the 'Becha' of the family decide over a jar of 'Zu' where to look for the tree called 'Se' (Sahi in Manipuri Language), a particular branch of which must remain bent or 'Kon' towards the East. After locating the particular tree, known as 'Sekon' ('Se' plus 'Kon'), the 'Tucha' and the 'Becha' of the performer inform the Priest. He is then led to the spot where the tree is found. The Priest then utters invocations at the foot of the tree. This act of propitiation is called 'Thingao-Lhai' or praying for the soul of the tree. In the process of such propitiation, the Priest sprays a mouthful of 'Zu' on the tree. He mutters some words in prayer for the soul of the tree. Thereafter, the Priest cuts the tree only once with an axe to symbolise that the tree can now be cut by others. Thus, the 'Tucha' and the 'Becha' of the family of the performer continue to cut down the tree. This done, its branches are hewn where necessary, the trunk is prepared in the following manner : The trunk of the tree is cut just above the branch which curves out towards the East. At the base of the topmost branch, the trunk is made like a soup-plate wherein the bones of the sacrificial chicken and other ingredients can be placed.

At this stage, the same procedure of informing the Priest, the killing of one cock etc. continue. In addition, the performer kills a pig, 'Vohchal-Tuh-Nga', meaning thereby a male-pig of the size of five-fists. This is known as 'Thiem-Lhah Na', which means, send-off meat meant for the Priest.

Meanwhile, the trunk of the tree is prepared and the 'Tucha' and the 'Becha' of the performer bring the same to the house. This day will coincide with the day of killing of the pig. Besides this, he kills a white cock (Ahchal Kang) and a 'Voh-Gol' or growing- pig, and all other procedures as were done during the earlier two stages follow. In case the performer is not ready with the done- up tree to be brought from the jungle, the 'Sekon' or the tree is not allowed to be brought to the spot for erection in the village. It is kept at the outskirts of the village. The tree- trunk is kept covered with leaves, so that birds and other animals may not defile it with their night-soil on it.

On the day the tree-trunk is erected, the spot where it is so be erected is first sanctified by the priest, who performs a 'Juphi' propitiation with a mouthful of wine sprayed at the proposed site. Thereafter, the Priest does the symbolical digging which is later made into a hole by others, and the trunk is pitched there. The trunk of the tree is then decorated and the following ingredients are used in decoration of it.

1. 'Vom Gui Khao' (a kind of creeper called 'Vomgui) is inserted in the hole provided earlier at the base of the branch that curves towards the East. As it is made to creep upward from the ground along the tree-trunk, it is arranged to do so anti- clockwise.

2. 'Thinghi-Tuoi (a growing tree which is not yet matured - the tree is called 'Thinghi') is erected along with the tree trunk.

3. 'Gopi-Tuoi (a very big and tall type of bamboo called 'Gopi'). This bamboo should also be in its growing stage, and not matured yet.

4. 'Se-Tuoi (a kind of tree called 'Se' which is still immatured).

All these are erected together with the 'Sekon' tree. The trees and the bamboo thus erected wear their leaves at the top whch is called 'Sawli-Boh'. Then the creeper called 'Vom-Gui' is crept up the trunk of the tree, which act is preceded by the ritual of the priest. The invocation of this ritual runs as follows :

> Thien Nu Thien Pa Kalhai Je,
> Vomgui Nampha Nasah Bangin Neisan,
> Thinghi Nampha Nasah Bangin Neisan,
> Gopi Nampha Nasah Bangin Neisan,

Free Translation :

> Praying to the almighty on high, I beseech Thee to bless me (the performer of Ceremony) as Thou doest to the 'Vom Gui', 'Thinghi Toi', 'Gopi Toi'.

This is followed by creeping the creeper, 'Vom Gui', anti- clockwise to the trunk of the tree till it reaches the branch of the tree where the Priest tucks the end of the creeper into the hole, being rolled anti-clockwise. With this the erection rite of the tree-trunk, called 'Sekon', is over.

Ankong-Tawl :

As has earlier been said, in the third stage of purification also one spotless white cock and one pig are killed and, as in the second stage, the son of the performer can join his parents in their self seclusion. The three of them can now eat the ritual food together. But the menu of the performer is not the same with that of his wife and the son. Details of the menu in each plate are given below :-

1. One plate of boiled chicken (a whole chicken) only for the performer.
2. One gourd of 'Zu'.
3. One plate of pork,
4. One plate of rice.

(Items 2–4:) For all the three of them.

In the plates of the wife and the son, the chicken item will not be included because of the fact that the man only had undergone the ordeals and the chicken signifies a higher social value than the other items. At the same time, it constitutes the main features of the ritual value which manifests the social standing of the three of them. The sitting order of the three members of the family at the dinner is such that the wife sits on the left- hand side of her husband, while the son sits on the right side of his father, in a triangular shape.

Before the food is taken, after all the items of the menu have been placed before them, the performer transfers his gourd of 'Zu' in front of his son's plate who, in turn, does the same to his mother. The wife again transfers her gourd of 'Zu' in front of her husband's plate. All other items mentioned above are rotated in the same manner three times. When all the items reach back to their respective places, as is originally meant to be, they start eating the ritual meal.

While eating the chicken, the performer does so very carefully so that the slightest portion of the bone is not broken. This is particularly so in respect of the chest portion of the meat. Thus, the performer is not allowed to touch any body parts of the chicken. After the meal, the Priest places the bones of the chicken on the tree-trunk of the 'Sekon' erected at the hole gnawed earlier. The priest, while placing the bones of the chicken, invokes in the following manner :

Thien Nu Thien Pa Kalhai je,
Ka Upthai, Chanu Chapa To Ka Upthai,
Damthei Phat Thei Toh Ka Upthai,
Thein Nu Thien Pa Kalhai Je.

Free Translation :

Praying to the almighty God,
I beseach Thee that Thou wouldst bless with many sons and daughters, and
That Thou wouldst bless him
(the performer of the ceremony)
With all kinds of blessings,
I pray Thee, oh, God, the mighty.

The priest then sprays a mouthful of 'Zu' on it.

Satumbu :

The pig of the size of five-fists thus killed is divided into two halves. One half is given to the priest and the other is cooked and eaten together by the people in general and relatives of the performer. The head of the animal, called 'Sapang', is separated from both the halves. The blood of the pig is baked along with rice-flour and then it is inserted in a rolled leaf, the ends of which are closed and bound tightly. It is then cooked and is called 'Satumbu'. Some portion of the mixture of the blood with rice-flour is again baked in the form of a dough or bread which is called 'Sa Changlhah', meaning bread made of meat, 'Sa Chang- Lhah' is eaten by the members of the family of the performer and also of the family of his 'Tucha and 'Bechas'. On the other hand, 'Satumbu' is used for observing the omen for testing as to whether the performer of the ceremony has been in luck or not. A bamboo is split into two and one piece is sharpened at the edge for cutting the 'Satumbu'.

The 'Satumbu' being ready now, the priest takes it out from the oven and holds it out by his left hand and asks the performer to hold the other half on his right hand. The priest then cuts it in two equal halves. It is then observed as to which half of the 'Satumbu' becomes swollen. Incidentally, before cutting of the 'Satumbu', the Priest recites some doggerel verses. The reason for cutting into two equal halves is that the Priest has all along been telling the performer the secret words, called 'Thiem Thu' and also the sacred rites, called 'Doi Thu' in the course of self-abstinance and purification of moral, physical and spiritual state of the letter. It is now assumed that the performer had sufficient time to learn the craft thereby has been fully equiped with the 'Doi Thu' and 'Thiem Thu' as good as the priest. Therefore, after cutting the 'Satumbu' in two equal halves, he will see if one half is slightly swollen. If it is so, whoever holds the swollen part will be considered as having a richer knowledge in 'Doi Thu' and 'Thiem Thu' than the other.

Half of the pig-meat meant for the Priest, including the head called 'Sapang', are combinedly called 'Sapi'. The following persons are entitled to eat the head portion, 'Sapang' of the pig.

1. The Chief of the Village.
2. The Council of Ministers of the Chief.
3. The clan representatives of the village.
4. The Thiempu or the Priest.

Whoever eats this meat is a witness to the ritualistic performances of the ceremony.

The other half of the pig is then cooked separately sans the 'Sapang' to be served to the laity, relatives, 'Tuchas' and 'Bechas' of the performer, including the whole village people. On the day of such feasting, the 'Becha' of the performer goes round each household in the village and invites them to the feast. The village women respond to the invitation along with a 'Jubel' each, which are shared together. Every lady bringing a jar of 'Zu' is entitled to have a portion of meat, especially set apart for them, which includes a portion of the intestine, the flesh, the bone mixed with flesh and fat.

When the food is made ready, the priest takes a portion of the liver and splits it into two with a bamboo called 'Gopi'. Each piece of liver is then eaten by the Priest and the performer. Before they do so, the 'Thiempu' performs certain rites, called 'Phuisam' or purifying the meat for health.

After the liver is eaten by the Priest and the performer and before the actual feast commences, the Priest invokes another propitiation by which a third piece of the liver is cut from the vessel and thrown away. This act of propitiation is called 'NU-Lhai Na', meaning, appeasing the greed of evil spirits, so as to protect the laity and the weak from harm and food pollution . This act of propitiation is the general practice in every feast and is called 'Kao Lhai Nai. But in the present case the grace offered by the 'Thiempu' in regard to food is termed as 'Nu Lhai Na', or appeasing the lady of the food and not 'Kao Lhai Na'. Invocation of such ritual in respect of 'Nu Lhai Na' is as follows : As the priest commences the invocation, he takes a piece of the liver in his hand which indicates shielding of all evil activities, thereby protecting the health of those who take part in the feast. The wordings are as follows :

Nu Kadal Nai,
Leng Suhnu Kadal Nai,
Leng Tounu Kadal Nai,
Phungpi Nu Kadal Nai,
Phung Chanu Kadal Nai
Khojet Nu Hem Kadal Nai.
Khovie Nu Hem Kadal Nai.

Free Translation :

I am protecting from the greed of evil spirits, from the ones that come flying down from above, from the ones that come from below, from the greed of lady-evil of the Community, from the greed of the daughter- evil of the Community, from the left and the right of the community location.

After this, he throws away the liver beyond and across the house of the peformer. Having done this, he announces that the feast may now be partaken . The eating procedure of the half portion of the pig is in the following manner and order of precedence :

1. The persons entitled to eat 'Sapang' mentioned above and the 'Tuchas' of the family of the performer eat first.

2. After taking the food, by the above categories of people, the 'Bechas' and the commoners can eat.

The 'Tuchas' are entitled to take before others. As per Kuki custom, the 'Tucha' relatives are supposed to serve the food to others. Thus, for the sake of convenience, and for maintenance of physical purity before defiling themselves when they serve others, such persons take food on a priority basis. In ordinary course of feasting. the bechas, being higher in the soical hierarchy than the Tuchas, should eat first but in the present case, the 'Becha' acts on behalf of the performer as the host. Therefore, the 'Becha' of the family and takes food with the latter group. Feast over, the time for the departure of the Priest comes.

As he proposes to go, he takes the half portion of the sacrificial pig set apart for him .But if the Priest happens to be a family member of the performer of the ceremony or is a close relative of the latter, he may not take the meat with him, but asks the meat to be cooked and eaten next day at the residence of the performer together with the family members of both the Priest and the performer, along with the 'Tucha' and the 'Becha' relatives of both sides. In case the Priest takes away the meat with him, he invokes a propitiation as follows , before he leaves.

Thien Nu Thien Pa Kalhai Je,
Kache Ding Ahitai,
Sumja Sieljan Eijui In,
Nimja, Changjan Neijui In,
Thien Nu Thien Pa Kalhai Je,

Free Translation :

Praying to the almighty, I am going, let all the riches and the paddy follow me. I pray to male and female benovolents.

Then, once again he sprays a mouthful of wine which is known as 'Juphi'. As he finishes this, he takes leave of the performer and departs.

At this stage, the performer offers the Priest a cup of drink. As the Priest drinks, the performer who has also become a Priest himself by now, having been more or less fully conversant with the knowledge of 'Thiem Thu' and 'Doi Thu', politely retorts the Priest in his ritual propititation. This becomes a test of knowledge between the two, for the two have already started competing in their quantum of knowledge of the 'Thiem Thu' and the 'Doi Thu'. In doing so, the performer of the ceremony invokes thus :

Thien Nu Thien Pa Kalhai je,
Kalho Nai Chanu Chapa Kalho Nai,
Sum Lha Siel Lha Kalho Nai,
Mim Lha Chang Lha Kalho Nai.
Thien Nu Thien Pa Kalhai je.

Free Translation :

Praying to the almighty, I ask the souls of sons and daughters to remain and so also all riches and crops. I pray to the almighty.

Saying this he sprays a mouthful of 'Zu' in front of the Priest. It is believed that in doing so, the performer has stopped all the blessings the 'Thiempu' had sought from God to go along with him. In other words, the performer has taken back the blessings supposedly taken by the 'Thiempu' along with him. As a reprisal, the Priest does the same to the performer again to take back all the blessings from the latter, who reacts in the same manner. Thus, the two parts their company in a spirit of competition.

On his arrival home, the Priest offers the meat to his relatives, 'Tuchas' and 'Bechas' of his family the next day, wherein the performer is also invited to the feast. In accepting the invitation, the performer joins the Priest at the latter's residence along with his own 'Tucha' and 'Becha' relatives. In doing so, they take one jar of 'Zu' in the name of the performer of the ceremony in addition to the 'Zu' each of his 'Tucha' and 'Becha' brought. The 'Thiempu' welcomes the performer, his 'Tucha' and 'Becha' relatives with a small jar of 'Zu'.

The competition at the time of their parting has two aspects. Firstly, it is the test of the new knowledge of 'Thiem Thu' and 'Doi Thu' acquired by the performer of the ceremony from the 'Thiempu' and, secondly, to test as to whether the fact that all the blessings of God for children, wealth, material objects, paddy etc, to the performer which are symbolically believed to have been carried away by the Priest in his last invocation before leaving the performer for his home could be stalled or not. This is the beginning of a life-long rivalry between the two. There, however, happens no love-lost between them.

Having successfully gone through all the hurdles that stand in the way of a person performing 'Chon' and a feast of honour having been given in the form of 'Sa-Ai' or 'Chang Ai', a person becomes eligible to perform any of the 'Chons'. Such vigorous tests and trials normally take no less than two to three years to complete. On completion, a man is supposed to attain a state of physical, moral and spiritual transcendency that makes him not only qualified to perform the 'Chons', but becomes also eligible to be a professional Priest.

In the whole process of the ritual trials of a person, every step of formality is seen moving through a certain set pattern of social norm which manifests the social structure of the Kukis.

IV. Sa-Ai Ceremony :

After attaining the eligibility of becoming a 'Tuolsuo Kigaw', through various rigorous tests, if a man prepares himself to perform 'Sa-Ai' ceremony, i.e. becomes an accredited wild-game hunter, he informs the fact to his 'Tuchas' and 'Bechas' along with the Chief of the village and also the Priest of his choice, be he of his village or elsewhere. These people decide the date and time for going ahunting and also other pre-requisites for this ceremony. A man who intends to do so has certain preconditions apart from the vigorous ritual tests already gone through by him. He must have killed a tiger, an eagle (Muvanlai), a wild-bear, 'Tnoche' and 'Vengke'. Even if he had not killed them all,he can add them to his credit. if his close relatives, such as, younger brother, elder brother, or nephew, etc, had killed them, to fulfil the apriori conditions. In the event of not killing a tiger by himself or his kinsmen, the same can be substituted for its kind, e.g. a 'Keisan'(red tiger) or 'Kamkei' (Leopard). Likewise, if an eagle has not been killed, the same can be substituted for 'Mubuong' (grey eagle). The tally of the wild games hunted must not be small in number. At least one tiger, one wild-boar and one eagle (Muvanlai) must be hunted, even if a deer or any other animal has not been killed. But the tally must not be less than two hundred, preferably it should be five hundred. In such head-counting of wild games hunted, he can include the games of his kinsmen.

On the fixed day, the performer of the festival offers a jar of 'Zu' to the young boys and girls of the village and his own 'Tucha' and 'Becha' relatives with a request to help him in the preparation of all the necessary arrangements for the occasion. This is called 'Acheh', that is, a request to help.

The pieces of stick tallying the number of wild games claimed to have been hunted by the performer of the 'Sa-Ai' festival are collected by the young boys. The sticks are of one fathom length each and is called 'Samol', i.e. sticks of the wild games. The 'Tucha' and the 'Becha' relatives of the performer of 'Sa-Ai' prepare one tree-trunk called 'Siel-Khuom', meaning, post of the Mithun. The 'Siel-Khuom' has to be made from a kind of tree called 'Sething' which must have three branches at one node of the trunk and not at different levels of it. There should also be two other posts with similar branches nearby it and just beyond the eaves (bilha) of the house. One of the trees chosen for the purpose must be of 'Sething' (Sahi in Manipuri) tree, while the other has to be necessarily of 'Ahthi Thing'. The number of sticks that tally with the number of wild games claimed to have been hunted by the performer of 'Sa-Ai' are placed in between the branches of the two posts erected. These two posts are called 'Samol-Khuom'.

Another tree is erected at the corner oppostie to the 'Siel-Khuom', but still further from the house which is called 'Nungbem Jel Na Khuom'. This particular place on the far end of the family lawn called 'Leituol' is known as 'Tuolmonglam'. The kind of tree selected for this purpose is a 'Se' tree called 'Sething'. Together with this are erected one young tree of 'Thinghi-Tuoi', one young tree of 'Se-Thing-Tuoi', one ordinary bamboo with its brancehes hewned clearly leaving the bush at the top that is made to rest on the post called 'Nungbem Jel Na-Khuom'. Two more bamboo poles of shorter height than the one with bush on the top that rests at the main post called 'Nungbem Jel Na-Khuom' are also erected. These are not necessarily of equal height. Thus, there are altogether two tree and three bamboo posts erected and bound together with the main post along with a number of bamboo sticks that should tally with the number of wild games claimed to have been killed. All these erected together are further tied together by a creeper called 'Vom-Cui' all along the trunk beginning at the base of the post. After completion of the binding, the village Priest sprinkles a mouthful of rice beer on the 'Nungbem Jel-Khuom' in ritual invocation.

The erection of the posts mentioned above is preceded by the erection of 'Siel-Khuom', the post of the Mithun. In the process of erection of the post, the Priest pours a little quantity of 'Zu' to the spot where a hole for the erection is to be dug. He then propitiates and sprinkles a mouthful of 'Zu' called 'Hi'. Then the 'Tuchas' of the performer of the 'Sa-Ai' festival do the rest, ultimately erecting the 'Siel-Khuom'.

After erecting all the posts, the performer proceeds towards the outskirts of the village called 'Khuomuol'. Prior to this, a skin of the tiger he is supposed to have killed, is placed on the top of two posts erected for the purpose of keeping the tiger-skin. On his arrival at the 'Khuomuol', the skin thus spread on the top of the two posts is removed. In his procession towards the 'Khuomuol', the performer is accompanied by the Chief of the village, the Priest, his wife and other important persons, and a number of villagers. 'Zu', rice and pork are eaten by the performer, the Chief and the Thiempu only, while the 'Zu' is distributed among the whole crowd at the 'Khuomuol'.

The performer of the 'Sa-Ai' is dressed in a woman's attire. He wears a lady's 'Lungi' called 'Puonve', his hair plaited into two and crossed in front above the forehead through the sides above the ears and given a double-knot called 'Samkop'. He wears a chain of beads called 'Khi' etc. On his arrival at the 'Khuomuol', the tiger-skin that had been spread earlier on top of the two posts is removed. Then the food brought is served to him. Before the food is taken, the Priest utters an invocation which runs as follows :

Thitou Touhing,
Na Ankong Ki Um In.

(Thitou and Touhin are the ancestors of the Kukis. So, in order to appease their souls the Priest invokes to the effect that the two souls of the ancestors should have the food that has been laid for them.)

Then the performer of the 'Sa-Ai' takes his food. After finishing his food, the performer of the 'Sa-Ai' takes the spinning needle called 'Muitul' and with it pinches the skin of the tiger saying :

Ka Ahtui Naso,
Ka Gancha Nadel,
Kengkou Sutlih Nahi Bouve.

(You have stolen my eggs, you have killed my domesticated animals. But I have not killed you. You are killed by a thorn called 'Kengkou'.)

The performer of the 'Sa-Ai' then goes back home, leaving the whole congregation behind at the 'Khuomuol'. On his return home, he changes his dress to that of a man. As he goes back to the 'Khuomuol', he is seen as a new brave man who puts on his turban on head, takes his gun on his shoulder and the bow and arrow on his back, along with the customary head-gear. In the meantime, the tiger-skin, which was removed from the top of the two posts, is placed on the ground in the likeness of a living tiger. He jumps ove three times eac the sham-tiger made out of its skin length-wise and breadth-wise. As he jumps, he mutters :

Nadung Kachop Chop Khop Lou,
Navai Kachop Chop Khop Lou.

Free Translation :

I can jump across your body length-wise, and do also breadth-wise.

He then stops and says as he jumps again :

Nangla Billou Nanuoi Nungin,

Keila Vanpi Kachung Nunge.

(You are the vanquished, while I am the victor and high as the sky above you.)

After this, the Priest invokes with 'Juphi' and then entire congregation proceeds towards the village. On their return home of the performer, his 'Becha' and 'Tucha' relatives welcome them with 'Zu'. Thereafter, the ceremony called 'Siel Buon Chou' is started. It is the wrestling with the Mithun. In doing this, all the able-bodied young bachelors and newly married men line up in a row. They first bend forward and rest their palms on their knees. While in this position, they bowl saying 'Ho,Ho, Ho,' in succession, thus producing a wave of sound that travels as they move to and fro, first to the right in one circle and then to the left in the same way. They do this three times and again say 'Li,Li, Li, Li, Li' in the same process, three times, with every round they straighten up and along with it say 'Ha,Ha, Ha,Ha,Ha'.

This is followed by wrestling with the Mithun by the youths three times. If they cannot wrestle and let the Mithun be thrown on the ground, they cannot proceed further with other events. They wrestle again. Only when they beat the Mithun, they start competing among the youths in jumping the Mithun. This is called 'Sielkal'. Whoever is good in high jump can join the competition, irrespective of age. If they can cross the

Mithun, the height- stick is pushed upward placing more layers of cloths to the extent they can jump, putting it on the back ridge of the Mithun.

After this, the village Priest asks the performer of 'Sa-Ai' whether he can do the 'Sa-Ai' again. If the answer is in the negative, the Priest pours 'Zu' on the Mithuns commencing from its head, and following the ridge ending at the tail (Amei Bul). He does it the same way back to the head from the tail and then back to the tail again. But if the answer is in the affirmative, the Priest pours the 'Zu' once only at the top-ridge of the midsection of the back of the Mithun. He then utters incantations and sprinkles the mouthful of 'Zu'. This is called 'Siel Jang Buch Phui Sem', which runs thus :

Vantham Jolla Hungkon Chun,
Sisep Ma Hung Chu Chun,
Daisan Pi Hin Hoh Lha Chun,
Hatna Kabol Mahipoi,
Daija Kabol Nahi.

Free Translation :

You are the mighty which comes from the heaven, lending at 'Sisep' and then to 'Daisan Pi'.

I have not done this to you because I am strong but because I am weak.

Then is followed the killing of the Mithun for the feast. The Mithun is killed by a senior member of the performer's family called 'Mi Upa'. The killing is done by way of piercing the heart of the Mithun with a sharp instrument through the armpit of the left fore-leg. The following portions of the slaughtered animal have significance in society :

1. Ating-Sung (flesh of the topmost ridge-inner portion). -two pieces.
2. Ating-Puo(flesh of the topmost ridge _ outer portion) - two pieces.
3. Akawng (the waist portion) - one piece.
4. Anah (the rib portion)
5. Amal (the right hind-leg).

6. Heart and liver.

7. Sengong (Neck portion).

The following morning, the Chief, the Priest, the performer and his 'Bepu' (Becha) partake the heart and liver as witness to the ceremony. The righ-outer-tompost-ridge-flesh called 'Ating-Po' is given to the senior member of the performing group called 'Upa'. The left side is given to the Chief. Likewise, the two pieces of 'Atingsung' are given to his brother-in-law by marriage of the two sisters called 'Anulam' or he may give them to anyone whom he feels close to him. The waist portion called 'Akhong' is always given to the female married relatives of the performer called 'Tucha'. It is the aunt's or sister's or daughter's husband. The rib portion is given to the 'Bechas' of the performer who represents the performer. The neck portion is the sole prerogative of the maternal uncle called 'Mipute' or 'Songgao'.

In contrast to the rituals performed during the preparatory period of the performer when he was under severe self-denial and seclusion, when pig-killing was an important act, the man may kill more pigs in addition to the Mithun, but those have no significance or importance. The Mithun killing occupies the highest position on such social occasion. The Priest is given a hearty send-off the next morning after partaking the witness meat (the heart and the liver) of the ceremony. The performer sets apart a special portion of the meat for the Priest. The portion in between the two hind-legs, including the genital portion, is given to the Priest. As regards the quests, a small piece of flesh each is taken out from the legs and is given as a token of thanks for joining the feast.

The right hind-leg called 'Amal' is given to the village youths. They arrange a feast with it, the following day of the main event. In case the performer is able to afford, he offers more by killing pigs for them.

A very great significance that deserves mention is that the day before the actual time of the festival bears immense implication. Every arrangement for the festival is done, but the 'Siel-Khuom', i.e., the post of the Mithun, and other 'Khuoms' are not erected yet. All these are done on the following day. The previous night is thus observed in complete wakefulness. By this time, the Mithun is located and it is tied to the post for the festival. This night of endurance test is called 'Sajan Hay' on the next morning, the erection work and other ceremonial functions are started.

V. Chang-Ai Ceremony :

A person who performs 'Tuolsuo' rites is called 'Ahkang Mul Totsa'. Such a person can only perform 'Chang-Ai' festival. But, according to custom, he does not publicise his intention of doing so willingly. His 'Becha' approaches the village Chief and the Priest to go along with him to the man who has in his mind that he will perform 'Chang-Ai'. They take a jar of 'Zu' with them. It is the custom that though the man prepares himself for performing 'Chang-Ai' undergoes vigorous rituals and restraints for personal purification through certain strict abstinance and living in seclusion, he should not divulge the fact that he is eligible to perform the 'Chang-Ai' festival. It is his 'Becha' who will do the needful, so that he, the village Chief and the Priest formally announce the decision to the public in general about the on-coming event on behalf of the performer. 'Chang-Ai' is a festival performed by a person who harvests paddy much above his requirements for more than a decade and expresses thanks to God for the bountiful harvest.

On the day of the harvest, the man who performs 'Chang-Ai', his 'Becha', the Chief and his Council of Ministers formally announce to the effect that on that day so and so would harvest his field. So, every able-bodied person in the village is to take part in it. Along with this announcement, they carry the wine prepared by the performer to the field together with the special wine called 'Phuol-Zu', which means the 'Zu' for the field. This wine is contributed by the 'Becha' of the performer. On their arrival, the village priest does his propititation of 'Zu' called 'Zuphi', signifying inauguration of a rich harvesting ceremony. This is called 'Chang Lha Kuona Zuphi'. After this, the wine brought with them is distributed for drinks after which the actual harvesting begins. A recess is given at mid-day during which they drink the wine contributed by the 'Becha' of the performer. Thereafter, they resume their work. On completion, they collect the paddy meticulously and perform a dancing about, which is called 'Sagol Phei Khai' and'Saipi Khup Suh', for three times. This dancing spree ends with a sound of 'Li, Li, Li, Li, Li', and 'Ha, Ha, Ha, Ha, Ha'. The dance is performed mainly by the elders of the village. While they dance, the young boys build one 'litter' or palanquine. At the time of dancing a song is sung in accompaniment with an instrument called 'Pheiphit'. This is a kind of musical instrument made of small bamboo pipes, one end of which is cut open at the mouth. There are several sizes of it and the different sizes of the slantingly cut mouth produce different sounds to harmonise with various notations of the songs. Then the performer of the festival is carried on the palanquine from the field to his house. As they march homewards, the whole gang harmonise their pace with a rhythmic quartet called 'Heijam Sap' all through the village.

On their arrival, at the outskirt of the village called 'Khuomuol', they start blowing the bamboo pipe called 'Pheiphit' till they reach the house of the performer of the festival. Having reached there, another three rounds of 'Sagol Phei Khai' and 'Saipi khup Such' dance accompanied with the bamboo pipe music is performed, which ends with the exclamation of 'Li, Li, Li, Li' and 'Ha, Ha, Ha, Ha, Ha'. This done, all the young boys march inside the house where they perform 'Sunglho' by which they all join their arms through shoulders rocking three times with the 'Li, Li, Li, Li, Li' and 'Ha, Ha, Ha, Ha, Ha,'. They then part for sometime to wash and to freshen themselves. Thereafter, they come back to the house of the performer of the festival where they are offered welcome-wine called 'Vailhun Zu'. Another pot of beer is offered by the performer at the main pillar of the house. This is called 'Chang Lha Lhaw Na Zu', meaning, the beer that appeases the soul of the paddy. This beer is taken by sipping, while the other beer called 'Vailhun Zu' is distributed in cups. Before sipping the beer, the village Priest performs his usual rites called 'Chang Lha Lhaw', meaning, appeasement of the soul of the paddy. In doing so, he removes the sipping pipe from the pot of the 'Zu' by closing the upper end of the pipe with his finger as he withdraws the pipe from the pot of jar. When the pipe is clearly out of the pot, he removes his hand from the tip of the pipe, thereby draining the beer inside the pipe. Everyone participating in the harvest is to take part in the sipping by turn as follows: The Priest starts the sipping turn.n. He then calls the Chief to do so, who is then followed by the 'Becha' of the family, then the performer of the festival and the lady of the house. She is then followed by all in turn, according to their status. Such sipping turn is overseen by the 'Becha' of the performer of the festival. This is the formal opening of the 'Chang-Ai' festival, i.e., the harvesting ceremony.

On the following morning, the performer offers beer to all the close relatives to make formal request to them to prepare rice- beer for the occasion and to help him in all sundry works. The lady of the house then distributes rice to all those ladies invited for preparation of wine for the 'Chang-Ai' festival. Before maturity of the beer thus prepared, the family of the performer sees to it that all the paddy harvested from the fields is collected and stored in the granery. A small portion of at least ten tins of paddy is left behind in the field in a make- shift granery. In the meantime, if the beer is found matured, the performer offers one pot of rice-beer to drink in which the Chief, the Priest and the leader of the Lawm get precedence. They sip from the pot through a pipe called 'Don'. One or two days after this, the 'Becha' of the family requests the people to carry the paddy left behind in the field. This announcement is done by the leader of the Lawm early in the morning. Before they proceed to the field, all the boys and the grils go to beating the drum and gong. At the sound of the drum they all gather at the outskirt of the village. Here, the Priest of the village performs his 'Zu' rite. Then they proceed towards the field. The procession is led by the drumer who beats the drum all along through the field, and is followed by the Priest of the village after whom the people go. On arrival, they form a circle called 'Lawmval Kuol', and dance 'Sagol Phei Khai' and 'Saipi Khup Suh' for three rounds and then everyone sings the popular exclamation 'Li, Li, Li, Li, Li' and 'Ha, Ha, Ha, Ha, Ha'. While they dance, the Priest performs his ceremonial rite called 'Min Lu Tuo' or 'Min A Luo Diu', meaning, repeating the genealogy of the family of the performer. In the process, he mentions every name of the family in a genealogical order and ends up with the name of the mother of the performer of the festival. This is then followed by everyone producing a sound like the neighing of a horse - 'Yiiiiiiiii'. They then bring the paddy from the field to the house. Each of them brings some quantity according to his capacity. The paddy thus brought is then strewn all along the way to the village. This signifies that the performer is rich in paddy and is symbolic of his/her status. This is also a symbolic invitation to the soul of the paddy showing the way to the house of the performer of the Chang-Ai feast. This is the manifestation of the nature of economy which has no place for saving for future. On their arrival, they perform the same kind of dance as was done earlier at the outskirt of the village for three times. Thereafter, the young boys go inside the house joining their arms together through the shoulders. At the same time, they spread paddy all over the house. This is called 'Sung-Lhaw'. They jointly jump three times inside the house, ending with 'Li, Li, Li, Li, Li' and 'Ha, Ha, Ha, Ha, Ha' sound.

Whatever food is prepared by the 'Bechas' and the 'Tuchas' of the performer is taken by those who went to the field to carry the paddy. After this, a pot of 'Zu' is offered which is sipped in a pair simultaneously through two sipping pipes. In the process, every married person is offered by the 'Becha' of the performer while the young boys and the girls are offered by the leaders of the Lawm. Every sipping turn is to be done by a pair, thereby signifying the performance of 'Chang-Ai'.

There is one post called 'Siel Khuom' where the Mithun for the occasion is bound. This is collected from the jungle by the 'Tucha' and the 'Becha' of the performer, while others are busy carrying the paddy from the field. This must be brought to the residence of the performer before the arrival of the group that has gone for carrying the paddy. While erection of the post called 'Siel-Khuom' is in progress, it is preceded by the usual rites performed by the Priest before digging the hole for erection of the post.

Thus, the 'Tuchas' and the 'Bechas' of the performer erect the post. In the evening, the announcer of the Village Council of Ministers called 'Khuosam Pa' announces that no one should go out of the village next day for any other business than the 'Chang- Ai', and that everyone should take part in the festival. Accordingly, every village lady from each household contributes one jar of 'Zu' as assistance to the performer. The 'Zu' contributed is either for drinking or sipping, which must not be started unless it is offered first by every household lady to the Chief and the Priest of the village. All other details of the festival are precisely the same as those of "Sa-Ai'.

As the Mithun is brought out, the lady of the house of the performer offers it salt as it comes out. When she serves salt, she says : 'Be not angry, my child, Mithun, you are going to be famous. ('Lung Phamo hih in, Sielcha, akithang ding nahi').

This is followed by the rites performed by the Priest. He sprays the wine kept in a small pot called 'Vai Khawn'. As he sprays the wine from the 'Vaikhawn', if the Mithun shows signs of trickling (Akithin leh aphapuoi), it is believed that it is not a good omen. Then the wrestling by the young boys with the Mithun called 'Siel-Bot' commences. The procedures of it are the same as those of 'Sa-Ai'. As the last phase of the Mithun fun with high jump competition is over, the Priest leads the performer and his wife to the spot where the Mithun has been kept tied to the post. As they come out, the Priest and the performer are adorned with the feather of eagle called 'Mivan Lai Ving' (the longest of the eagle wing, which is usually the topmost of the feather). As they come down, the performer speaks to the Mithun saying - 'Do not regret or be grieved, it is for the fame of us both'. This is followed by the Priest who takes one 'Vaikhon' wherein 'Zu' is kept. He propitiates and sprinkles the 'Zu' on the Mithun. This is followed by piercing of the Mithun by a senior clansman of the performer through the foreleg armpit of the Mithun on the right side aiming at the heart of the aminal. When the Mithun is killed, all the boys and girls, perform a dance called 'Siel Pang Lap' when they encircle the Mithun and sing a song called 'Sielpang Lap La', which runs as follows :

" Siel Lha Hungo E,
Vungson Te Siel Lha hungo E.
Chang Lha Hungo E,
Telngoh Te Hungo E.
Siel Lo Hungloi Yo,

Kapun Khulla Napen Pi.
Hongjoi Pha Nabol Peh Nange,
Siel Lo Hung Loi Yo.
Chang Let No,
Jouloi Ya Lomtang Kaina Leh Chango Letno.
Sielpang Lamme,
Kajou Jang Som Siel Kalo Leh Siello Lamme."

Free Translation :

"Come, Mithun's Soul,
Vungson's Mithun Soul, Come.
Come, the soul of paddy,
Come, the Telngohs.
Come soon, oh Mithun,
You came along with my ancestor from 'Khul'.
I will prepare a good place for your living,
Come soon, oh Mithun.
May paddy overflow granery,
In the field the Lawm work for you,
May paddy overflow granery,
So that dancing beside the Mithun
May be performed again,
The best of my Mithun
May perform the dancing."

The neck portion of the killed Mithun is given to the maternal uncle of the lady who performs the festival. The shares of 'Tuchas' and 'Bechas' are kept apart from the entitlement portion of the animal killed, being its waist and the rib portions respectively. The elder member of the family is, as usual, given the flesh of the ridge portion called 'Ating Sa'. All the guests who come to join the festival are given a small piece of the flesh of the slaughtered animal as a token of appreciation of their participation and co-operation. The pieces of such flesh are necessarily three. The boys and girls of the Lawm are given a leg which they cook and eat with fun and frolick in accompaniment with rice-beer for the whole day and night.

VI. Siel Pang Lap :

This ceremony is performed after the killing of the Mithun at the time of 'Chang-Ai' and 'Seil-Ai'. The village Priest having observe all the formalities and the ceremonial rites, the Mithun is killed. Before the meat is dressed for cooking, all the able- bodied married male persons form a circle joining their hands through the arms and over their shoulders. As they do so, they start singing a song called 'Siel Pang-Lap-La'. While they sing the song, they bend their knees slightly and straighten them again as they move their bodies sidewise in waves. This is symbolical for the farewell of the soul of the Mithun. The song sung runs as follows :

Siel Lo Mange,
Sah Le Lhang Tenga Thangsa,
Siel Lo Mange.

Siel Lo Mange,
Khovai Pheilam Siel Kalo Leh,
Siel Lo Mange.

Siel Pang Lamme,
Thangbon Sonlou,
Siel Pang Lamme.

Siel Pang Lamhu Te,
Kajo Jangsom Siel Kalo Le,
Siel Pang Lamme.

Free Translation :

Mithun, You are dignified,
You are already well known far and wide,
Mithun, you are indeed famous.

Mithun you are dignified,
Despite all humiliation,
Mithun, you are indeed dignified.

Mithun, you are magnificient even in death,
Irrsespective of fame and infame,
Everyone dance in praise of thy greatness.
Let us all dance beside the Mithun,
The Mithun of my Father which I have slain

Come, let us all dance
To commensurate its magnificience.

They sing the above song moving in a circle and end the singing with a sound, 'Li, Li, Li, Li, Li' and 'Ha, Ha, Ha, Ha, Ha'. Then 'Tucha' and 'Becha' relatives take away the Mithun for dressing and cooking for the feast.

VII. Lou Mun Vet (Agricultural Rituals):

The main system of cultivation is 'Jhum' or slash- and -burn system among the Kukis. This is essentially due to their ecological condition. Thus, at the approach of the annual cultivation season, every man of each house-hold in the village would go out in the jungle to locate a site for cultivation within the area of cultivation earmarked for that particular year by the Village Chief and his Council of Ministers. In the process, each man makes his markings at various places at regular intervals by the side of a tree by cutting a little portion of its trunk. This marking operation is called 'Loụ Chan'. Such sign-marks are much respected as they indicate that the particular portion or portions of land covered by such markings are already in possession of someone. Markings done, a man proceeds to cultivate his land. The man first erects two small posts within the area claimed by him and ties the tops of the two posts pitched with a piece of string. At the middle portion of the string, one wooden rice-spoon called 'Khalhei' is hung as a sign to ascertain whether the land would yield a good harvest or not. This sort of divination takes place at night. On the following day the man goes to the place to see if anything happens to the spoon. In case the site is good and would yield a bumper crop, nothing happens to it. But if it does not augurs well, sometimes the wooden rice-spoon is found to have dropped on the ground, or the head of a lizard or heads of other small insects are found hanging on the string. In such circumstances, it is believed that demons living in that jungle do not like the cultivation to be done there and, therefore, the place is abandoned and a new place is selected. When the new site is selected, the man starts cutting the trees and bushes for clearing the portion. He leaves the cleared things of the jungle for some days to dry up. When these are sufficiently dried, the fuels are set ablaze, so that while the cultivation portion is cleared of all the trees and shrubs the ashes of the burnt down things serve as a manure to the soil. After this, a ceremonial rite is performed. For doing this, the Priest and the man who selects the land go to the site. The rituals called 'Daiphu' are done in the following manner. The Village Priest makes images of clay of the following objects, each being made ten in number.

1. Mithun - 10
2. Beads - 10
3. Thoche - 1 (It is a kind of Squirrel. It has its area of land beyond which it does not go).
4. Vengke - 1 (It is a wild bird which also has a specified area of land beyond which it never goes).

These are indicative of appeasing the demon called 'Gampi Gampa' (the owner of the jungle) of the land earmarked for cultivation. The above items are added to the following other items in the offerings by the Village Priest for propitiation of the devil.

(i) Elephant Trunk - 1

(ii) Gong (Big Size) - 1

(iii) A group of small gongs - 1 Set.
comprising of three such gongs called 'Dohbuituo Khat'.

(iv) Sohlong (a kind of log of Sohhel Tree). - 1

(v) Silver Coin - 10

The man constructs a field-shed almost in the middle of the proposed land for cultivation, which is called 'Buh'. The above items are kept at a place below a tree near the field-shed. The aforesaid nine items of images of clay are placed in a circular order. In the middle of the circle, a kind of bamboo-family called 'Laothe' is put to which the following herbs are tied:

1. Daikham,
2. Loudai
3. Loudong.

But some people disagree with the above items and claim that they are the following herbs :

1. Daikham
2. Chonbeh
3. Luonglao

This bamboo which is erected is made pointed on both ends. While the one end is inserted deep in the ground to make it firmly fixed, the other end is used for placing an egg. The pointed side of the egg is slightly broken and the opening is inserted to the pointed end of the bamboo spike so that the egg slowly leaks all through the bamboo down to the ground where the images of the items mentioned above are placed. The Village Priest then chants Mantras which are as follows :

Daikham Kaphu Bangin Dai Yin
Loudai Kaphu Begin Dai Yin
Siel Som Kapeh Kalhai Na Nahe,
Dah Pi D-ahbu Kalut Na Nahe
Khichang A Kalut Na Nahe,
Ka Ahpi Vom Tui, Ka Ap Pi Bong Tui A Kalut Nahi.
Hiche Lou Munna Eisu Sedinga Dai Yin,
Mim Lha Chang Lha Kakou Na Ahi
Tidam Ludam Kakou Na Ahi.

Free Translation :

Be in peace like the herb (Daikham) I plant.
Be in peace like the 'Loudai' I plant.
In prayerful, I offer you ten Mithuns
The gongs, small and big, are tokens of submission.
Beads are also tokens of surrender.
My black hen and grey hen eggs are token of tribute
Kindly do not be harmful to my paddy-field.
I am asking for the souls of paddy.
I am praying for health and longivity.

Thereafter, the Priest sprays a mouthful of 'Zu' from his mouth as a token of offering. Then he cuts some young trees nearby, called 'Thing Tuoi' and erects them all around the items mentioned above, the top ends of which are bound together. This done, both the Priest and the man on whose cultivation land the above rites are performed return home. In the evening, the man takes one jar of 'Zu' to the house of the Priest along with his 'Tuchas' and 'Bechas' and offers the same to the Priest. This 'Zu'is called 'Daiphu Zu'. The Priest also invites his own 'Tuchas' and 'Bechas' as also some close neighbours and friends. The process of this drinking is not formal, as is done on other occasions. It is sipped by turn. A song proclaiming the value of paddy called 'Chang La' is sung on this occasion. It is as follows :

Ja Chang Thang Kadei Lot.
Kalmo Lammah Kavan Ngei Til Ngonne.
Sum Minthang Kadei Lot,
Gam Vengke Band Sietlei Thai Ni Gonge.

Free Translation :

So much is what I want paddy that I encourage My children to cultivate my paddy field.

Inasmuch as I wish to earn money.

I work ceaselessly like 'Vengke', (the kind of bird known for its hard labour in search of food).

VIII. Chang Nungah (Paddy Diety) :

This is a kind of paddy that is grown sparingly in the field. These paddy plants never sprout flowers nor fruits. People believe that this type of plants help increase fertility of the field, and also augments production. When such paddy plants grow in the midst of the actual paddy plants, these are very carefully preserved, even after the harvesting. This particular paddy plant grows very rarely. If by chance such a plant grows, it is properly treated and certain rituals are observed in order to appease the 'Diety' in charge of paddy. Such plant is called 'Chang Nungah', and it is worshipped. The genesis of 'Chang Nungah' diety worship is very interesting and the story in this connection runs as follows :

There was an orphan boy who lived all alone in the corner of a village. He was very poor and did not have enough to eat. As a result, he often starved. One day, he went into the jungle. While wandering, he saw a particular tree called 'Nake Tree'. On its branches perced up a flock of parrots. He stealthily went near the tree and observed them for sometime.

Standing beneath the tree, he shouted all of a sudden which frightened the parrots, and they flew away. One of the parrots, however, was carrying in its beak a paddy plant called 'Chang Nungah'. As all the parrots flew away, this particular parrot dropped the paddy-plant on the ground. When the 'Chang-Nungah' fell, it turned into an old lady. But neither the old lady nor the boy could see each other. The boy went back to his house. The old lady was very grateful to the boy as due to him she was saved. Otherwise, she would have been eaten up by the parrots. She told herself that she must find out the boy and do him a good turn. Accordingly, she enquired of the boy in the jungle. Her search having turned abortive, she went to the village to search the boy out. In the village, she went round the houses, but none could throw any light on the whereabouts of the boy. But though she did not express, she knew who the boy was. So, at last she entered into a hovel house in one corner of the village. She met the boy and asked him if she could be his guest. The boy welcomed her saying apologetically that he had nothing to offer her to eat or a good place to sleep in. The boy slept himself in the 'Sawm' or youngmen's dormitory. She said that she did not mind for such petty discomforts and stayed in the house. When the boy returned next morning from the 'Sawm', he found the old lady cooking the breakfast, although there was nothing in the house. He was surprised to find very aromatic food-stuffs being cooked. He questioned her and she answered that she collected something here and there on her own. This affair continued for two or three days. The boy grew suspicious about the lady's finding the foodstuffs and lay in wait to explore the mystery. One evening he pretended to be slightly indisposed and informed her that he would not go out to the 'Sawm' that night. He spent his night at home. At dawn, he found the lady preparing the breakfast. The boy pretended to be sleeping, while she was busy cooking. He was stealthily peeping through his quilt to watch her movement. He saw that as she began to cook, she put the rice from her right hand fingers, while the millet came out from her left hand fingers. The boy then understood that the old lady was not an ordinary person. He requested the lady to stay with him permanently. She told him that in case he wanted her to remain in the house, he would have to cultivate a paddy field to earn their livelihood. The boy agreed. She told him that he should cultivate the portion of land where the kind of tree called 'Nake' was present and that there should be a heap of earth where white-ants called 'Lhemlhung' live near that tree. The area he would cultivate should include these two. Accordingly, he looked for a place where he could find both. When the time came to clean the paddy field in order to protect the paddy, the old lady told him that he should make the field very clean and that there should not be even a blade of grass. So, the boy tried to clean the field as instructed. Despite his cleaning, there still remained a small blade of grass. On his return home, the old lady told him that his paddy field had certainly not been properly cleaned as her teeth had began to ache. She, therefore, asked him to go again to the field and check up whether there was any grass left. The boy, therefore, went there and found one stump of grass between two rice plants. He removed the grass and returned home. On his return , he found her relieved of the tooth-ache. This was an attempt on the part of the old lady to indicate to the boy that she was not an ordinary human being, and she could make him rich being the queen of the paddy corn.

The paddy field he claimed was hardly fifty square yards. Before the harvesting she warned the boy that no one should burn the straw which the boy meticuously followed. When the harvest was over, the collection of paddy for the size of the field was found to be disproportionate. The produce far exceeded the expected quantity. One day the old lady asked the boy to go to the field along with her and they went. On reaching there, she told him that he could then set fire to the straw which she forbade earlier. He arranged to burn the straw accordingly and as it began to produce flames she covered her head and face with cloth and ran towards the ant-hill of the white-ants. The boy caught hold of her saying not to leave him alone. She replied, "My child, do not tarry me. I must go. My time is up. If you really love me, you will have to do as I tell you now for next harvest. When you cultivate the field again next year, in the midst of the paddy plants in the field, you will find that there will grow one distinct paddy stalk which will remain green even when others become yellowish and ready for harvest. You will have to construct a small field-shed close to the green paddy plant. You will also have to fix up a platform placing one comb, one gourd of hair-oil, one water container made of bamboo called 'Tuithei' on it, and you will have to perform a rite with one black-hen inviting the soul of paddy. On that day, I shall come. Do not worry." So saying, she vanished into the round of the earth, called 'Lham Lhung'. Next year, the boy did exactly what she said to do, near the one green rice-plant that grew in the midst of the field. For performing the other rituals, he sought the help of the Priest. In the process, he and the Village Priest went near by the shed constructed by the green paddy plant, called 'Chang Nungah'. As they sat there, a man with a bag of paddy collected from the field came towards the field-shed. As he approached the shed, the man with the load of paddy shouted, "May I be thy guest" The owner of the field responded enquiring as to whether he was a good guest or a bad one. The man answered that he was a good guest and he had come along with all the blessings for prosperity and a bumper paddy crop. A warm invitation was extended to him by the owner. As the man entered the shed, he put down his burden on the floor. The man thereafter walked out of the shed, and came back once more saying the same thing he uttered earlier and was greeted with the same answer from inside the shed. The man who carried the paddy was the 'Tucha of the owner of the field. Thereafter, the Priest started doing his rites of propitiation. He killed the black-hen and placed it on the platform constructed near the field-shed. His incantations run as under :

Kolte Tolla Chang-lha Hungin,

Tuihat galla Juthel Nu Changpoh Changlha Hungin.

Free Translation :

May the souls of paddy from Burma come

May the souls of paddy from beyond the river which flows with strong current come.

Saying this, the Priest sprayed a mouthful of 'Zu' and ended the ceremony. They then flayed the hen for cooking. When it was cooked and about to be eaten, the Priest offered a piece of the meat to the unseen devil by throwing away the same before they ate the meat. Thus, it is believed that wherever the said paddy plant called 'Chang Nungah' grows in the paddy field, it is a sign of prosperity and good fortune. Since then the plant has become the paddy-diety. In doing so, the rituals of the diety are followed as were done by the boy who was blessed by the 'Chang Nungah Siem'. This paddy-deity worship was done by Sounpu Chongloi while he lived in Tamenglong. In his paddy field this paddy plant with divine power grew and so he worshipped the diety. While performing the worship of 'Chang Nungah Siem', his next door neighbour, Jangkhothang singson, was made to carry the paddy load for three times. It was said that when he propitiated the 'Chang Nungah' diety, Sounpu always had sufficient paddy to eat. In fact, he had more paddy than he needed.

IX. Khuongchoi Ceremony :

This concerns the religious rites involving young boys and girls directly in competition with the evil spirit, called 'Thilha', in order to earn fame for the 'Lawm' or young organisation of the village, which combines with a sense of festivity. The boys, the girls and the Priest involved in this ritual activity are transferred into a world of mesmerised behaviour. In a sense, it is a competition with an abstract thing in order to test their own sense of discipline, restraint and conformity to a set rule framed for their own behaviour. This is called 'Khuongchoi'. When the young boys and girls of a 'Lawm' decide to perform 'Khuongchoi', the leaders of the 'Lawm' go to the Chief of the village seeking his permission to allow them to do so. They take a pot of 'Zu' with them in token of their prayer. The Chief, in turn, enquires from them whether such a thing can be undertaken in view of the bad economic condition of the village. If there are not sufficient number of rich families with a good harvest, the proposal is not entertained. The proposal involves a great amount of expenses. Therefore, the Chief asks them to name the number of villagers who are prepared to associate themselves with the performance. 'Khuongchoi' means that the 'Lawm' young boys and girls of the village have to go to work in the paddy field of some families who can afford to offer them a midday meal and sufficient quantity of wine throughout the day, which requires no less than ten to fifteen pots of 'Zu' during the day. The 'Lawm' boys and girls, while working for the whole day in the field observe certain rules. Their working is punctuated by dancing and singing in the field, which are part of certain religious rituals, they rythm with the best of drum for which a man is set apart. The priest does the propitiation in his own way. Thus, 'Khuongchoi' is a very expensive and risky affair. The 'Lawm' leaders must ensure that there are not less than ten such able persons to meet the expenses in the village.

On getting permission from the Chief, the priest along with the leaders of the 'Lawm' come to the residence of the village Chief where the 'Thiempu' offers propitiation of the 'Khong' or drum of the 'Lawm'. In doing so, the leaders of the 'Lawm' bring their own drum, called 'Lawm-khong', along with a new 'Mithun' horn which has not earlier been used for drinking wine and also as a musical instrument at the time of singing and dancing. The drum, called 'Lawm-khong', and the horn, called 'Siel-Ki', are bound together. The priest then offers prayer and sprays a mouthful of wine on the face of the drum after invoking some incantations which is called 'Khongmai-Lhai'. In his invocation, he prays for the health of all the villagers, so that no misfortune befall on any of them during the period of seclusion of the drum. After this, the drum and the Mithun-horn bound together are hung up on top of the floor in the mid-section of the house at a place called 'Inting'. Hanging of the drum and the Mithun-horn is for a fixed number of days, during which period nobody is to touch it nor to beat it. This period of seclusion of the drum is considered to be a period of purification of the drum, after which the drum is brought down for use in the competition of the boys and the girls with the 'Thilha'. The number of days during which the drum and the Mithun-horn are to be kept hanging is decided by the Priest and the leaders of the 'Lawm' in consultation with the village Chief.

On completion of the period of seclusion of the drum, the same is taken down from the top of the floor where it remained hanging at the mid-section of the house of the Chief of the Village. For doing this, a spotless white cock is used by the Priest for propitiation of the drum. The Priest then observes omen from the signs of the legs of the strangled cock. This is called 'Ah Kanga Pathien Lhai', i.e. praying to God by sacrificing a white cock. With the taking down of the drum, the performance is permitted to be started. In the meantime, the 'Lawm' leaders will contact the persons selected to partonise the 'Khong-choi' in their field. They also will decide about the order of precedence of going to the field where the performance is to be held. Everything arranged, the 'Lawm' members all along practice the details of the steps to be followed minutely. The slightest mistake in the procedure of performance will entail danger to whoever commits the mistake, including the drummer and the Priest. Thus, in order to avoid mistakes, an elaborate and thorough rehearsal is carried out by the 'Lawm' members for a long time.

As everything is made ready for the performance of 'Khuongchoi', the 'Lawm' members also become ready to go to the paddy field. They then inform the person in whose field they are supposed to go. The man, in return, gets himself ready by arranging their mid-day meal and 'Zu'. The 'Tucha' and the 'Becha' of the man are also informed. They make everything in this regard ready, and carry them to the field to entertain the 'Lawm' members who would work in the field. The owner of the field also informs the Chief, the Priest and the Council of Ministers of the village.

The 'Lawm' members select from among themselves some boys to beat the drum. Such persons are to beat the drum ceaselessly on the day of the performance. They would also sing a song repeatedly and continuously along with the sound of the drum, right from the 'Khuomuol' or outskirt of the village, throughout the day till the end of the 'Khuongchoi'. The 'Lawm' members would also select some boys and girls to dance. These dancers must not have any defect, physically or morally. The girls are expected to be virgins.

The selected boy is expected to sing the song faultlessly. The same also applies to the beater of the drum. In case of any mistake on the part of the singer or the drummer, there is every possibility of being liable to suffer any kind of misfortune. The song runs as follows :

(i) Kalenchon Toh Somil La Vai Lou Konning Eitam Lhang be Lhanghui Thin Na Lethen.

(ii) Eitan Lhang Se Lhanghui Thin Na Lethen Langchom Pa Toh Nithnom Mol Kho Songe.

Free Translation :

(i) As I start going for work to the field at Khuomuol, along with my drum, may all devil and other devil agents that may harm me be swept away by the wind.

(ii) May all the devil and other evil agents that may harm me be swept away by the wind, so that I might fulfil with success my desire to have a good time with my drum.

As he keeps on waiting while singing the above song in accompaniment of the drum beating, others, such as, the Chief, the Priest, the Council of Ministers, the owner of the field and his 'Tucha' and 'Becha' relatives, as also the 'Lawm' members, start congregating at the 'Khuomuol'. Having thus assembled, the Priest starts his invocation for appeasement of the 'Khuomuol', called 'Khuomuol Lhai'. After propititation, he sprays a mouthful of 'Zu' at the 'Khuomuol'. This is followed by formation of a circle by the 'Lawm' members. As they do so, the selected boy for the dance comes in the middle of the circle with a sword in his hand and start dancing, brandishing the sword. The selected girls then join him in the dance. Then all the Lawm members who form the circle start singing and dancing. Their song is as follows :

(i) Somol khang khai Ido Leh Senna Gol
Vai Lou Knon Leh Phei Phung Khai Nan Lomme.

(ii) Vai Lou Kon Leh Phei Phung Khai Nan Lomme
Sang Mang Lu Leh Lai Lu Lap Nan Lomme.

Free Translation :

(i) Friends, the platform we built at Khuomuol is indeed befitting to the occasion.

(ii) The platform we built at Khuomuol is indeed befitting to the occasion and so also for hoisting the heads of our enemy.

As they sing and dance to the tune of the drum, they prepare themselves to proceed towards the field. The procession is formed in such a way that they are led by the drummer beating it incessantly. He is followed by the Priest, the Chief and his Council of Ministers and then the owner of the field and the Lawm members forming the tail end along with the 'Tucha' and the 'Becha' of the owner of the field. En-route the field, the 'Lawm' members exhibit their dancing skill at three places - the spots of which depend on the drummer. As they start the dancing by the selected boy and the two girls, the accompanying song runs as follows :

Mitha Gal Naang Saa In Bon
Muvan Laai Ving Atotne,
Pupa Changlam Phei Ya Bon
Jaitha Alvan Abomme.

Free Translation :

Even a man who kills his foes himself having been seriously injured, put on the headgear of honour and prestige with the feathre of eagle, so also the man of fame and honour on his own merit is honoured and venerated by all, even by the Burmese.

While the 'Lawm' members and the drummer continue dancing and singing on the way at intervals, the Chief, the Priest, the host and his 'Tucha' and 'Becha' relatives, however, overtake them without waiting them. As a rule, a small hut is constructed in the field for being used as a resting place or a make-shift called 'Lou-buh'. On their arrival, the Priest, the Chief and others would wait for the arrival of the 'Lawm' members whom they left behind.

As the young boys and girls reach there, and before entering the borderline of the paddy field, called 'Lou Chin',they perform another dancing session accompanied with song which runs as follows :

Haosa Gamlei Navang Si Selang Jon,

Neihoi Ven Lang Khannou Gol Neihoi Ven,
Neihoi Ven Lang Khanńou Gol Neihoi Ven,
Kumtin Lutsiel Kachoinȧ Tong Neh Hen.

Free Translation :

Oh ! Chief of the village,With your protective wing we have the field whereon we cultivate for our livelihood. We beseech Thee every year with our Mithun.We pray Thee that thou wouldst continue to bless our Chief and so also all of us so that we might continue to live happily in the years to come under Thy care and protection.

Here also, they dance thrice, after completion of which they proceed towards the hut in the field, called 'Lou Buh'.

As the 'Lawm' members come close to the hut, they dance and sing once more for three rounds. The following is the song sung :

(i) Kabuh Tolla Joujam Leng Sonang San
Dei Babilla Chullou Din Appamme,

(ii) Joujam Ba Hin Pan Hih In Kaphungte
Kadei Genu Toh Tenge Lung Jonne.

Free Translation :

(i) The beautifully blooming red 'Joujam' (Cock's comb).

How valuable it is not to be put on the crest of my lover.

(ii) How valuable it is not to be put on the crest of my lover, do not ever attempt to pluck it by any one of you, my people, for it remins me of my lover.

The song and dance finished, they sit in the field-hut, called 'Buh' or 'Lou-Buh' for a while. They come out of it, being led by two boys and two girls of the 'Lawm'. They then enter the field in a single file. In the middle of the file, a set of two boys and two girls each is positioned being followed by others and then another set of two boys and two girls each in the rear. Having formed a single file, they start working on the field. As they work, they gradually form a circle, the two ends of the file closing on each other. No one is allowed to,talk while they work. As they complete their work for each round they perform dancing in accompaniment with the song which runs as follows[1]. This is done three times.

Jinga Kaphu Jinglei Lam Dinna,
Nao Khalla Limlou Honjol Na,
Sichanga Valeng Lui Oe.
Palla Khuva Thathei Tolla Limlou Honjol Na
Lam Cheng Adet Tolla Kholle,
Lamvui Akai Nan Phahe.

As they complete the circle three times, it becomes the time for their proceeding towards the field-hut. After the performance of dance, they all produce a sound like whining of a horse - " Bru ...ru...ru...ru". It is believed that the 'Thilhas' can do whatever a man can do, but they cannot do the whining sound. This is the only wanting item by which mankind, including young boys and girls, can beat the 'Thilhas' in their competition. They make this sound for three times. This is followed by singing and dancing. The song runs as follows :-

Neotajong Simbeng Chalchah Bangin Neotajong,
Hangtajong Khoimuchang San Cha Bangin
Hangtajon E.

Free Translation :

Though I may be as small as 'Simbeng' (a tiny animal),
I am as brave as a ferocious type of male-bee called 'Khoimu'.

Then the members on extreme right of the filing lead the group towards the 'Buh'. As they come near the hut, the 'Becha' of the host, hands over a small packet of rice to the leading man. He passes it on to the one behind him. This becomes a continuous process till it reaches the last men who then shouts - "Dathang in pao tan atie" (Dathang says, you can talk). As he shouts this, they are at liberty to speak once again. The rice packet that moves from hand to hand is called 'Buchun'. On entering the hut, they are received by the 'Becha' of the host who offer them the

1. This song was believed to have been composed at a time when mankind could communicate with 'Thilhas' directly, and, as such, no one could give me the translation, the language being too old.

mid-day meal. They eat together with the people who come along with them, i.e., the Thiempu, the Chief, the man of the day with his 'Tucha' and 'Becha' and the Council of Ministers. After the meal is finished, they are served with 'Zu' while they take rest. They are now free to talk. Then, they enter the field again for the second round of work as was done in the morning shift in a single file. It must be noted here that while working in the field, they are forbidden from killing any insect or touch stumps in the field. It is believed that the 'Thilhas' may come in disguise of insects, snakes, lizards, etc. and that they might be killed by accidents. It is further believed that the 'Thilhas' are omnipresent but are unseen. Even some might have taken their position on the stumps to watch the boys and the girls working in the field. That is why no one is allowed to kill the insects, snakes, lizards, etc., or to touch the stumps.

The working method by forming gradually a circle from both the ends of the single file is still to be observed. With every round of such circle being completed, the 'Lawm' members perform a round of dancing and singing. For this, the selected two girls and one boy will dance only one round. While the 'Lawm' members work, two selected girls serve them 'Zu' - one from the one end and the other from the other end. The girls chosen for this job must have an unblemished body and morals, and must have not lost their virginity. The cup with which the 'Zu' is served is not replaced. Every member has to drink from the two cups used by the two girls.

On arrival at the outskirt of the village, 'Khuomuol' the Lawm members sing and dance once again, which is soon followed by a ritual propitiation from the Priest. This marks the end of the day's ritual activities. Since the 'Lawm' leaders have earlier arranged as to who and how many persons are to perform the 'Khuongchoi', the same procedures that have been followed in the first occasion are repeated.

These ritual activities concerning the young boys and girls are one of the most complicated and risky ones and, as such, very few people dare perform the same. The risk is involved equally with the Priest, the drummer and all the members of the 'Lawm' of the village, who take part in it. In case the Priest commits mistake in his ritual invocation and stumbles in his propitiation at any stage, he runs the risk of getting into misfortune, even to the extent of death. The same is true with the drummer. If he makes mistake in drumming to the tune of singing and dancing, he is liable to run the same risk as the Priest does. The 'Lawm' members are no exception to it. Therefore, great care and caution is taken to perform their individual part faultlessly which is considered a challenge to the evil spirit.

On completion of three rounds of work punctuated by singing and dancing of the two girls and one boy, the time for winding up the work comes. Thus, they stop their work by coming towards the field hut. Before leaving the paddy field, the Priest invokes a ritual propitiation in the same manner as he has done at the time of proceeding from the 'Khuomuol' of the village in token of biding farewell to the evil spirits 'Thilhas' believed to be living in the forest. As they come towards home, the 'Lawm' members perform dancing on their way home at the same places where they danced on their outward journey towards the field.

Prior to crossing the borderline of the field for home and after the Priest invokes his ritual propitiation, the dancing and singing of the 'Lawm' members are once again performed. The song is as follows :

(i) Kabuh Tolla Nompe Bang Kajil Le
Jang Leng Khu Van Sen Gol Umang Khole.

(ii) Ken Jong Sen Gol Um Tuyang Kakholle
Jang Leng Khu Va Te Sangin Katam Joi.

Free Translation :

(i) As we spend our time so happily at my farm, the wild pegion makes it a place for merry making in great number.

(ii) As the wild pigeon does, if I also collect my relatives they will far exceed the number of wild doves.

As the rites continue to progress one stage after another without mistakes, the act of propitiation and the sound of the drum beating go along in complete harmony with songs at different stages accompanied by dancing. But, if the rites are not done correctly and mistakes are committed in the rythm, the sound of drum becomes more and more blunt and flat and does not bring harmony with the songs and dancing.

This is one of the few celebrations in which not only the Priest takes part but the laity also, especially the young ones of the 'Lawm', actively involved, and the Priest is subjected to a great stress and strain of the proceedings which sometimes continue for more than fifteen days.

All the rituals described above are closely linked up with the performance of religious rites in respect of 'Khuongchoi'. It is believed that, the singing of songs and the beating of the drum will be more rhythmic and pleasant, if the boys and the girls can win over the 'Thilhas'. In case they commit mistake, it will be manifested by the flat sound of the drum in the process of the competition. In such event all participants are likely to face the same misfortune as already mentioned above. The drummer, the dancers and the singers, therefore, have to be careful not to commit mistakes at any stage. It is also believed that the health of the whole community of the village will improve if the performance is faultless.

On completion of the elaborate rituals in all the fields of the ten or fifteen patrons, the Priest performs his last rite at the 'Khuomuol' to signify the closing of the performance. While going to the 'Khuomuol' for the last rite, the 'Thiempu' is accompanied by the village Chief and his Council of Ministers, the patrons and also all the boys and girls who worked in the fields. In doing so, the young boys and girls take 'Zu' with them, in small pots to be served there.

As usual, there is dancing and singing and then it takes the form of a social gathering without much formality. Any young boy or girl desiring to dance can do so to the tune of the songs so selected for the occasion. In this connection, a particular song was composed, and is now very popular. The name of the composer is Hoilhing of Bolkot village. The song has become synonymous with the 'Khongchoi' rites :

Len Lhang Kolni Asoh Tai Kalom Gol,
Somol Lungdei Chong Jinang Galhao Te.
Somol Lungdei Chong Jinang Galhao Te.
Theisen Lomgol Ngoilli Bang Lhingkit Hen.
Vang Kholai Ya Lenchong Gin Kajah Leh,
Golpi Lenkhong Choi Lai Jin Kabolle.
Golpi Lengkhong Choi Lai Jin Kabolle,
Phungmang Lenkhong Somilla Gingkit Hen.

Free Translation :

The sun has arisen from the east,
Let us bid farewell to our beloved
'Khuomuol' where we danced,
Let our childhood friendship be replenished
And filled lika a lagoon which never dries.

It reminds me of the days of 'Khuongchoi', which makes me feel still as if in the midst of 'Khuongchoi' ceremony.

I wish if the drum of the Chief 'Khuongchoi) is beaten again at 'Khuomuol'.

Just before starting for the homeward journey and in front of the field hut, the boys and girls once again dance and sing for three times. The song is :

Mukho Thimbang Jing Ta E Golgenu,
Josing Lambang Jong Ta Te.
Taikho Mei Bang Val Ta E Gollhangpa,
Majopma Khabang Cheta Te.

Free Translation :

My girl friend, it is becoming dark,
Let us go to our father.
As the day breaks,
It is time to go to the field,
Let us go for work.

As soon as the 'Khuongchoi' rites are over, the drum and the Mithun-horn are immediately packed together and hung up at the same place wherefrom those were taken. Those will remain therefore, not less than three years without being touched. Only on the expiry of three years, another 'Khuongchoi' can be performed. Prior to that, the drum and the Mithun-horn must not be touched.

'Khuongchoi' is a competition with the devil, called 'Thilha' which is represented by a kind of serpent known as 'Lhangnel'. No one is allowed to take the hoe, dao, etc. upside down during the 'Khuongchoi' ceremony, and the work done at the field is also without any implements but with bare hands only. This is done as a precautionary measure against any accidental killing of even a small insect which may represent the 'Thilha'.

The mistake committed in dancing or singing in the course of the competition is immediately noticed, as the reaction of the 'Thilhas' to such mistakes is made manifest. 'Lienkholal, the Chief of Khaochangbung village, said that while they performed 'Khuongchoi' in 1941, when he was then a just grown up boy at Khaochangbung village, it so happened that as they started to sing a song during the performance of the dancing in the field, the leader made a mistake in starting the song. Instead of beginning the song with the first verse of the song, he started with the second one. Immediately the clouds around them thickened and they were surrounded by a rainbow. The leader quickly realised the mistake and corrected the song. As they did so, the clouds disappeared gradually and the rainbow cleared. In another instance the reaction of the 'Thilhas' was that when the ceremony was in progress in the field at Bolkot Village, one of the leaders of the group became drunk and fallen into a deep sleep. Even at the time of leaving the field, he could not be roused from his sleep. Then the Priest suspected it to be the handiwork of the 'Thilhas'. The Priest asked a youngman to compose a song to awaken him. While composing the song, the young boys sat around the sleeping youth leader. The song was as follows :-

(i) Setlei Ya Long Godlo Khalhet Soh Tah,
Lheo Kong Sih Tui Gollo Killim Sellin.

(ii) Heokong Sih Tui Gollo Killim Sellin,
Jouva Chang Najeh Bangin Kilham In.

Free Translation :

i) Our friends is lying as dead as a log without life,
May the sprinkling of water on him be felt as is being fallen on all partss of the juncle leaves when heavy downpour falls on them.

ii) As he feels such sprinkling water, may he be awaken from the bondage of much devilish handiwork as the jungle banana sprout germinates very fastly releasing itself from the thickly covered banana skins.

As he composed the song, he let the young boys sing it three times, while standing around him. After such singing, he sprinkled water to the head of the sleeping man. As he did so, the man woke up immediately. The young boys asked the Priest whether it was a magic he played with the wordings. The Priest replied that the song itself was the magic.

X. Indawi Diety Celebration :

The 'Indawi-Diety' has its origin in a story in which a couple lost their daughter. The story runs as follows :-

Kimchal Hangsing, while living in the Chin Hills in a village called 'Muolphei', where 'Thilhas' were believed very active and aggressive, had a daughter whose fame for beauty spread far and wide. This beautiful girl was the centre of attraction of many young men. Even the 'Thilhas' were interested in her. The name of the girl was Japhal. One day, Japhal did not return home from the Jhum field of the family at a place called 'Sisep'. Frantic searches were made to trace her out, but in vain. Her parents, out of love and affection for their daughter, and having nothing else to do, cried bitterly in grief. Seeing the condition of the parents of the girl, the 'Thilhas' who stole away the girl revealed themselves in the dream of the girls, father and admitted that his daughter was taken by them. He said :

> .... cry not, and be not worried. We, the Malphei villagers were responsible for the loss of your daughter. We have taken her as the bride for our son. She is living fine with us, and she will not be harmed. Instead of worrying and crying for her, be happy. In the morning, when you get up from your bed go out of your house and look up at the bushes of the tree, called 'Se'. You will find in the bushes of the tree, 'Seboh', some ingredients at the branch of the said tree. Worship the said elements contained therein, so that you might live in happiness, and prosperity will be yours so long as you worship the said elements which is known as 'Indawi'. This also will serve as a covenant between you and our people.

The night he had the dream, the sound of many Mithuns, moving below the floor of the man's house was reportedly heard by the neighbours. The next morning, the man looked up at the bushes of the tree called 'Se' nearby his house, and found the said ingredients at the base of a branch of the tree. He took the 'Indawi' and worshipped it. Thereafter, he became rich and he amassed great fortune, as was told in the dream. His other relatives followed suit and ultimately 'Indawi' worship became the main religious diety of the Thadous and their cognates. The following ingredients are contents of the 'Indawi':

1. Vohpi-Lu (a female pig-skull),
2. Kelki (horns of a he-goat).
3. Khaokol (bamboo bangle) -7 round each (double),
4. Peng (small gourd) 2 pieces, one for 'Zu' and one for seeds. (one each of the round type and the long type)
5. Tengdop (spear).

6. Chemkol (Dao),

7. Belval (a circular stand for a jar made of bamboo split - differs from clan to clan and is being used by Singsons alone).

These items are bound together with a creeper, called 'Khaopi'. 'Khaokol' is a ring-like cord made of bamboo, called 'Gopi'. Splits of 'Gopi', peeled and thinned, called 'Gopi-naang' are used for binding together the spear and the dao with seven rounds on each side in a bangle-shaped fashion. Likewise, the gourd is used for two purposes- one as a container of 'Zu' and the other as a container of the seeds.

Worship of 'Indawi' is done once a year compulsorily . But, in some exceptional cases, when illness and other exigencies demand, it can be worshipped as many times as necessary. The above mentioned ingredients tied together are called 'Indawi'. These are bound together and placed at the inner portion of the roof of the portico, called 'Hongcha'. This is the place where the rice pounder called 'Sum' is placed and the poultry of the family called 'Ahgil' is constructed. The portion of the house where 'Indawi' is kept is called 'Biching'. The end of the creeper used for binding the 'Indawi' is not cut. The entire length of the creeper is used and the remainder is tucked in together.

When 'Indawi' is worshipped, the performer has to kill a female pig. The Priest of the village officiates the rite to propitiate the deity. He goes early in the morning to the man and does the 'Juphi' propitiation by spraying out a mouthful of 'Zu' in and around the house. This act is called 'Inthenso' or cleansing of the house. Thereafter, he goes back to his house. Meanwhile, the 'Tucha' and the 'Becha' relatives of the performer catch a female-pig to be sacrificed before the Priest returns. The pig is to be killed at the portico. Nothing is done inside the house in the case of 'Indawi's worship. As the pig is about to be sacrificed the 'Indawi'is taken down by the Priest and placed near the pig. Before the killing, a gourd is arranged and the same is broken on the head of the pig. The act of propitiation before the killing of the pig is called 'Ganlha Lhai', appeasing the spirit of the pig. Then, before killing of the pig the following invocation is made:

Molphei Kho Nasah Bangin Neisan,

Vohpi Dokon Nasah Bangin Neisan,
Peng Jom Phe Nasah Bangin Neisan,

Kelchal Kiheh Nasah Bangin Neisan,

Chaokol Pha Nasah Bengin Neisan,

Tengdop Pha Nasah Bangin Neisan,

Khaopi Toipha Nasah Bangin Neisan,
Chemkol Pha Nasah Bangin Neisan.

Free Translation :

Bless me as Thou blessed Molphei village
Bless me as Thou blessed the pig (female) to its full growth.
Bless me as Thou blessed the big gourd (round and long)
Bless me as Thou blessed the he-goat
Which grows its horn to the fullest and curly length.
Bless me as Thou blessed the wristlet
Bless me as Thou blessed the pear
Bless me as Thou blessed the 'Khaopi' (a kind of creeper).
Bless me as Thou blessed the Dao.

After this invocation the Priest sacrificed the pig with a spike of sharpened bamboo piece, called 'Gopi-Tul', by piercing it through the left armpit and aiming at the heart. The pig is placed in such a way that the head of it is turned towards the place where 'Indawi' is hung, which normally runs parallel to the hearth of the house-hold. The performer and his wife who sits on the left side of her husband face the priest and the front of the house. Both the Priest and the performer with his wife sit on their legs without any support.

As the Priest piecres the pig with the sharp bamboo spike, it dies instantaneously. The blood that stains the bamboo spike is smeared by the Priest on the forehead of the man, with his forefinger. Then the 'Bechas' of the family take charge of the pig for dressing and cooking it. During dressing, the left portion of the hindleg is separated as the share of the Priest. The neck portion upto the point where the head joins with the body is also taken out for the performer himself.

Prior to the propitiation by the Priest, the performer brings, as he comes to sit in front of the Priest, one gourd-cup filled with water and spills over the ground spreading round the pig. It is symbolical significance of family problems, illness and misfortunes that the performer was supposed to have brought with him before the 'Indawi' deity for which propitiation is invoked. As the water is spilt over the pig, it is said that all that contains in the gourd-cup has been transmitted from the performer and his family to the pig. Thereafter, the Tucha of the performer comes and smashes the gourd-cup into pieces with his leg, signifying that all the illness and misfortunes of the family are completely done away with. Likewise, the performer brings a ring of bamboo-split of around three diameter fitted to the mouth of the pig. He inserts the bamboo-split-ring to the mouth of the pig. Since the mouth of the pig is pointed at the end, with the slightest movement of its mouth, the pig pushes out the ring that covers the mouth. As it pushes out, it is said that the entire calamities of ill health, misfortune and badluck which befall the family have been taken out in much the same way as the ring comes out. The floodgate of a bright furture, good health and better fortune is thus opened.

The pig, after sacrificial ceremony, is dressed by the 'Bechas' of the performer. The 'Tucha' relatives burn the pig to cleanse it properly, and then hands over the same to the 'Bechas' for dressing and slicing it into pieces, so that they might be able to set apart differrent parts of it as shares for individual categories of relatives of the performer. Thereafter, the portion to be cooked is given to the 'Tuchas', who cook it for a feast to be served to the invitees. The different parts of the body of the pig are divided in the following manner : the 'Tucha' relatives have to dress the intestine of the pig. Before, the 'Becha' relatives cut the pig into pieces, the Priest instructs them to take out a portion of the nitch immediately that lies next to the head, but without the neckbone. There is another portion to be set apart for God. It is the left foreleg. The portion is taken out in such a way that the foreleg is sliced without completely severing it from the body. The skin of the two sides upto the waist will taken inside the house and kept hanging at the midsection pillar of the house by the Priest. No other person should touch it. The entire portion of the waist is taken out and is divided into two halves. The right half containing the tail is given to the senior 'Tucha' or 'Tubul' relative, while the other is given to the junior 'Tucha'. Along with this, the intestine portion, called 'Angoi' is divided into two halves. This portion meant for the 'Tucha' relatives of the performer is then cooked. The cooking area should not be far off from the place where the Priest performs his rituals, which is called 'Huongcha'. This portion of the meat must not be mixed with other portion cooked for the general consumption. As the meat is cooked, the priest enquires so to whether the meat has reached properly cooked-stage. He will be informed that the meat is at the boiling point. At this, the priest goes inside the house, picks up the foreleg hung up inside, and puts it on the boiling pot without being out into pieces, wherein the waist portion of the meat for the 'Tucha' relatives is being cooked. The priest assumes that the portion given to the God or 'Pathien' must have also been cooked and is at the boiling stage. Therefore, the portion thus meant for the 'Pathien' should also be included among the meat for the 'Tucha' relatives. Thus, the waist portion, the intestine called 'Angoi' and the share for the 'Pathien' having been boiled without chopping into pieces, are fully cooked. The pot of meat is taken down from the oven when ready and then it is cut into pieces. The alice is divided again into as many shares as there are 'Tucha' relatives of the performer. After the distribution is made of the respective shares, if there still remains some more, that will also be taken to their home by the 'Tucha' relatives. Such portion of the 'Tucha' must not be touched or eaten by any other relative or persons.

The portion of the meat for the ccommoners is cooked outside the house, i.e., in the lawn. This is cooked after cutting the meat into pieces before boiling and is called 'Sapi'. the cooked meat is then separated from the soup. The soup is cooked again separately as an item, mixing with rice and is called 'Mepoh'. The 'Sapang' or head portion is meant for the Chief of the village and his Council of Ministers, the priest and other elderly persons of the village representing the cross-section of the social stratum, including the performer of the 'Indawi' worship.

The menu for eating 'Sapi' or the meat meant for the commoners is comprised of two items - one of soup mixed with rice, called 'Satui Poh' and the other is the meat portion prepared as an item of curry in the normal course of cooking. It is mixed with salt and chilly and is divided into as many shares as possible to give each participant in the 'Indawi' worship a share of not less than three to four pieces of meat as a second item of the menu, in addition to the soup item mixed with rice.

Out of this 'Sapi' meat, the priest and his 'Becha' on the one hand and the performer of the 'Indawi' worship and his 'Becha' on the other are made to eat separately. The sitting order is as follows :

The commoners eat outside the house, while the four persons mentioned above eat inside, at the midsection of the house. They eat from one big plate made of wood. They sit facing each other in square shape. The performer of the 'Indawi' worship sits towards the inner house, facing the front door of the house, while the preist sits opposite the performer and facing the backside of the house. Facing each other are the 'Becha' of the priest and the 'Becha' of the performer, respectively. The meat given to them has no share. A quantity of meat, sufficient enough to satisfy them, is given. In the event of their inability to eat the whole quantity, the remainder is divided equally among them and they take the same to their homes.

The 'Sapang' portion is eaten by the Village Chief, his Council of Ministers, other elders or selected persons, the performer of the 'Indawi' and the priest. The portion of the meat included in the 'Sapang' is the head of the pig, the heart, the liver left after cutting the other portion and splean.

This is eaten at random with their shares equally divided according to the number of persons entitled to take the meat.

The eating procedure mentioned above is preceded by the completion of the 'Indawi' rite performed by the priest. After having ameared the forehead of the performer with the blood of the sacrificial pig, the priest who had earlier taken down the 'Indawi' at the commencement of his propitiation from the roof of the house, now places it at the 'Sekon' branch, if the performer has earlier performed the religious rite of 'Sekon Tun' or erection of 'Sekon', a kind of tree called 'Se'. In case the performer has not performed the 'Sekon' rites, a small branch of a tree of about three to four feet high, representing 'Sekon', is erected in front of the house parallel to the place where the 'Sekon' is usually erected. The wood thus erected is only a replica of 'Sekon'. On it the ingredients of the 'Indawi' are placed, being covered with a basket, in order to protect it from destruction. The 'Indawi' thus taken down from the 'Biching' remains there for three days.

Propitiation of 'Indawi', is followed by the sacrificial feast of the ceremony. Before the feast is partaken, the priest calls the performer inside the house. The former makes the latter sit near the hearth of the family in the house, while he himself site facing the performer. He invokes incantations and hands over the ring-like neck portion of the meat. At the same time, the priest offers the performer a piece of the meat to eat. The rest is eaten by the performer, as and when he likes it, but within three days.

After the meat is offered, the priest advises the performer not to cross the area beyond the portion where he had earlier performed the 'Indawi' rites during the period of three days, on the expiry of which the 'Then Hon' rite is to be performed. He also gives instruction to the 'Tuchas' of the performer that they should keep some undefiled water drawn beforehand in the morning before the chirping of the early birds, called 'Vavom Te Nupa'. They should keep it in a new bamboo container, called 'Tuithei'. Then he leaves the place for home.

On the third day, the priest goes early in the morning to the residence of the performer of the 'Indawi' rites. Prior to his arrival, and as per his earlier instruction to the 'Tuchas', the undefiled water is kept ready. The priest gives it to the performer in a cup. The remaining quantity of the water is sprinkled by the priest all over the floor inside the house. He does so upto the portico of the house whre he had earlier performed the 'Indawi' rites. This act of the priest is called dedication rite or 'Thien Hon Na'. On this occasion, the performer offers a jar of 'Zu'. The Tucha and the Becha relatives of the performer of the 'Indawi' rites, as also the officiating priest of the rituals, the Village Chief and his Council of Ministers do the same. All the 'Zu' jars will be put together and served to all present. They will all sip the whole day in a body. The order of precedence of sipping is done in accordance with their social standing. While the priest and the Village Chief sip the 'Zu' served in the name of the performer of the 'Indawi' rites, the sipping is followed by the performer of the rite and others at random, according to their convenience.

After the sprinkling of water is finished, the 'Indawi' which was earlier placed on the 'Sekon' or on a branch of a stick in the likeness of 'Sekon', is taken down and placed at the 'Biching; inner portion of the roof and slightly above the caves of the porch of the house where it is thrust into the thatch. By doing so, the priest propitiates it by spraying a mouthful of 'Zu'

It has been observed that throughout the rituals in connection with the 'Indawi' worship, each individual performs his part well enough and precisely. Unlike other religious rites, 'Indawi' rites manifest the individuslistic nature of the rite. Every household has to perform the 'Indawi' worship, and it is not done on a community basis. Even in the same family, when a son has a separate family and wishers to have his 'Indawi', he has to go the whole hog of performing the rites. The father observes the rites for his family which may consist of his dependent sons. In the case of the eldest son, the same 'Indawi', which is installed by his father is to be taken as his own. No new 'Indawi' is required for him only

The word 'Indawi' literally means 'house-magic' or 'witchcraft', and is the name given to the diety of individual household. It is , therefore, a family diety, though the community is invited to take part in various phases of its activities, when a particular man performs 'Indawi' worship. But the invitees or the community never take active part in it. Instead, they are more observers in fulfilment of their social obligations in associating with the elaborate rituals. The only active participant, besides the performer, is the priest who officiates in the ritual ceremony concerning the religious aspect of the rites. The 'Tucha' and 'Becha' relatives of the performer, the Village Chief and the wife of the host are active in so far as the fulfilment of the individual social role is concerned. As could be gathered from Hose and McDougall's work on the 'Pagans of Borneo', the 'Indawi' worship is very similar to the 'Siap Aioh' of the Kenyahs. Every family that worships 'Indawi' should have one 'Indawi' diety which is also said to be very similar to the 'Sanamahi' diety of the Meiteis of Manipur. But in case a younger son, who is termed as 'Naopa', establishes his primary family, after marriage, he cannot depend on the 'Indawi' diety of his father any longer. The same has to be passed on from father to eldest son as an inheritance. The younger son has to acquire it with the help of his father and elder brother or 'Upa'. The procedure to be observed and things to be done have been enumerated in the foregoing paragraphs. The contents of ingredients of 'Indawi' as the writer records, are different from what Shaw (73-74 :1929) has described which includes:

> A piece each of the 'Sething' and 'Thinghi' tree, small bits of 'Gopi' (a garden bamboo), 'Vomgui' (creeper), goat, pig, fowl and egg. Also small portions of a gourd, 'Khaopi' (a tree the bark of which makes excellent rope), and 'Hailhi' (a particular species of gourd). A sword, a spear and a women's brass wristlet called (Ghao' have to be produced .... Then the Thiempu taking a very small bit of each of the above with the spear, *dao* and wristlet in his hand says :

'Pathen; bless so and so (the person whose Indawi is being made).

Bless him, as you blessed the 'Shetoinampha', i.e., the best of the 'Shething' tree (to be the Indoi of man).

Bless him, as you blessed the 'Thinghitoinampha' (the best of the 'Thinghi' trees).

Bless him, as you blessed the 'Copichengnampha' (the bamboo), 'Vomguipha' (the creeper), 'Vohpimaikem' (the pig), 'Kelchalkihe' (the goat), 'Pengjompa' (the round gourd), 'Hailhipha' (the long gourd), 'Chemkolpha' (the old dao), 'Tengmunpha' (the spear), 'Chaoveipha' (the wristlet), 'Khaopithosom' (the tree whose bark makes rope), 'A tolngo' (the white fowl) and the 'Katuilungtheng katui Lungva' (the clean and the clear egg).

> The priest then carries on the invocations praying that the householder may have many sons and daughters, riches and power and a long life. After this, the genealogical tree of the householder from 'Chongthu' has to be repeated in full and the priest asks Pothen to exempt the present maker of an 'Indoi' from the consequences of the sins of his forefathers. So saying, the bits of articles enumerated above are put into a small gourd and hung up on the outside of the front wall of the house near the top, usually above the door and out of the way of chilren and fowls searching for something to play with or for food. Thus, the ceremony ends and there is much drinking and eating. there is no special animal to be killed; that merely depends on the circumstanes of the person performing the ceremony. The 'Indawi' thus made is carried with him by the maker wherever he does until he dies, when his son or sons have to repeat the ceremony

if they intend having an 'Indawi' also. The house-god, therefore, is apparently only for the protection of the person for whom it is made, which is also evident from the ceremony given above.

While the invocation rites are identical, except for the properties of the 'Indawi', which are different in their composition, a great deal from what I gather together from almost the same groups of Thadou and their colletaral cousins, as were collected by Shaw some fifty seven years ago, the differences still persisted with that of the information collected by Hutton, almost at the same time as Shaw did it. Hutton's information appeared to have closer identity with what are now being collected. Hutton (153-54 :1929) said :

> The Indawi is the 'house-magic', a bundle of charms which is made either by the Thiempu or by anyother person who has the requisite knowlege of what is required and of the signification of the objects used and of the formulae used in putting them together. It consists of seven objects bound with a single cord to a bamboo spike, some of the objects being ornamented with feathers from a white cock. The spike is thrust into the thatch in the porch of the house.

It is interesting to note the explanation given by Hutton - of the physical propeties of 'Indawi'. Every ingredient of the 'Indawi' is impliedly given to have carried definite meaning to the magical properties of 'Indawi' to justify the worship of the same. His explanations are as follows :

1. A pig's skull, to confer vigour and ferilty like that of the fabled sow of 'Lheival' (the place of origin of man), which had ten bonnives at a farrow, and which rooted up and rooted down, overthrowing great trees even as disease shall be uprooted and cast forth from the bodies of the owner of the house and all that dwell therein.

2. A goat's horn, to confer beauty and vigour like that of the goat of 'Heilhongipi' (the rock that 'eats all water' and stands in the sea where the rivers flow into it), with curly horns and silky hair.

3. A miniature gourd ladle to confer plenty in all that can be lifted in a ladle - water & wine (i.e., rice-wine), grain, etc.

4. A miniature gourd, complete, containing water and seeds, to confer rapid increase, prosperity and perfection like that of the gourd, and wealth in cattle, crops, and all else, that shall never dry up.

5. A 'Belval' (i.e., a circular stand for a jar, but it is represented in a purely conventional manner by a fragment of split stick with a coiled silver of Bamboo peel) to ensure that all wealth acquired by the owner is encircled and bound with a 'Belval', and cannot escape or be lost.

6. A minute bamboo Dao (Chempong) of Kolthi (it should be 'Kolthih', i.e. iron of 'Alva'-Burma) to ensure that even as such a 'Dao' will cut through everything there is high up or low down (kol-sa Kol-lhang) it should be as 'Kolsah Kol-lhang), so all evil spirits that bring disease or misfortune shall be cleft and driven away from the body of the owner of the house and all that dwell therein.

7. A minute bamboo spear-head (Theingcha) (it should be 'Tencha') to ensure that even as from one horizon to the other (Kolas Kol-lhang) the spear is used of all men for slaying and killing, and there is nothing that is not pierced by it, so all misfortune and disease and ghosts (Pughao Paghao- it should be Pu-gao pagao), i.e. ghosts of cognates and ghosts of agnates (the interpretation of the meaning should be rather the curse or sins of fathers and forefathers) shall be pierced and driven off.

The above seven items are bound together on a single cord fibre made of the plant 'Khaopi' and with the cord bound fast to a bamboo spike. The spear-head is at one end of the cord, the 'Dao' at the other. On the two gourds articles and feathers from a white cock are fastened with wax.

8. The bamboo spike is cut from the cultivated bamboo only and confers vitality and straight and strong growth like that of the cultivated bamboo and ensures prolific increase, like the green shoots which the bamboo puts forth early.

9. The cord ensures that, as the plant came from the earth and has ten layers of cortex, so shall the owner of the house and all that dwell there be strong and that even as it is bound about the bamboo spike, so will be the diseases, misfortune and evil bound fast and prevented attacking the owner of the house and its inmates, and that the same will happen to the cattle, crops and all forms of wealth bound together, so that they cannot escape him.

10. The white chicken feathers ensure that as the white cock of 'Molkoi' recalled the sun after the 'Thimzin' and restord the light dispelling the darkness, so shall all disease, misfortune and evil be cleared away from the persons and the owner of the house and the dwellers therein.

These are the explanations that could be gathered from elderly people in modern times also, though there are certain variations here and there in the number of items of 'Indawi' which do not tally with those I have gathered.

Physical properties of 'Indawi' differ slightly from clan to clan. Hutton said that the Singsons do not use cock's feathers and gourd ladle due to the fact that in the past the priest of the particular clan was chopped by the enemies during the performance of the ceremony and before its completion. But it should be mentioned here that feathers of white-cock or only cock are not necessarily to be included. Feathers of cock are used only when the performer of 'Indawi' has earlier performed a ceremony of 'Sa-Ai' in the process of which he erected a kind of tree called 'Sekon', signifying his fame, popularity and bravery as ornaments of decoration in his Cheadgear. It is, therefore, not a permanent ingredient of 'Indawi' for all the clans worshipping it. A basket is also attributed to the 'Indawi' of the Singsons, as the recognised fee of the basketful of grains for the Thiempu. But in the areas that have been studied, the inhabitants disown this fact and attribute the basket to signify a particular clan called Haokip who, though worshipping, 'Indawi', use basket in the belief that it represent a kind of diety called 'Selseo', meaning Python'. So, they said that a basket in 'Indawi' is indicative of onlv the ceremony of the'Haokip' clan. As for 'Belval', it seems to have a great variety of usages among the kukis, who worship 'Indawi'. Some use 'Belval', while others do not. Whatever may be the variation, the fact remains that the worship of 'Indawi' is peculiar to the culture of the Thadou kukis and their cognates, such as, the Hangsing, the Chongloi, etc.

XI.

It is very clear from the above desription that the monotheist kukis, in olden days, were happy with one God - the All Creator - who had no anthropomorphic form to appear before the people, demanding any special worship or offerings. But a few minor mischievous spirits have already occupied their vast supernatual Pantheon and it is they, in many cases, who demand rituals along with other formalities, like offerings and sacrifices. This colourful display of the rituals, through ceremonies, have cut across the familian cult and his covered, rather involved, other people for such specific purposes to reinforce the group solidarity through bindings and obligations. It is quite discernable that the less affluence, leisure and freetime of the people and their movement from one place to another, have practically set the people with limited world view and thus they have capsulised their group identities. So, they have very minimal scope for proliferation. Rather, Chieftainship which compelled the group to be ruled by one and only spiritual head, the 'Thiempu' or the priest, had to brave all supernatural and spiritual confrontations through offerings, sacrifices and ceremonies. Their nature of offerings are less, items of worship are small and esoteric charms or incantations are not prolific to make everything more colourful, rhythmic and vibrant. However, procedures to overcome diseases and sickness, through magic, divination and with occult practices are still in vogue and all these be cloud their mind and manifest it in the action patern ; and thus their monotonous life has dazzled with rituals and ceremonies. But, slowly and inevitably, the force of conversion to Christianity proselytized the society drastically, though some have retained it through their rituals and ceremonies.

CHAPTER 9

CONCLUSION

I Reconsidering the Background :

The North-Eastern territory of India, comprising several States, has some distinctive geo-physical features. The lofty Himlayas standing as a rampart of the Indian Sub-continent, the highest rain washed region of Cherrapunjee, the series of rolling ridges and undulating and arid unplands, the unfathomable deep forests of different species of trees and creepers presenting indescribeable sylvan beauty and the criss-crossing and gargling rivers and streams of umteen numbers have in totality created a panoramic view in this border region of India. Politically too, this region has strategic importance of immense import, sometimes with Burma, sometimes with China and at times with the sister country, Bangladesh. As a result, the north-Eastern states occupy vitally strategic position in the matter of integrity, security and defence of India.

Here, the important racial concentration is 'Mongoloid', though , in the past, there were slow penetrations of other racial elements in this vast tract. Though these fertile valleys girdled with rivers, movements of motley people followed the course of hard rocky serpentile paths, which eventually ended up in the conglomeration of varied groups in different places of the region. On the face of it, the region appeared at first to be difficult and inaccessible terrain. With the passage of time, these difficulties were overcome. Discovery of tools of the Stoneage through excavation, which reflect a neo-lithin type of civilization, indicates its existence roughly between eighteen and twenty thousand years B.C. It also indicates that these groups of people possibly come from the South-Eastern tract to this region with the typical 'Gelt' culture, with enumerable shouldered 'celts' (T-shaped polished celt, used as an axe or adze or plough or hoe share) for cultivating land and felling trees, to initiate agriculture. They then followed South-Westerly direction of the presentday Bengal-Orissa border of the manland of India. Hence, were ascribe it to 'Austric' culture, which ultimately formed the bedrock of Indian culture and civilisation through assimilation and blending. Thus, the question of non- interaction with the mainland cannot be accepted as true.

Again, in the historical testimony we find that many other elements slowly penetrated. In the Mahabharata (Pan-India) age also,we find glaring examples of Chitrangada, Nag daughter - Ulupi and Kiratas, who held very important position in the building up of the epic account. This reflects the idea of Indianization in this sub-continent of Bharata. However, with these tardy processes of interaction, involvement and endemic amalgamation, still this region shows occasional expressions of identity crisis, which have gained momentum in recent past. It is true that this geophysical region with many identifiable groups, speaking different languages and owning heterogeneous cultures, are living in this region tied to a narrow and emotional attachments which have brought them to a stage of holding divergent mentalities. Coupled with these and other factors, they exposed the indegenous groups of people to a feeling of discord, dissatisfaction, dissension and grievance, which ultimately accentuated the ever increasing crisis for ic ntify.

The British Colonial administration, by their misinterpretation of the genuine terms and amalgamation of many groups into a derogatory nomenclature etc., hightened the mental enguish and bitterness of the people concerned. Of course, the striking physical differences of the people of the mainland exist, and these easily establish the indelible distinction between them and the other people, their cultures and languages. As such, a hiatus has been created having natural reminfication on all sides, sometimes eroding many precious and prized human values and sentiments .

The area, did not, in the past, encourage visitors from outside and, therefore, a thorough investigation and analysis of the people and their culture could not be undertaken in a systematic way. Very few anthropologiets and social scientists did venture to work in this place to get a detailed account of the inhabitants here. Thus, the area remained an unexplored mystery. During the British rule, we find the spread of Christianity vis- a-vis spread of formal education of the local inhabitants. But this alienated them from their fellow brethren and the ethnocentricism was disturbed among them. In such a confounding situation, a thorough study and examination of men and things was felt an imperative necessity, so as to project the actual state of affairs of the people and their culture. With this end in view, this study has been conducted with a slant on the historical analysis of positions . Due to rapid Christianisation, most of the people forget their own history, nay, their culture, which interlaced the people with ecology, environment and their manifestations through the march of time.

II Ethnography

Due to rapid conversion into Christianity, spread of eductaion and employment opportunities in various whitecollar jobs, and due to staying in various placess to get education, the peole in general formed the habit of moving towards the greener pastures. Obviously, such a situation would present immense difficulty to undertake a systematic ethnography of the people nor such an attempt was made. Sporadic references here and there have been made, and legends, fables nd facts stated orally by the inhabitants have been pieced together to focus the cultural background of the people. With all this collections and from the wealth of memory of the people living in distant villages, an ethnographic profile had been attempted for restructuring.

The British Colonial administration used the term 'Kuki' for some groups of people, which the latter are still resenting. In the list of Scheduled Tribes of Manipur State, there is no categorisation of the people bearing the term 'Kuki'. The clans/groups of kuki have their separate identities to have constitutional status, through which benefits accrue. Traditional kuki social system is based on various social institutions. The present monograph very clearly records the details of these institutions functioning through 'Tucha-Becha-Songgao' relationships. These relationships establish a man's position, status and role in dealing with the traditional social activities. They have specific duties, obligations, privileges, formalities, procedures and finally all these are meant to link up people in a cohesive whole. Special types of duty and obligation demand particular terms, and even during ceremonial feasts and festivities certain portions of meat of the sacrificial animal are presented to certain persons only. And those are distributed as per rules set by the social system. In the same way, mother's brother and sister's son have specific duties and obligations to perform in the society.

The labour organisation, called 'Lawm' includes all the able bodied members who are generally employed in agricultural activities. There are four tyupes of 'Lawn' among the kukis, with specific duties and roles for them. many festivals are associated with their activitiesand certain games are also arranged. Such as, hunting, etc., 'Pon kaap' is an occasion when fun and merry- making is done among the 'Lawm' boys and girls. The prevalence of inter-tribal feuds made the existence of young boys dormitory system called 'Sawm' essential though later the same had taken to a decentralised form of organisation due to exigency of defence requirements. This system served as the institution of informal education for the young boys. Birth, puberty, marriage and death have all separate and elaborate ceremonies, and in these ceremonies *Tucha-Becha* relations become prominent. Formal bride- price is paid in marriages and some associated ceremonies are performed in this connection. A pregnant woman has to abide by many taboos and restrictions. After the birth of a child, many prohibitive activities are practised by the lactating mother. In these matters, the 'Thiempu' or the village priest has a distinct role to play. After death, burial is the rule and for this also there are a series of ceremonies relating to the departed soul.

The political organisation is constituted with a Council of Ministers headed by the Village Chief. Practiclly the Village Chief is a very respected person in the whole community. Theoretically, he is supposed to provide food and protection to all the villagers under his chieftainship. Enforcement of the executive orders, proper maintenance of social practices and customary laws are the *reison d' etre* of the village administration under the Chieftainship and the Council of Ministers. The office of the Chief is hereditary and it is handed down from the father to the eldest son, who otherwise is known as 'Upa' or the senior member. The entire set-up of the administration is known as 'Semang Upa' or 'pachong'. The office of the Chieftainship is known as 'Haosa' The villagers have to pay annual payment to the Chief by means of 'Changseo' which means a basketful of paddy and other tributes, such as, Saleng (Samal), Khuotha, etc.

Recent changes in post-independene era have ushered in new situations in Manipur where Village Authority Act, 1956 has been introduced. As a consequence, the Village organisation under the leadership of the 'Haosa' has changed in its structure and content. Besides, the Chief cannot now officially or openely enjoy its age-old prerogatives, like 'Saleng' (Samal), 'Salu', 'Changseo', 'Khuotha', etc.,

With regard to their supernatural beliefs and practices, the kukis traditionally believe in one God - the Supreme Beig, called 'Chung Pathien'. He is omniscient and omnipotent. He does not, however, want any propitiation, worship or appeasement. But the kukis believe in some other evil spirits or soul of persons meeting unnatural deaths. These spirits cause diseases, misfortune, etc. and for these they require appeasement through sacrifices and offerings. For religious purposes, the kukis have the 'Thiempu' or priest whose office is often hereditary from father to any son who has the aptitude other than the eldest son. Of course, his position depends on his capabilities and successful taking of initiative. He has to act as per dictation through oneirology during dream at night. Some doggeral verses are used as incantations to appese the gods or the spirtis to gain their favour. 'Maicham', the 'holy platform' is a part of the religious formalities, and blood of the sacrificial animal is offered on it. It is believed, offering of sacrifices to all the evil spirits causing harm to the community is the way to pacify their wrath.

Many rituals and ceremonies have made the life of the kukis colourful. During sacrifices, a special set of persons are there to participate and to renew their mutual obligations and formalities. Music, dance, incantation, etc, reflect their vibrant life while interacting with the supernatural powers on varied occasions at different seasons.

Practically, the kuki life is governed by the Chief who maintains the law and order and allows the formalities to continue, and the 'Thiempu' or the religious head, is there to interact with the supernatural powers when needed, as also to conduct all other religious performances for the group.

III. Changing Scene

Change being the unchanging law of nature manifests in human societies; it may appear in different degrees at different situations. These changes are automatically changes in the life- style of the people, i.e., in their cultural contour at different situations. In the life of the kukis, changes began while they started migrating in search of food and shelter, with the changing ecology and environment. Other cultural groups have had interactions while they faced each other. In the pre- Independence British days, slowly and surresptitiously changes crept in their action pattern , mutual outlook and relationships. Spread of Christianity and formal education pitchforked them from their narrow world of individual outlook to a broader and wider would view, and this opened up many new vistas of higher education and never types of hjob opportunities through interactional scenes. The king of Manipur and other ethnic groups came closr to each other and tardily, after Independene and establishment of democratic rule, more developmental activities re-shaped the region with marked progress.

World view was extended, new jobs came their way and, thus, this group of people became a part of the bigger economic system. Through this and in conjunction with the spread of christianity, people began to orient themselves to the new directions whence traditionalism or the historic manners and customs began to lose grip over them. Thus, a new situation developed and fresh mental make-up started growing to buttress the entire changing processes while absorbing them in their stride or better civilisation.

IV. In Search of Identity

On various occasions a new dimension of awareness was noticed among the two important groups of people called the Nagas and the Kukis. Among the Nagas, it appears to be the cementing force of unification through alignment of many groups in many parts of this region. It had even succeeded in enticing some tribes, such as, Anals, Marings, etc., of the old Kukis to their fold.' Among the Kukis, however, while some groups staunchly espoused for adherance to the conventional nomenclature of 'Kuki', despite its complete deletion from the list of the recognised tribes of Manipur, for a common identity of all the Kuki tribes, other groups propounded the 'Chin' theory with an avowed policy of creating a 'Chinland' for all the Kuki tribes on the plea that the term was being used in Burma for the same groups of people who were known as Kukis in India. Yet another group advocated 'Mizo' as the most acceptable appellation with an argument that the other terminology - Kuki - was obsolete and, therefore, unacceptable, and that the second terminology, 'Chin' being used in Burma, it was as good as a counterfeit term.

Every effort to bring all the erstwhile Kuki tribes uner the banner of one nomenclature having failed, more confusing new ideas came up for consideration, and some people advocated the term 'Zomi'. Another sect advocated a new nomenclature which had the accommodative element and the most compromising identity in favour of a phraseology 'Chin-Kuki-Mizo'. The latest exponents of a common identity for the Kukis were those who professed the term 'Chikim', in an acronym form 'Chi' from Chin, 'Ki' from Kuki and the letter 'M' from Mizo. CHIKIM is now a word conveying the literal meaning of 'Complete Tribes' or 'All Nations'. But this term has not yet gained much currency.

It may be noted in this connection that the term 'Mizo' is a new terminology adopted with some political motivation. If the term 'Kuki' is rejected on the grounds that it is derogetory and foreign to the people to whom it is applied, there are similar grounds for rejection of the term 'Mizo', which is a derivative from the words used by the Sailo Chiefs to denote their subjects as 'Mizotute' or 'Mizote' in a derogatious sense that 'Mizote' or 'Mizotute' were the people dependent on the Sailo Chiefs and their wealth. Subservient as they were to their Sailo Masters, the subjects recognised the terms thereby accepting the Sailo authority and their subordinate position as a 'People depending on others". Secondly, not to speak of its derivation and its ultimate implication, the term 'Mizo' has a literal meaning which indeed is rediculous. 'Mi' means 'Man' and 'Zo' means 'Hill'. Therefore, the term 'Mizo' means 'Man-Hill' or ' a man who looks like a hill'. It is also a fact that in Mizo language, 'Hill-man' is called 'Tlangmi' and 'Son of the hill' as 'Zofa'. If such terms are to be used in the same way as the term 'Mizo' is coined, 'Tlangmi' and 'Zofa' are to be termed as 'Mi-tlang' and 'Fazo' which carry entirely different meanings, if not a total cipher. Hence, nobody says 'Mi-tlang' and 'Fazo', but 'Tlangmi' and 'Zofa'. Thus the term 'Mizo' is no less derogatory and foreign than 'Kuki'.

Indeed, it is admirable that despite such a situation wherein different ethnic groups, being prisoners of indecision, are clamouring for a new identity, the Thadous and their cognate tribes stick to their traditional nomenclature - 'Kuki', without any inhibition or the slightest concern as to what does the term mean. The nomenclature matters very little to them. Recognition and advancement of the people have nothing to do with the terminology being employed to denote them. What matters to them was the unity and outlook of the groups of people who bear the terminology as their common identity. Undue importance given to the terminology employed to denote the tribes or ethnic groups only manifests the abyssmal narrow mindedness and parochialism in approach. In as much as beauty is only skin-deep, so is clamouring for terminology superficial and negative to unity. Fanaticism cannot bring glory, and is divorced from pragmatism and far-sightedness which forfeits political sagacity and statesmanship. It is, therefore, clear that, while the Nagas are united under the Naga identity with each tribal group maintaining its separate entity, the Kukis are engrossed with the problem of finding a common identity, being in doldrums to accept the term 'Kuki' as such. It may be said that there are three factors that contribute to such differences in acceptability or otherwise of the term - 'Naga' and 'Kuki'.

The prime factor is environmental influence. Every Naga tribe occupies a compact, well-knit, well-demarcated and well-defined areas contiguous to the other tribes.The Tangkhul areas are exclusively occupied by the Tangkhuls and no other Naga tribes of significant number mix with them. Likewise, the Mao, the Maram and the Kabui Naga tribes occupy their respective areas without mixing with other Naga tribes. However, their physical proximity makes it possible for regular social intercourse among themselves. Thus, while maintaining their identity separately, social mobility and fusion are possible among them. They are also not very much subjected to outside influence to entertain variegated opinions.

Unlike the Nagas, the Kukis are scattered all over the hill areas of Manipur. Hudson (1911 : 2) said :

> ... for various reasons, economic and political, Kuki settlements exist not only in the British districts of the Naga Hills in the vicinity of Henema but also far away on the North- East of the Manipur State, in the neighbourhood of Melome and Lapvome ... Indeed, the Kuki is to be found almost everywhere in the State, except in the territory occupied by the Mao confederacy.

To emphasise the nature of their scattered habitation resulting from their nomadic habit, Hudson quoted a Kuki who told him :

> ... We are like the birds of the air. We make our nests here this year, and who knows where we shall build next year.

This observation speaks of the condition of the Kukis who are possibly subjected to the influence of alien communities and tribes with whom they had long been living together. In other words, the Kukis have been greatly influenced by the people with whom they have come into contact through time and space in their approach to their ethnic identity.

The Thadou and their cognate groups live in the North, East and West in Manipur among the Nagas, apart from being preponderant over other groups of Kuki in the South and South-East. They also live in pockets of Nagaland and Assam, and are being influenced by the examples of their Naga neighbours. These groups of the Kukis are the exponents for continuance of the term 'Kuki' as a common identity. The Hmars and the Paites are the second and the third major groups of Kuki who are found mostly in the South. They have constant social intercourse with the Chins of the Chin Hills State of Burma and the Mizos of Mizoram. The influence from the Chin Hills State of Burma and the Mizoram has in no small measure contributed to their variegated opinions on the question of common identity. The smaller tribal groups, such as, the Gangte, the Simte, the Vaiphei, the Zou,etc., are sandwiched in between the Thadous and their cognates on the one hand and the Hmars and the Paites on the other. These groups are often influenced by the bigger groups on either side of them, and are, therefore, non-averse to adopting any of the controversial nomenclatures for a common identity, provided such adoption gives all the ethnic groups of the erstwhile Kukis a sense of solidarity and unity.

There are still smaller Kuki tribes, such as, the Aimols, the Anals, the Chirus, the Koiraos, the Koirangs, the Kom...They live side by side with the Thadous and their cognates, mainly in the Chandel district (South-

East) and the Sadar Mill Sub-divisions of the Senapati District (North). There is no denying the fact that the culture, tradition, customs, manners, language etc. of these tribes are closely allied to the Thadous and their cognate groups than any other Kuki tribes, except the Hmars with whom some of them, especially the Koms, the Koiraos,the Koirangs, can converse in their respective tribal dialects.

It, therefore, goes without saying that the influence of the Thadous over them in regard to the common identity was visibly great. However, non- inclusion of the term 'Kuki' in the recognised list of the tribes and emergence of the Nagas in the political arena in the whole of North-East region during the fifties and the sixties, under the leadership of Phizo attracted some of these smaller tribes to taking shelter under the political banner of the 'Naga' identity. Kabui (1985 : 50) thus illustrated the Anal Kukis :

> No tribe in Manipur has faced the problem of identity as the Anals. The situation in which they are now put into may have been caused by the natural desire of a minority to have an identification in community status, political aspiration with one major group or the other. The Anals and smaller groups, like Mayon, Monsang, Lamkang and Tarao by their habitats occupy such a geographical situation that they are sandwiched between the Nagas in the North and the Kuki-Chin in the South. This naturally produces constraint on their group identity. An element of complication about the identity problem was injected by the British administrators who were themselves not sure of the identity of the Anals in relation to the bigger neighbours, Nagas or the Kuki-Chins. The British Colonial Rulers applied a broad yardstick of grouping a tribe within the Naga or Kuki fold. The British officials who wrote on the tribes of Manipur were confused about the major identification group of the Anals. While someone called them Nagas, others called them as 'Old Kuki Tribe'.

Second factor is the tribal political institutions. While the form of government among the Nagas was democratic in nature; the Kukis had the autocratic form or despotism. Carey and Tuck (1932 :3) observed :

> The Government of the Naga tribes is distinctly democratic. Their Chieftainship do not necessarily pass from father to son, but are practically dependent on the will of the tribesmen, and the Naga chief are therefore without much individual power and their rule is based on the general approval of the clan. The Kuki chiefs, on the other hand, invariably inherit their position by the right of birth and take

initiative in all matters concerning administration of their clansmen, by whom they are respected and feared.

Similarly, Hudson (1911:21) was emphatic in his tacit remark :

We are sometimes able to distinguish a Kuki from a Naga clan by the development of the Chieftain in the former instance into a secular leader who takes only a ceremonial part in the tribal rites, and in the latter case by the diminution of the secular authority as the GAON-BURA,who remains the religious head of his village. Perhaps the evolution of the secular authority of the Kuki chief is due to the urgency of the need among such communities of strong administration unimpeded by "turbulent priest"

Indeed, the nature of forming such absolute authority among the Kukis by the Chief is susceptible to his becoming a despot to which Carey and Tuck (1932—2001) further observed :

The Chief may be wanting in qualifications and there may be many of other families his superior in ability; but, unless he is physically quite unfit for his position, there is no danger of his being supplanted, and the usual course is for elders and advisers to assist him in his rule.

The Nagas having been under the democratic form of Government did not find anything strange in the change brought about by the dawn of independence in India. As a matter of fact, having had the spirit of a democrat, a Naga readily adjusted to the situation. True to his tradition, the leadership moved through the public and their opinions. But in the case of the Kukis the situation was a nightmare. Their mode of thinking, being dictated by individual authoritarianism, commensural to the type of Government under which they had been brought up, was misfit to the changed circumstances. The traditional leadership of the Kukis mainly provided by the Chiefs and their Clansmen could not adjust to the new situation. Conversely, the common people who saw a new horizon for commoners to move in their social heirarchy welcomed the changes that came about and asserted themselves through organised ethnic activities. This attempts came in direct conflict with the traditional leadership which led to the variegated opinions on the question of common identity. While some tribes wanted to assert themselves by maintaining their separate identities and led their people through organised activities of their ethnic groups, the traditional leadership and their clansmen who constituted the bourgeoisie wanted to retain their leadership status. This posture of the dominant groups incurred the displeasure of the proletariat who wanted to get rid of the former by separately identifying themselves. Thus, the emergence of nomenclature like, Chin, or Zomi, or Mizo, or Khul, etc. was counterproductive of the posture of the traditional leadership and their clansmen, on the one hand, and the politicisation (Betteille, 1969:139) of the tribal society by the proletariat groups on the other.

Thirdly, language factor has a great role to play. Examplary to their political wisdom, and as witness to the process of assimiliation, the Nagas are able to evolve, at the height of linguistic diversity, a common language called Nagamese, a pidgin Assamese, at the National level. Encouraged by such evolution of Nagamese, the Tangkhul Nagas of Manipur set a rare example by adopting Ukhrul dialect as the language of the Tangkhul Nagas. The peculiar situation of the Tangkhul Nagas is that almost every village, big or small, irrespective of physical proximity, has its own dialect. Two villagers belonging to different villages could not communicate to each other in a common dialect. One dialect was almost Greek to the other. Their linguafranca used to be the 'Meitei-Lon', language of the Meiteis of Manipur. The possibility of evolving such a common languages among the Tangkhul was due to constant social intercourse among the various dialect-groups which made assimiliation and fusion favourable mainly due to Ukhrul being the centre of political, social, religious and economic activities since the days of British India when the seat of administration was established there.

In contrast, the Kuki tribes while using their respective dialects or one of the dialects of the tribes, can communicate among themselves as in the biblelical penticostal days. Robert Raid (1942 : 3-4), the then Governor of Assam, thus observed that the Kukis,

> . . . form a mingling of clans, speaking so far as I know, dialects of the same language, who are known to us by various names, Kookies, Lusheis, Pois, Shendus, Chin, etc. . . .

Thus, the extreme case of language similarity among the Kukis is that of the Thadous and their cognate groups who speak one and the same language popularly known as the Thadou language. Both the groups accepted the term without demur till the dawn of Independence in India as an expression of solidarity. Now, the situation is changed. Instead of accepting it as a common language and as an expression of solidarity, it has unleashed disunity, enmity, tension, conflict and social disharmony among them.

The Thadou group says that the language has been known as 'Thadou Language' from time immemorial. It belongs to them, and should, therefore, be called 'Thadou language' and nothing else. On the other hand, their cognates claim that the language is not the exclusive possession of the Thadous alone. It is as much theirs and, therefore, should be called 'Kuki language'. At a time when social tension was at the peak, the Government of Manipur issued an order to the effect that Thadou language be read upto Primary stage in schools[1]. This was, however, contested by the other groups. Conceding the counterclaim of the other groups, the Government of Manipur issued another order[2] which superseded the earlier orders deleting the term 'Thadou', replacing it by 'Kuki'. The result of such action of the Govenment had done more harm than good. A Pandora Box had been opened for all concerned.

It is of conspicuous peculiarity to the Kukis that unlike the Nagas and other communities whose tribal identifications are of impersonal connotations, ethnic appellations among the Kukis bear personal names. Thus, Thadou is the name of the progenitor of the Kipgen, the Haokip, the Singson (Singsit) and the Sitlhou. Thadou is the younger brother of Doungel and the elder brother of Chongloi, Hangshing and Touthang. The decendants of Thadou being preponderant over the others as also being more famous in reputation, colloquially 'Thadou' has been used to denote all the groups mentioned above collectively. But as time changes, the thinking of the people changes. They have become more conscious of everything including their identity. Thus the term 'Thadou' being a personal name meant for the decendants of Thadou alone, other groups have refused to be so identified since recent past for it carries a deeper social value than superficially taken for granted. Such colloquial usage of the term 'Thadou' has quickened the process of distintegration among the Thadous and their cognate groups. It has, indeed, become the main issue of identity among the Kukis, and has, therefore, become the centrifugal force which drives homogeneous people into divergent tribal groups.

The main contention of the 'Thadou' protogonists is that 'Kuki' being the nomenclature denoting other othnic groups of Kuki who do not speak 'Thadou language' as well should not be misused, by calling it as 'Kuki language'. The scope and coverage of the nomenclature 'Kuki' must on

1. Government of Manipur, Secretarit : Education Deptt., Orders No. 17/1/72-SE dt. 22-3-1977.

2. Ibid : dt. 3-1-81

no account be made narrow and limited. In the event of the 'Thadou' language' being called 'Kuki language', the term 'Kuki' automatically excludes other ethnic groups of erstwhile 'Kukis' and would, therefore, relegate the nomenclature to the level of group appallations which constitute the term 'Kuki'. The term 'Thadou' which is a personal name must not be treated synonymous to the term 'Kuki' which is a political nomenclature having a far larger meaning and wider scope than the term 'Thadou'.

As against this, the term Naga has assumed the centripetal force which unites heterogneous tribal groups that converge around the Naga axis, while at the sàme time maintaining their separate identity zealously. Establishment of the Naga National Council, the ascendency of Angami Zapu Phizo in the political limelight of the Nagas which took them to the path of secessionist movement in the fifties and the subsequent creation of Nagaland State in the sixties, gained momentum to propound that the term Naga was not a tribe, but a Nation. The term Naga became a prestigious ethnic identity for many small tribes of erstwhile Kukis, such as, the Anals, the Marings, etc., of Manipur in particular and the North-East India in general.

In the past, till the end of British rule in India, different ethnic groups did not object to being identified as Kukis when inter-tribal feuds were the practice of the time.The term 'Kuki' gave security and protection, and was an expression of solidarity and ethnic identity. In a resurgent India after Independence, the lofty ideals of equality, fraternity, justice, liberty, etc., of the Constitution provides special provisions for growth and development of the weaker section of the people to bring them at par with other advanced communities. In doing so, certain backward groups of people were listed as Scheduled Castes and Scheduled Tribes. These groups no longer feel the necessity of being called 'Kuki'. The security and protection they needed having been provided by the Constitution of India, the much required expression of social solidarity by being identified as 'Kuki' was no longer felt. They feel that they should avail to the fullest extent possible of the privileges being accorded to them by the Constitution of India. The total sum result was that while recognised tribes wanted to maintain their separate identities, other tribes who have not so far been recognised created situations craving for the attention of the Government for according them the status of recognised tribes through organised ethnic activites.

The nature of conflict and the divergent opinions in regard to their common identity among the Kukis speak of the close ethnic affinity among them and also reflect maladjustment ot social values among the conservative Kukis as against the adaptability of the Naga tribes to soical change. Non-conformity of the conservative Kuki tribes to social change resulting in conflict, tension, disunity, etc., is hightened by the arbitrary and haphazard categorisation of tribes by the Government of India for which Bhowmick (1980 : 28) observed :

> The criteria relied upon by the Government in determining whether a group is a tribe, and those used by the academicians, do not tally with each other. Thus a disharmonious categorisation is found to prevail with regard to the definition of a tribe.
>
> The same group of people may be considered as Scheduled Tribe in one 'State' and is not considered to be so in a different State. Instances are galore. We may give one example. The Bhumijes of West Bengal are not considered a Scheduled Tribe, whereas the Bhumijes living in the adjoining State of Bihar are regarded as a Scheduled Tribe.

The above observation is exactly the same as is being meted to the Kukis of different States. It is interesting to note that while the different tribes of Manipur, such as, the Haokips, the Sitlhous, the Hangsings, the Gangte, the Vaipheis, the Guites, the Khawhlangs (Hmar), etc. are put together as tribes under the heading 'KUKI' in the lists of Scheduled Tribes in Nagaland, Meghalaya, Mizoram, the same people living in Manipur have not been so treated which had in no small measure contributed to the crises in the identity of the Kukis in Manipur, for which Bhowmick (1980 :2) attributed categorisation of tribes as having been done without "Valid scientific definition applicable to a tribe".

V. Blending Process

With all this background, a good number of people are now thinking over a new dimension. Changes are inevitable when science, technology, modern education and new job Opportunities have brought all the people together to a greater world wherein ethnic identity should not be overemphasised. Besides, Christianity has cut a deep gorge into their life-style and the people have no other altenative but to roll down in it by embracing Christianity. At the same time, Indian Democracy in constitutional form has opened up many opportunities and, as such, people are not simply confined to its narrow cell; but many think that the good elements of cultures which have so long been sustaining the group together, affiliated them with the nature and established friendships with many through rites, rituals and celebrations, should not be discarded. Rather, these will take them to a glorious history of the past, which all the time favoured them with cultural touches and retouches in order to shape the profile of the group. India is a land of many groups having diverse origin and identity. It is an epitome of the *Mahabharata*, i.e., Pan-India where Naga, Kuki, Kirata, Asura and other groups mingled among themselves to form a confluence of eternal unity in diversity. The traditional dance and festivals of Manipur are such examples which continue even today in the life of the people for their identifications so that these may be allowed to vibrate in the symphony of Indian culture. Unity in diversity with a feeling of nationalism, which is the only binding force for group identity, may be allowed to imbue the life and culture of these colourful people of ancient India.

INDEX

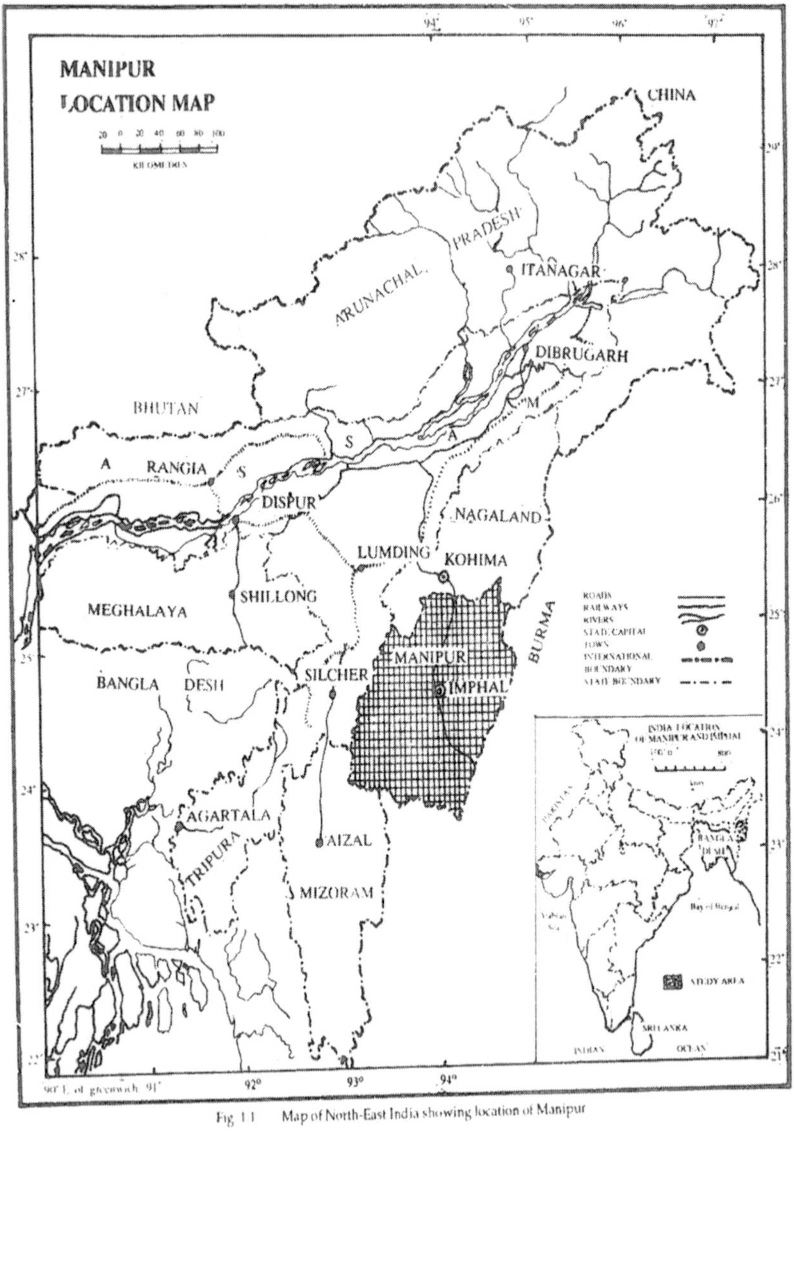

Fig. 1.1 Map of North-East India showing location of Manipur

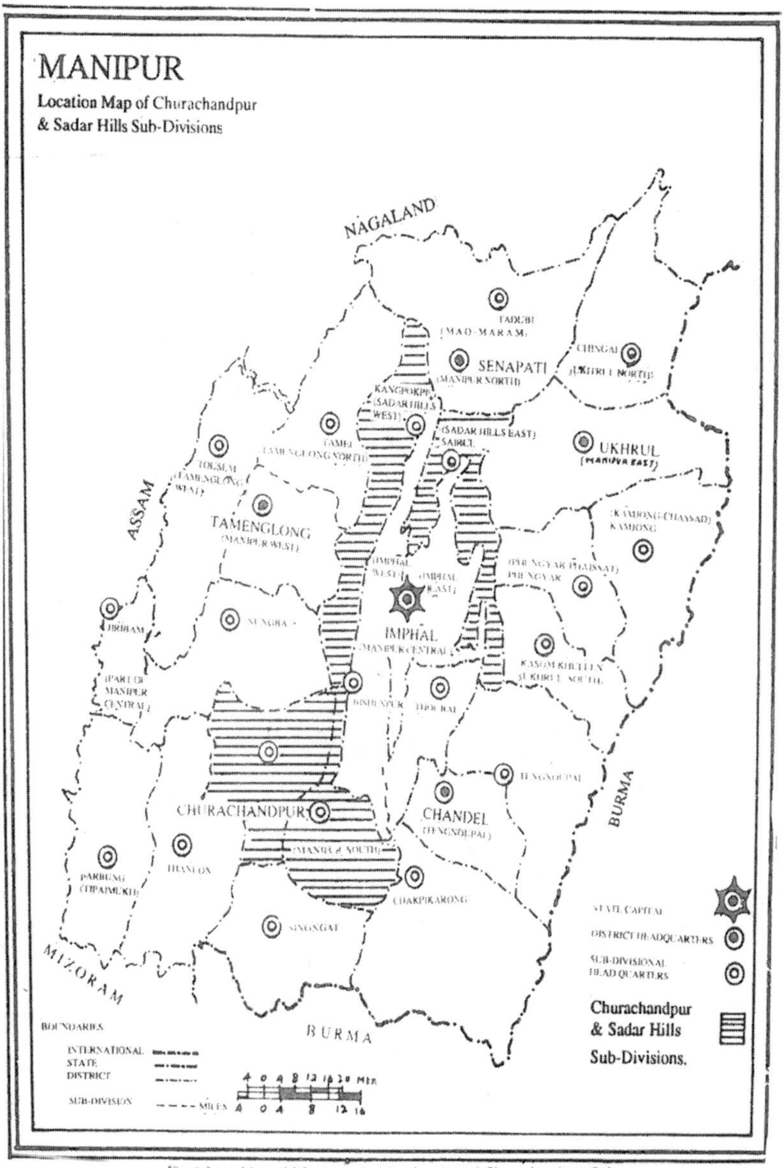

Fig. 1.2. Map of Manipur showing location of Churachandpur Sub-Division of Churachandpur District and Sadar Hills Sub-Division of Senapati District.

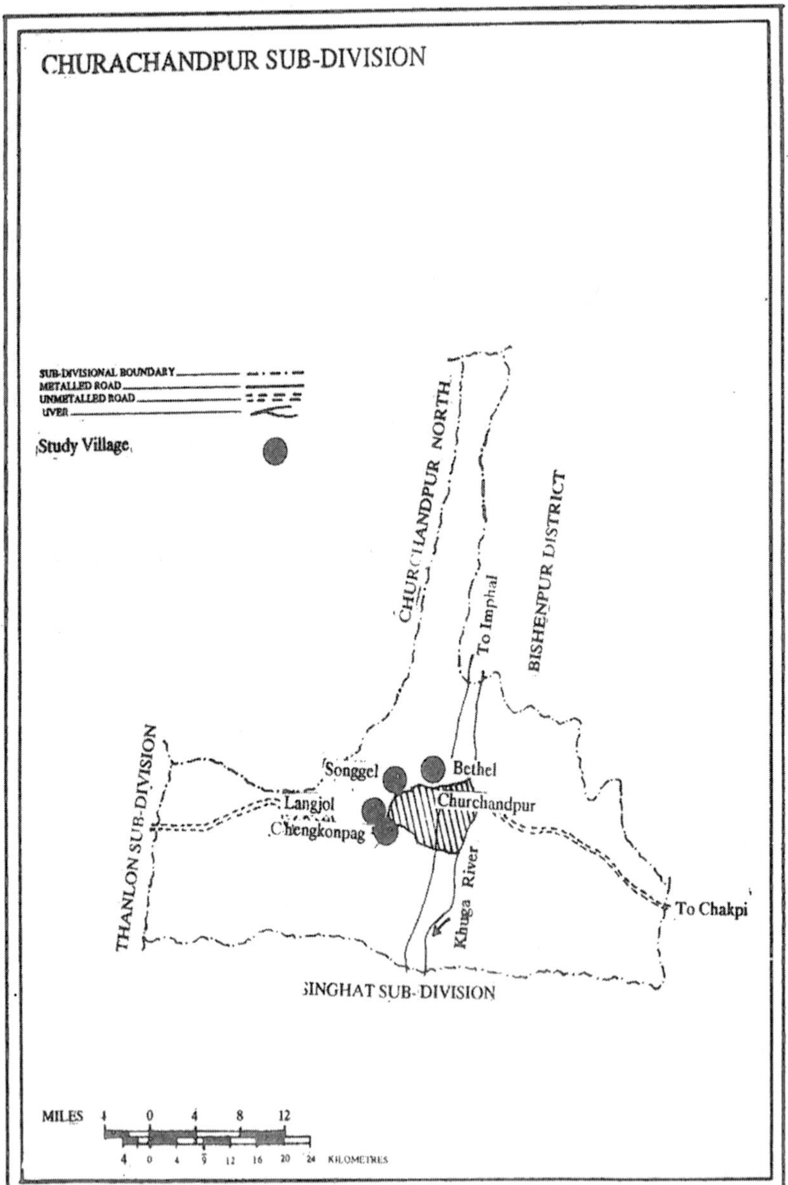

Fig. 1.3. Map of Churachandpur Sub-Division of Churachandpur District showing location of the four villages under study.

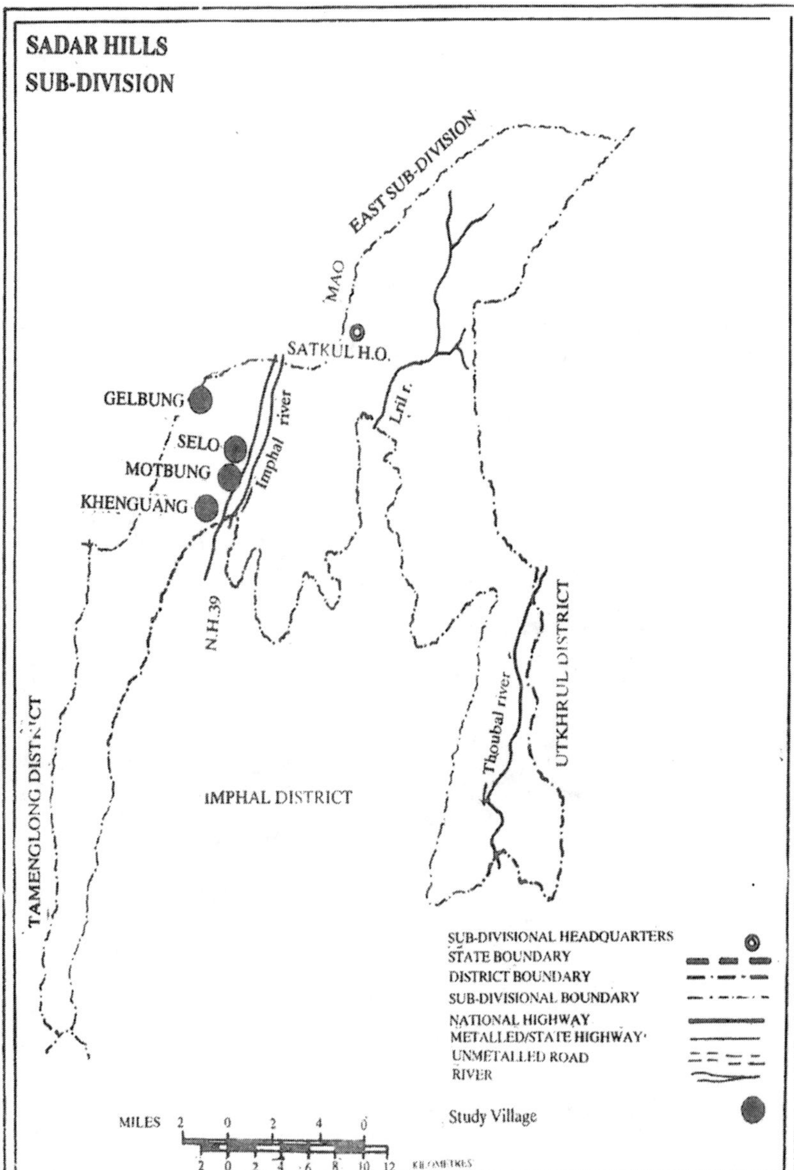

Fig. 1.4. Map of Sadar Hills Sub-Division of Senapati District showing location of the four villages under study.

ILLUSTRATION SHOWING DISTRIBUTION OF MEAT TO RELATIVES

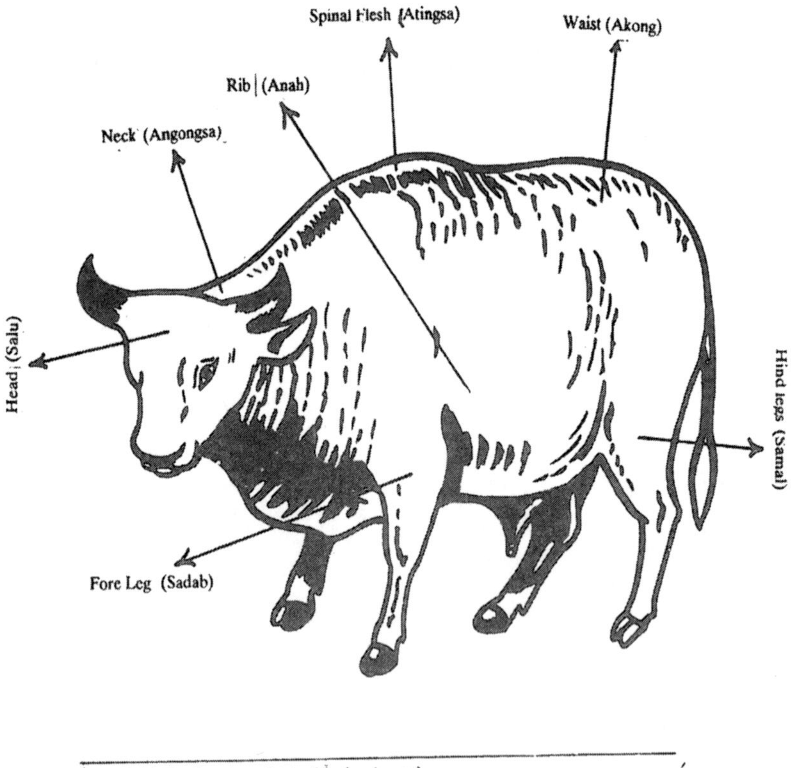

MITHUN (Bracketed words stand for local name).

Illus. 1. Mithun showing distribution of meat to relatives.

Thanghlunkim Gangte, Chura Chandpur District, in a combined traditional dresses of 'Gangte Puondum' lungi, 'Thadou Thangnang-Puon' shawl and 'Hmar Blause'.

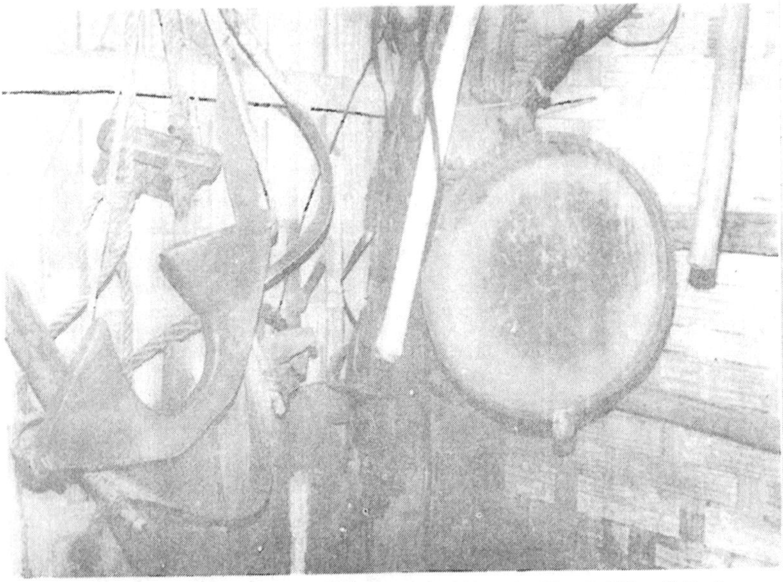

Picture showing kuki indegenous wooden-plate (round), man's cable called `Nam-Kol' and woman's cable called `Nam' for carrying basket.

A lane of Motbung village along the National highway.

The author with his elder son, Lienchungnung, daughter-in-law, Thanghlunkim, second grandson, Mangjahao, on his laps and grand-daughter, Nenghoikim.

Over-view of Bethel village from the Office of the Deputy Commissioner, Churachandpur.

A group of boys and girls of khengjang village.

The Chief of Khengjang village, Thangkh'osei Chongloi, and his wife, Chongkhokim.

A Kuki couple of Khengjang village in their traditional attires.

Lower part of Churachandpur town ship Street with T. Tomba Singh standing on the roadside.

The upper part of Churachandpur street running towards the South.

The author with his mother, Thangkhoneng on the left and his wife, Lhingjaneng.

A traditional Kuki cane container called 'Lel' wherein valuable things and clothings are kept. Alongside is seen a bamboo basket for paddy container called 'Koh'.

A bamboo basket called 'Reng' with its cable for carrying the basket used by male alone called 'Nam-Kol'. The basket is used for carrying firewood.

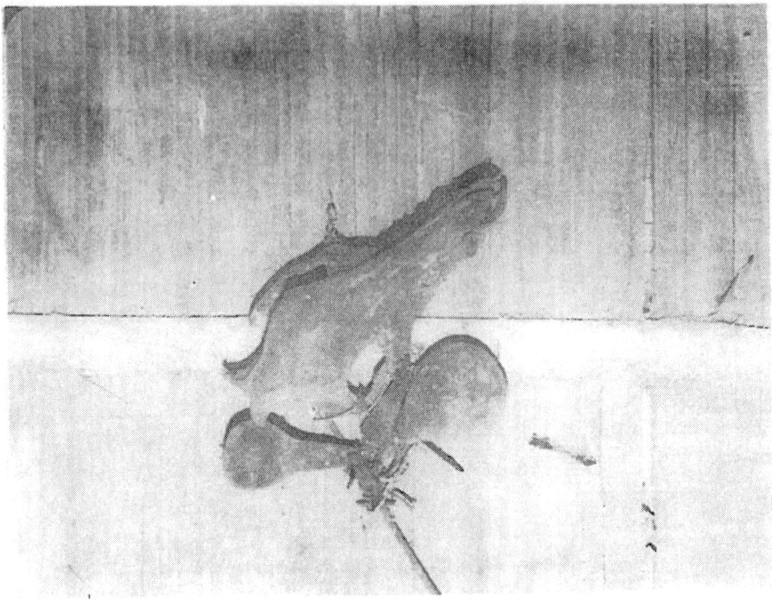

'INDAWI' snapped placing on a bamboo wall to show its various ingradients.

Modernised hearth of a Kuki house called as 'Thuh'Khuh' and 'Cap-leng'.

Some village children of Bethel village playing on a Mango tree grown in the village orchard.

Lalhmingmawi, the daughter of the Chief of Bethel village in a traditional dress putting on a 'Khamtang' (Thadou) lungi and a necklace of beeds.

The author and Surendra, Vice-Principal, Liberal College, on the road between Song-gel village and Bethel village.

The autor, Tomba Singh, Principal, Nambol L. Sanoi College, Surendra and Mr. Achou Singh on the bridge over the small stream that runs on the borders of Song-gel village and Bethal Village.

A closely-knit cane basket called 'Beng used by women only'.

Modernised two girls from khengjang village on their new design attires. The lungis worn by them are of modern designs.

Kampu Gante, Chief of Chengkongpang village and his wife, Sangi Gangte, in their Gangte tribal costume.

Office of the Deputy Commissioner, Churachandpur District.

Central lane of the Song-gel Village.

Motbung village church that stands near the residence of the chief.

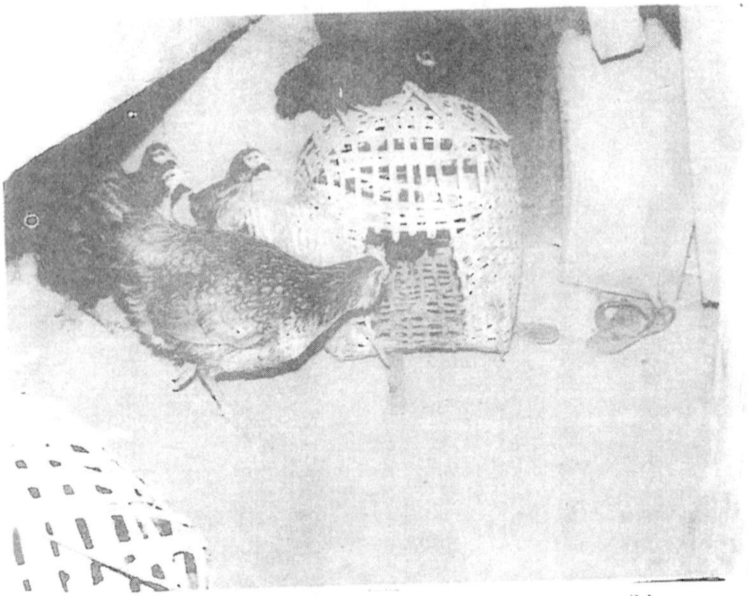

Coop of the Kukis meant for a hen with her chicks where they sleep at night until they are grown upto be able to fly to the poultry raised about 5/6 feet at the portico. The picture shows the hen about to enter the cane-basket poultry being followed by her chicks.

The picture showing the hen inside the coop with her chicks around it trying to enter inside.

Some women villagers and their children of Song-gel village on way to their village after attending a meeting at Bethel village.

A bethal villager taking bath from the village water-point that stands between Bethel and Song-gel commonly used by the villagers of the two villages.

'HAOKHOSEI SITLHOU' snapped while sipping the 'ZU' from the 'Jar' while trying to help himself to pour water from a 'Mithun-born'.

INDAI' spapped from its original position where it is normally hung from the thatched roof at the portico of the house.

The cheer of khengjang village, Thangkhosei Chongloi, seen arranging for the snap-shot of the baskets.

A typical Kuki house with slight modifications.

Mother of the auhor with a `Gangte Shawl'

Churachandpur District Headquarters Government employees' colony-Part I with a Community Hall in the centre.

Electric Colony of the Churachandpur District Headquarters with Dampi range in the background.

Churachandpur District Headquarters Government employees' Colony-Part II showing the street, a Church, on the right-hand side, the District Council Complex and the District Munsiff Court at the far end of the Streett.

Some villagers of Song-gel with the author.